Sasha Ayad, Lisa Marchiano and **Ste**▓▓▓▓▓▓▓▓▓▓▓
with extensive experience and refreshir▓▓▓▓▓▓▓▓▓▓▓
addition to consulting with thousands of families, they have worked
together on several important initiatives. The three helped found
GETA, an international association of therapists who aim to provide
thoughtful treatments for legitimate mental health concerns, without
pushing an ideological or political agenda. In addition, Stella is
the founder of Genspect, an international alliance of professionals,
trans people, detransitioners, parent groups and others who seek a
healthy approach to sex and gender.

'Parents of children who announce a transgender identity often find themselves in a world of confusion and contradiction. These brilliant, clear-eyed authors – all with extensive clinical experience – have written the emergency survival guide for families'

Abigail Shrier, author of *Irreversible Damage: Teenage Girls and the Transgender Craze*

'This compassionate and evidence-based book is an essential counter-balance to the ubiquitous "trans child" narrative that has misled so many loving parents into unwittingly harming their gender-distressed children'

Helen Joyce, author of *Trans*

'There is perhaps no subject today that is more complicated, fraught, and confusing than the sudden rise in gender dysphoria among young people. Parents encountering this issue for the first time will be hit with a tidal wave of conflicting opinions, theories, and "experts" that, however well meaning, are guided by an incoherent and potentially harmful ideology. The book could not have come soon enough. Its authors are leading figures in the effort to bring sense and rationality to the conversation. Moreover, they are experienced clinicians who understand that gender dysphoric youth deserve meaningful psycho-therapeutic treatment, not blind approbation on the internet. For any parent embarking on the gender journey, *When Kids Say They're Trans* should be the first stop along the way'

Meghan Daum, host of *The Unspeakable Podcast* and author of *The Problem with Everything: My Journey Through the New Culture Wars*

WHEN KIDS SAY THEY'RE TRANS

A Guide for Thoughtful Parents

Sasha Ayad, Lisa Marchiano
& Stella O'Malley

Swift

SWIFT PRESS

First published in Great Britain by Swift Press 2023

1 3 5 7 9 8 6 4 2

Typesetting by Tetragon, London
Printed and bound in Great Britain by CPI Group (UK) Ltd, Croydon, CRO 4YY

A CIP catalogue record for this book is available from the British Library

ISBN: 9781800752641
eISBN: 9781800752658

MIX
Paper | Supporting
responsible forestry
FSC
www.fsc.org
FSC® C171272

To every mother and father who loves their child and wonders what their gender distress is really about. And to parents who feel they've had nowhere to go with their worries. This book is for you.

CONTENTS

The one thing parents can do for their children is live their lives as fully as they can, for this will open the children's imagination, grant permission to them to have their own journey, and open the doors of possibility for them.

—JAMES HOLLIS

PREFACE

This is a book for parents, and it is explicitly pro-parent. We are three psychotherapists, two of whom are mothers, who have each consulted with hundreds of parents over the course of our careers. Recently, parents have been getting a remarkably bad rap, especially when it comes to hot-button cultural issues such as gender. We recognise that there are some truly terrible parents in the world. It is difficult to be a therapist and not be aware of this fact, as many come into treatment to deal with childhood experiences that have left them traumatised or struggling. And yet the vast majority of mothers and fathers are good parents who love their children and sincerely want what is best for them. In general, parents or carers know their children better than anyone else – better than doctors, teachers, therapists or sports coaches. Parents also love their children more than anyone else. There is usually no one on the planet who is more invested in seeing their children thrive than them. When something goes wrong in children's lives, it will be their parents who show up and do the potentially painful work of helping them put the pieces back together. When something goes well, no one is more thrilled, happy and proud than the parents. If you are a carer or an extended family member looking after a child, you will also feel highly invested in their well-being and want to guide them to make the right choices, especially if the child has a history of trauma.

When children are small, parents are generally the best authority on their children. Parents have a sense of the child's history, challenges and struggles. As children grow to independence, they will become the experts on themselves, but this takes time, and it is helpful to have scaffolding and guidance from someone who knows them well. When doctors, therapists, schools or other institutions intervene between a child and their parent, the result is usually not optimal, except in extreme (and thankfully unusual) conditions.

The first rule of this book, then, is that parents must trust their own instincts – that deep, inner knowing we often have about a situation. By 'instincts', we distinguish between impulsively reacting to an emotional trigger and taking into account the small, insistent voice that tells us what is right for us. Much of what is being promulgated about kids and gender invites parents to ignore or silence this instinctual knowing. We are told that our female-bodied child is a boy, and that we have never realised it before. We are asked to surrender our authority to others, including strangers on the internet who may be no older than our child. And we are ridiculed or demonised for not abandoning what we know about our child and about reality itself.

You are the world's leading expert on your children, and you likely know more about them than anyone else. You certainly know more about your child than the three of us do! In the following pages, we've gathered advice and information based on the most current research, as well as our own experience with gender-questioning young people and their families. This may not all be a perfect fit for your family or your child. Take what feels right, but don't let anything here supersede your instincts about what you or your child need.

The debate around the social and medical transitioning of children is evolving quickly. New research adds to our knowledge almost weekly. After spending several years working with gender-questioning young people and their families, talking to academics and researchers, and familiarising ourselves with all aspects of the debate, we believe that socially and medically transitioning a child is not advised, given the current knowledge about risks and benefits. As things stand, the medical transition of adolescents is, at best, experimental.

Medical transition damages the body. Taking cross-sex hormones comes with risks both known and unknown. If a natal (biological) female transitions in adolescence or young adulthood, she may be looking at taking testosterone for many decades. Transgender surgeries destroy healthy tissue and biological functioning. Whatever one thinks of cosmetic surgery, and we are certainly concerned about any such surgeries being performed on young people, transgender surgeries – sometimes referred to as 'gender confirmation' surgeries – tend to be more invasive and may render someone sterile or with impaired sexual function. Breast augmentation doesn't usually have such damaging outcomes, although we would recommend extreme caution with regards to a young person undergoing that procedure, as we know adults can come to accept a physical feature that, to their teenage self, was an unacceptable flaw. Justifying invasive medical procedures that permanently harm the body requires proof that benefits outweigh harms. The claim that your child is the opposite sex from the one you know him to be and that he requires life-altering procedures to thrive is not supported by good evidence, much less the extraordinary evidence such a claim demands.

When science can't give clear answers regarding children's health, parental judgement becomes even more important. You deserve to be given all available information about possible treatments and afforded the respect to take your time and make the decision you believe to be right for your family and your child, without fearmongering, threats of dire consequences, or undue influence.

We recognise that some parents of gender dysphoric children and adolescents will decide that undertaking social and medical transition is the best option. This book might be helpful to you as you are considering your options and trying to decide which course to take. Fair warning: the evidence in this book will generally steer you away from transitioning your child. If you do decide to pursue your child's transition, this book won't be likely to help you much. There have been many books written for parents who are facilitating a child's gender transition, but there are few if any books for parents who decide that social and/or medical transition is not the best option for their child. Many who have taken this approach have been vilified in the media and online. They have been told their children will become suicidal. There have been few places where they could find support.

This book aims to redress this balance. It is explicitly a resource for parents who want their children to flourish but who do not believe hasty medicalisation is the best way to ensure their health and well-being. It is a book for parents who would like to support their child's exploration of identity but who do not believe it is advisable to concretise such exploration with irreversible drugs and surgeries. It is a guide for parents who affirm their child's wonderful, unique personhood without believing 'gender identity' should be privileged over other aspects.

There are holiday clubs, summer schools, organisations, workbooks, Facebook pages and clinics for parents who want to affirm a child's chosen gender. If you want the help of a professional to assist in socially or medically transitioning your child, you will have your pick. If, however, you would like to slow down a child's rush to engage in life-altering medical procedures or to ensure a child has engaged in a thorough process first, you may find professional help in short supply. Every day, the three of us are contacted by desperate parents seeking therapists who will help a child to examine all potential outcomes of such a decision.

But helping your child to learn about themselves is not a job you can outsource to professionals. Parents who have successfully helped their children navigate gender distress without resorting to surgery and hormones have done so by authoritatively taking the reins, not waiting until they found the right therapist or doctor. You can do this. You are the person most invested in your child's flourishing. You have the widest perspective on his or her future and past. Because there aren't a lot of resources *now*, you will have to become your own expert. This book will help you do that.

In the chapters that follow, we'll explore gender identity, also referred to as 'gender'. How do we understand the increased interest in this subject in recent years, and how is this affecting children and young people? We'll look at what is currently known about interventions for gender dysphoria (a discomfort with the sexed body) and offer advice on how to navigate these choices.

We'll consider the impact that having a gender-questioning child has on a long-term partnership or on your relationship with your ex-partner, on siblings, on friendships, and on the extended family. We'll explore best strategies for parenting and look at all the potential outcomes. Finally, we'll offer suggestions for how to weather the storm.

We've also included a resource list at the back of this book where you can learn how to find more information.

The three of us each have unique stories that brought us into this world of gender, and we have a lot of experience of working with parents. Since 2021 our organisation, Wider Lens Consulting, has offered in-person retreats for parents of trans-identifying children where we help them replenish their energy, bear witness to their experiences and offer them practical help with managing their child's gender issues. Our work with parents has afforded us valuable insights into the experience of parenting a trans-identified child.

Stella is an Irish psychotherapist who had her own intense experience with gender as a child, and the resolution of her gender distress has made her curious about the wisdom of early intervention. She was the presenter of Channel 4's documentary on the topic, *Trans Kids: It's Time to Talk* (2018). In addition to facilitating a parent coaching site that provides practical help to parents who are navigating their child's gender-related distress, Stella is the director of Genspect, an international organisation that offers a healthy approach to sex and gender.

Lisa is a US-based psychotherapist and Jungian analyst. Noticing parallels between gender exploration and other social phenomena, Lisa began investigating what might be contributing to the rising number of trans-identified teens. In her private practice, she has worked with dozens of parents of trans-identified young people and has also worked with clients who were detransitioning and regretting their medical gender interventions.

While working as a school counsellor, Sasha started her school's first GSA (gay–straight alliance) to create a safe space for LGBT kids to discuss their evolving sense of identity and sexual orientation. She noted that, in some cases, gender dysphoria emerged after young people adopted a trans identity, rather than the other way around – especially following heavy social media and internet use. She began her private practice in 2016, which has been exclusively dedicated to gender identity concerns ever since. Sasha also runs a robust online membership group to help parents navigate their child's identity exploration with discernment, wisdom, and compassion.

The three of us have counselled hundreds of families, dozens of gender-questioning young people, and numerous detransitioners. We offer a compassionate, evidence-based approach to parenting a gender-questioning child. This approach draws upon the most up-to-date research and also relies on age-old wisdom about what it means to be human.

A word about language: we don't believe there is such a thing as a 'trans child'. There is no evidence that children can be born in the wrong body, or that some children are born with an innate gender which is misaligned with their sex. We do know there are some children who suffer from gender dysphoria, and we recognise that medical interventions are offered in the belief that these will alleviate their distress. Nevertheless, it is not possible to change sex. Because we do not believe there is a separate category of people who are innately transgender, we use sex-based pronouns. We refer to children's sex and not their gender identity, and we do not use terms such as 'trans boy', preferring the accurate term 'trans-identified female'. We note that the term 'trans children' is not used in the Cass Review, the NHS's commissioned report on gender services for children in the UK: 'Some children and young people will remain fluid in their gender identity up to their early to mid twenties, so there is a limit as to how much certainty one can achieve in late teens.'[1] Many young people identify as non-binary, gender-fluid or something else other than 'transboy' or 'transgirl'. We use the word 'trans' to cover any and all gender identities.

Some people thrive after transitioning. We passionately believe trans-identified people deserve rights, protection, compassion and dignity. Nonetheless, we believe such a drastic intervention should only be considered by adults whose brains have reached emotional maturity. Furthermore, comorbidities (pre-existing mental health conditions) and any history of trauma should be taken into account when helping people discern whether medical transition will be right for them. Being human is an extraordinarily complicated affair, and we celebrate the myriad, creative adaptations people make to live as fully as they can. Like any intervention, however, transition may solve some problems and create new ones. Anyone considering such consequential procedures deserves a neutral space in which to consider all aspects of such a decision and access to solid information about possible risks and benefits.

Through our work, we have all become close to trans adults. Their wisdom informs our practice, and we are grateful for it. Many trans adults have joined with us in expressing alarm about the rapid medicalisation of children and young people. They have added their voices to the growing chorus of individuals from all walks of life and all parts of the political spectrum who champion children and young people in their wholeness and complexity rather than reducing them to a constricting, medicalised notion of gender. Their support has enriched our understanding of this issue, helping us to bring important insights to you.

This book celebrates parental love as a power that creates the foundation children need to move out into the world. Eventually, you must let your children find their own way and make their own mistakes, but as they grow to maturity, you are best suited to be their guides and support.

1

IS MY CHILD TRANS?

'It came in like a rocket,' said Jason, father of fourteen-year-old Clara. 'One day she was a quirky kid, a little lonely, mad about anime, without any signs of gender issues, and the next day she was in tears, declaring that she was a boy, had always been a boy, and needed hormone treatment as soon as possible. It was the most bewildering moment of my life. If Clara really is trans we will support her all the way, but how can we know if this is truly who she is?'

These days, this is how it often happens: gender-related distress among teenagers arrives seemingly out of the blue, with few warning signs, and parents typically respond with a sense of shock and astonishment and an intense determination to seek out the best possible options for their child. The problem is that when a child comes out as trans, the emotional fallout can be considerable on everyone. In today's heightened political atmosphere, gender issues have become so controversial that it can be very difficult for parents to ascertain the most suitable response.

The number of teens and young people medically transitioning has exploded across the Western world in the past decade. It is coming to light that clinicians have been providing these medical interventions without sufficient evidence that they are helpful or necessary.[1] It appears that large numbers of young people, many of whom are gay, lesbian, bisexual, autistic or suffering from complex mental health issues, are being harmed. This is an unfolding medical scandal of unknown proportions. If you are reading this book, we assume your family has been caught up in this powerful cultural juggernaut.

WHAT DOES TRANS MEAN?

As psychotherapists working with gender-related distress, we are frequently asked by parents whether we believe their child is 'truly trans'. Hidden in this question is an implicit assumption that we subscribe to gender identity theory: the belief that some people have an unknowable, unfalsifiable, inner essence that makes them 'trans' and which may require the person to transition before they can be happy (see more on this in Appendix 1: What Is Gender?). We don't view gender dysphoria in this way; instead, we have a developmental understanding of this phenomenon. There are a wide variety of reasons for a person to develop gender-related distress, and likewise there are many ways this distress can be alleviated. We see medical transition as a life strategy that comes with certain costs. The decision to medically transition is an attempt to adapt – whether it is the best strategy available is open to debate, and will differ from person to person.

Parents often find the terminology involved in gender issues confusing, and it can be valuable to learn the various terms so this doesn't become an impediment to connecting with your child. While our 'sex' represents our natal bodies, our sense of 'gender identity' describes the range of characteristics pertaining to femininity and masculinity that a person might experience. To further complicate matters, the concept of gender identity also encompasses those who feel they operate outside the binary of feminine and masculine. Readers who would like to know more can refer to the Glossary at the back of the book. The six Appendices also clarify key concepts, co-occurring mental health conditions, and terminology.

Assumptions that everyone has a gender identity and that gender is an innate quality are new and unevidenced theories that often ignore other factors that may be contributing to a person's gender dysphoria. Some believe that once a child has a clinical diagnosis of gender dysphoria there is no other option but to medically transition, but this doesn't follow. Studies show that most kids grow out of it: gender dysphoria is resolved naturally during puberty or early adulthood for roughly 80% of children.[2] We have worked with many clients who have moved beyond gender dysphoria, and as mentioned earlier, one of us suffered from it in childhood. Some found therapy helped with an acceptance of their body and their place in the world. Others found that an absorbing interest in other aspects of life reduced and eventually eliminated their dysphoria: deeper friendships and loving relationships are often mentioned. Many people who have medically transitioned are happy they have done so, but others regret it and seek to reverse the process by detransitioning (see Glossary for definitions). Some people learn to live with their gender dysphoria, like millions of people with other conditions, and use different strategies to regulate their emotions so they can live a fulfilling life.

It is highly questionable that a person needs lifelong medication (which is what medical transitioning entails) to be their 'true self'. Many trans-identified young people focus on concepts such as 'my true self' and 'let me be who I really am' and 'I was born in the wrong body.' But none of us have been 'born in the wrong body'– we are born in and as our bodies; there are no alternatives. We die when our bodies die, and what happens after that is up for debate. There is no evidence to suggest we had other bodies to choose from.

Moreover, who is your true self? Is it the person you were at sixteen? Or thirty-five? There is little consensus. The English psychoanalyst Donald Winnicott used the term 'true self' to describe the authentic self: our 'false self' is created as a defensive facade, which can lead to the individual feeling dead and empty inside.[3] Meanwhile, the American psychologist Carl Rogers focused on the 'real self' (that embodies the individual's true qualities) and the 'ideal self' (the characteristics they aspire to have): the gap between our real and ideal selves is where our conflict lies. It is worthwhile for you and your children to know about these theories, as they offer rich opportunities to explore the nature of the self. You may be able to use these ideas to spark conversations with your child that can open up a deeper understanding. Plenty of gender-distressed individuals benefit from a psychological and philosophical analysis of human nature, the conscious and unconscious mind, and the options available to tackle any distress. No matter how intense the suffering, a thoughtful and compassionate exploration of who we are and who we want to be is often valuable.

So, is your child trans? If you mean does your child have an innate, untestable, inner quality that requires him or her to undergo social or medical transition to survive and thrive, the answer, we believe, is no. On the other hand, your child's gender-related distress is likely real and acutely felt. Your child may well meet the criteria for a diagnosis of gender dysphoria. But what exactly does this mean?

WHAT IS GENDER DYSPHORIA?

There is a difference between clinically diagnosed gender dysphoria and being trans. The word 'trans' is employed as an umbrella term to describe people whose gender identity is not the same as, or does not sit comfortably with, their biological sex. Being 'trans' is not a diagnosis, and anybody can identify as trans, whereas gender dysphoria is a diagnosable mental health condition. But nothing about this topic is simple, and different organisations take different positions. Essentially, in layperson's terms, gender dysphoria is the distress related to being uncomfortable with one's body and/or the associated stereotypical roles associated with one's sex.

Gender dysphoria is not just one thing. Why a person develops gender dysphoria is the subject of a lot of debate. For example, the experience and presentation of gender dysphoria will look different in a middle-aged heterosexual natal male and an adolescent same-sex-attracted natal female, or between a small boy who loves to flounce in dresses and a teen girl with multiple mental health problems and a diagnosis of autism.

The condition will likely look different in different populations. We've included more information in the appendices about how gender dysphoria is conceptualised in different ways, as well as how our understanding of this condition has evolved in recent years. For now, it's important to note that there are many theories related to 'gender' as a concept, and that the criteria used to diagnose gender dysphoria rely on outdated sexist stereotypes.

Some hold that all people have an innate sense of gender which may or may not be the same as their biological sex. This innate gender identity is said to be the origin of gender dysphoria, or a trans identification, when it doesn't correspond with biological sex. However, there isn't any robust evidence that all people are born with an innate gender identity. We believe gender dysphoria is the result of a complex interplay of biological, psychological and social factors, and its causes, manifestations and effects vary considerably from one sufferer to the next. People who hold this developmental understanding of gender dysphoria tend to view identity exploration as an important stage that unfolds during adolescence and needs to be tackled if the person is to become a fully functioning mature adult.

When Chloe suddenly identified as trans at fifteen, never before having shown any signs of gender-nonconformity, her parents were worried she had landed on the wrong solution. So they decided to slowly but surely speak about different aspects of their nationality, race, religion, sexual orientation, social class, thoughts, beliefs and experiences in a bid to show Chloe the significant impact these can have on identity. Chloe was mixed-race and had never before given much consideration to this part of her persona – and an online test that traced her DNA to India and Brazil widened her perspective on her sense of self and reduced the obsession and distress over gender.

IS MY PREPUBERTAL CHILD TRANSGENDER?

Prior to the recent explosion in teens coming out as trans, gender dysphoria showed up most often in two groups – middle-aged natal males, and young, prepubertal children, especially natal boys. There has always been a small cohort of children – Stella was among this group – who strongly reject their biological sex when they are very young. As with other age groups, gender dysphoria in young children can be influenced by biological, social and psychological factors.

When a child has childhood-onset gender dysphoria, the whole street knows about it. This typically emerges between three and seven, when the child has come to realise that society has gendered expectations but before they have become overly self-conscious. Children this age often engage in magical thinking, and so it is relatively easy for them to believe they are the opposite sex. Their ability to take on the role of the opposite sex can be impressively insistent, consistent and persistent, and yet tends to rely upon outdated stereotypes. The strength of personality in many of these children can be a defining reason why some parents take it so seriously.

We believe gender-nonconforming children would feel much happier if they were allowed to wear whatever they pleased, and play with whatever took their fancy. We look forward to the day when a boy can dance around in a princess dress without being commented upon. Sadly, these days boys in fairy dresses and girls with short hair are often asked their pronouns by well-meaning adults who expect them to identify as a 'trans kid'. It's hard to be a gender-nonconforming child today, perhaps even harder than in previous generations. In a world where we are increasingly focused upon diagnoses, categories and frameworks, many find it difficult to remain ambivalent – the adults often seek to label a child as 'trans' or 'gay', but this might not suit a little boy who just wants to have a tea party wearing a princess crown. The world of make-believe can feel to children like a sacred space where they get the chance to expand their consciousness to the outer limits. Heavy-handed adults coming in with their grown-up perspectives can break the spell.

We believe it is inappropriate to ask children to state their pronouns or how they identify. As mentioned above, various studies have found that roughly 80% of these children outgrow their gender dysphoria by the time they are adults. Not only that, but a large majority of them end up being same-sex-attracted.[4] Although puberty can be challenging, it can bring about a reckoning and a sexual awakening in the gender dysphoric individual, and this can lead them to a place of self-acceptance.

Some children, though, continue to feel profoundly self-conscious about their gender-nonconformity. Many experience mental pain because they are not the sex they want to be. If this is severe, parents might seek professional help. But given that the diagnosis of gender dysphoria relies upon regressive stereotypes (see Appendix 3), it might be more useful to bring gender-nonconforming role models into our children's lives, rather than seeking professional help for what is often a societal problem. This way, they can learn there is no right way to be a boy or girl. Parents of young children could introduce their child to figures from history and literature – for example Joan of Arc, Grace O'Malley, George in *The Famous Five*, Jo Marsh in *Little Women*, Pippi Longstocking and David Walliams' *The Boy in the Dress* all offer different ways to expand our understanding of gender roles. Some of these stories are over a hundred years old and yet feel more liberated than much of the content offered to girls today. On the other hand, the stark lack of representation of feminine boys in literature, notwithstanding more recent trends, suggests how deeply entrenched gendered expectations have been for young boys.

Parents can help by providing children with ways to answer adults who seek to impose categories on their identity. Answers to 'What are your pronouns?' can be sassy, such as 'I don't do pronouns, I'm still a kid,' or more formal: 'No thank you, I don't feel the need to label myself.' Whatever way the child prefers to handle this should be considered, but it is the parent's role to ensure their child doesn't become exhausted by constant questions about their identity, so a friendly word in the ear of adults before events such as summer camp can be valuable.

Parenting gender-nonconforming children in the age of trans kids

Lisa Selin Davis, author of Tomboy: The Surprising History and Future of Girls Who Dare to Be Different

My daughter was three when she first asked to wear a tie and a button-down shirt. This was not her father's daily uniform – he went to work in frayed jeans and a T-shirt – nor mine. But somewhere she'd gotten the idea that this was how she wanted to dress, and we consented. My mother gave her a dapper hat. My stepmother gave her my little brother's old blazer. She emerged as the nattiest dresser in preschool, one who mostly played with boys.

Then she asked for the same kind of short haircut that her male preschool friend had. To be honest, we were, by this point, a little confused, and even a little bit worried. Though I had been reared in the 1970s and 80s on the gender stereotype-busting record *Free to Be You and Me*, and myself wore short hair and unisex clothes as a kid in the golden era of the tomboy, there seemed to be no other girls like my daughter anywhere around us. I didn't understand what was happening, or why she was so different, or what we were supposed to do.

Neither, I realised after many years of research into the science, psychology and history of gender-nonconformity, did anyone else. This was before the debut of Jazz Jennings, before the cultural battles over what to teach kids about gender in schools, or whether and how to medicate gender dysphoria, before children were asked to name their pronouns in school – or before schools hid pronoun changes from parents. Our doctor was fascinated, always asking our daughter if she felt like a girl or a boy. The parent coordinator at school asked if she wanted to change in the boys' locker room. She was seven years old by then.

I did not know then that they were asking if my daughter wanted to socially transition; that wasn't part of my vocabulary yet, not part of the cultural lexicon. Their offers struck my husband and I as kind, but also as strange. Why were they assuming that a short-haired kid who played baseball and wore sweatpants wanted to disavow her sex? We had several butch lesbians in our family. My daughter had models of female masculinity. She wasn't unhappy or uncomfortable. But it was incredibly difficult to navigate a world that seemed to have absolutely no understanding of a girl who was more like a typical boy. No one had advice.

A decade has passed since then, and in that time so much has changed – including the word transgender, which has expanded to include young kids with no gender dysphoria but who don't hew to the gender norms and stereotypes associated with their sex. Sometimes parents of these kids write to me. They tell me their daughter wants short hair and trucks and to wear boys' clothes, or their son likes dresses and dolls and nail polish. They want to know what is happening, or why their kid is so different, or what they should do.

So here's what I tell them – and what I wish people had told me ten years ago.

First, we have to insulate them against the messages that their sex will or should determine their interests. They will learn early and often by cultural osmosis that pink – and kindness, sensitivity, dolls – is for girls and blue – and sports, exuberance, anger – is for boys. We have to remind them they need not limit themselves in what they explore or cotton on to because of what kind of body they have. Clothes, toys, colours and nail polish have no sex. We don't have to reinforce and play by our society's rules about what's for boys and what's for girls.

We also have to accept and facilitate our kids' nonconformity, allowing them to present as they please, and not shame them for their natural proclivities – while keeping them rooted in the reality of biological sex. It takes about eight years for kids to understand gender constancy, that their body is what makes them a boy or a girl, not what they like to wear or do or play with. Before that, they don't always understand the difference between sex and sex stereotypes. If we keep talking about those differences, that will normalise their non-adherence to stereotypes. We can also make sure they have models of gender-nonconformity, of feminine boys and masculine girls, even though you might have to watch old Jodie Foster movies to locate them.

The other thing we have to do is fortify our children to navigate a world that doesn't understand them. Though many feel the current gender revolution makes room for gender-nonconforming kids, I'd argue it actually pathologises them. Telling a stereotypically boyish girl that she can be or is a boy doesn't allow an ambiguous space for her to occupy. Telling a feminine boy that his mannerisms and tendencies make him a girl, or affirming his fantasy that he is one, tells him he's doing boy wrong, that there's no room for him in the category he naturally, biologically belongs to. I think this not only creates more shame, but can lead to very serious medical interventions.

Other than that, I don't think there's anything we have to *do* when our kids present as gender-nonconforming. Many parents want to know what their child's gender-nonconformity signifies, if they have a child who is trans, or a child who will be gay later. They're eager to slap a label on. I get it. I was very confused when my child acted so differently to all the other girls we knew, and so were all the professionals around us. But there is no way to forecast the future from a child's gender atypicality. Gender-nonconformity in children is not predictive of any one outcome.

When we practise being comfortable with ambiguity, when we don't immediately make meaning out of their gender, we leave room for exploration, for growing understanding, for shifts and changes, for a child to become a person. And then we can absorb the miracle of children like this: children so secure in themselves that they march against the grain, no matter how it unsettles the adults around them. All they needed to say was, 'Congratulations on having a kid who is immune to stereotypes! Let's check in down the line and see what happens.'

There's research showing that the more a child rejects strict gender roles, the better they do academically and in other areas of life.[5] Many women who were serious tomboys got better jobs later, because their comfort with men and masculinity allowed them to pursue male-dominated fields.[6]

Gender-nonconformity is a gift. If your child is this way, you don't need to fix them. Let's try to make room for them, and in the meantime, let's make them resilient with our love and understanding. They are perfect just as they are.

IS MY TEEN OR YOUNG ADULT TRANSGENDER?

Beginning around 2006, psychologists and researchers at gender clinics around the world started to notice an unusual pattern – more and more teens were beginning to complain of gender dysphoria and seeking out medical interventions to help them transition – and most of them were female.[7] This was a significant change from previous decades, when most people with gender dysphoria were either young boys or middle-aged men. Nowadays, gender dysphoria among teens is common. Does this mean they are all trans? Once again, we note that 'being trans' suggests a belief in an innate gendered essence. There is no evidence base showing that teens who identify as trans have an essence which makes them inherently different from their peers and requires medical intervention. As with prepubertal children, the complex forces at work can shape a teen's experience of mental suffering, and gender-related distress in teens can be influenced by biological, psychological and social factors.

Biological factors

Some people think gender dysphoria is a result of some sort of physical condition – for example an influx of hormones during pregnancy could theoretically lead the foetus to having had exposure to more testosterone (or oestrogen), which could eventually lead the individual to feel more or less feminine or masculine. Although some studies using brain imaging scans showed that the brains of transwomen were shifted towards their gender identity, these studies typically don't factor in sexual orientation – gay men also have brains that are shifted towards being more female.[8] Our brains are malleable – some women are masculine and some men are feminine – and if we could expand our understanding of how males and females 'should' act, then perhaps many people would feel more liberated to behave as they please.

We have noted in our work that polycystic ovary syndrome (PCOS), a condition which can cause irregular menstrual periods, excess hair growth, acne, infertility, weight gain and other issues, can contribute to a young person's trans identification. Girls with PCOS may not ovulate and may have high levels of androgens, usually thought of as male hormones. Other medical conditions, such as the very rare differences of sexual development (DSDs), may play a role in some young people developing gender dysphoria. As with all things related to gender, there is little research and a lot of theory.

Disorders such as anorexia or body dysmorphic disorder (BDD) tend to be somewhat heritable, suggesting that there may be a genetic component to them. Both eating disorders and BDD appear to overlap with gender dysphoria, making it plausible that individuals may have a genetic predisposition to develop gender-related distress. BDD can sometimes masquerade as gender dysphoria. Body dysmorphia is a mental health condition where the individual spends an inordinate amount of time worrying about perceived or real flaws in their appearance.[9] Anyone can develop this condition, but it is more common among teenagers and young adults. Many parents report how their teenage daughter has come to despise her breasts and seek to flatten them using a binder. Equally, teenage boys might become obsessed with their body hair and spend hours removing all trace of it. Many parents report that their child has identified as trans but appears to be experiencing BDD. You can help with this by reading about BDD, so you understand what might be going on for your child. We offer more information on conditions that are commonly linked with gender dysphoria in Appendix 6.

Psychological factors

Gender dysphoria can give expression to various kinds of psychological distress. These days, it often arises at the beginning of adolescence, which can be a difficult time for many. Childhood is usually filled with magic and make-believe. Then, somewhere around the age of twelve or thirteen, many teens are faced with the brick wall of reality. No longer are they in a world where the good guy always wins. High school is not the fun place promised in the movies – it can be joyless and often brutal. Many teenagers we work with can feel deeply disappointed by their adolescence, and it can tip them into an even deeper realisation that life can often be difficult, unfair and lonely. For many young people, there are no sleepovers filled with warm heart-to-hearts with their peers, no great romances. If your child is neurodiverse or has any additional challenges, the support can fall off a cliff at around this time – it's suddenly deeply uncool to be receiving extra help, and many teens shun it. The schoolwork tends to go up a gear, and extracurricular activities typically become more focused and competitive during early adolescence.

Loneliness, anxiety, depression and other mental health concerns can emerge or worsen at this time, leaving a child susceptible to also developing gender dysphoria. Obsessive–compulsive disorder (OCD), attention deficit hyperactivity disorder (ADHD), depression, anxiety, eating disorders and other conditions appear to make teens more vulnerable to developing gender dysphoria or understanding themselves as transgender. Gender-related distress may emerge as a result of trauma, and the young person may find gender dysphoria to be an effective unconscious defence against further vulnerability. For example, a girl who has been abused might want to become a boy to be able to fight off further aggression.

Neurodivergent kids can find gender a welcome explanation for their experiences of difference. While intense fixation, fantasy and rigidity are developmentally normal for most adolescents, they are even more pronounced for children with autism spectrum traits, from childhood through adolescence. Your autistic daughter may have very concrete ideas about being perceived as male, despite your attempts to inform her about biological reality. Your son may have constructed an elaborate fantasy of how happy he will be when he is 'seen as a woman', while in practice his poor hygiene and masculine appearance couldn't make him any *less* feminine-looking. Why the disconnect? Autistic teens have greater difficulty not only in reading the perspective of others, but in imagining how his or her own perspective may change in the future. They also tend to fixate obsessively on their passions, and if gender transition has captured your teen's attention, you may find it extremely difficult to broaden his or her interests.

Young people may find that a trans identity offers a sense of belonging or an acceptable explanation for experiences of difference of all kinds. It appears that gifted kids are adopting trans identities at disproportionately higher rates. In her 2018 paper that first described rapid onset gender dysphoria, Lisa Littman found that almost half of the young people described in the sample had been formally identified as academically gifted.[10] This could be in part because these kids are deep thinkers, but being very smart can lead one to feel out of step with one's peers, and so gifted kids can struggle socially. Identifying as trans may offer a comforting and much-needed tribe of other quirky, misfit kids that is also socially valorised in many schools.

A trans identity can do other heavy psychological lifting as well, giving voice to unconscious conflicts with parents and providing a way to separate from them psychologically. During adolescence, individuating from parents is a key task as we begin to sort out who we are and how we are different from our families. Some kids recruit a trans identity to help them with this task.

Social factors

The extraordinary rise in the number of teens identifying as trans in the last decade has not happened in a cultural vacuum. A perfect storm of social phenomena has occurred, a confluence of apparently random events: the arrival of social media (YouTube and Reddit came into being in 2005, Twitter in 2006, Tumblr in 2007, Instagram in 2010, Discord in 2015 and TikTok in 2016); a rise in the popularity of identity politics and a corresponding surge in social justice activism; 'diagnosis creep' (widening definitions of disease so that more people are diagnosed) and the tendency to self-diagnose via the internet. This confluence of events has resulted in an unexpected consequence: thousands of young people across the world have suddenly and intensely come to believe they need to medically transition into a different person. In Appendix 2, we have included some more information on social and cultural movements that influence many young people.

The conflation of sexual orientation with gender identity

Same-sex-attracted adolescents may experience gender dysphoria as they come to terms with their sexual orientation. Many detransitioners have stated that they experienced shame and discomfort as they grew into an awareness of their sexual orientation, and that this is part of what fuelled their desire to transition. Internalised homophobia seems to be a significant contributor to the growth of teens identifying as trans.[11] We have included a fuller discussion of this important subject in Chapter 3.

RAISING A GENDER-NONCONFORMING CHILD IN THE TWENTY-FIRST CENTURY

Not all gender-questioning kids are gender-nonconforming. Many trans-identifying teens have no significant history of early gender variance or distress. However, some kids who identify as trans have struggled to fit themselves to society's gendered norms. For these kids, navigating distress can be especially complicated. Despite the emphasis on gender identity, sexual orientation, inclusivity, diversity, Pride marches and flag-waving, it seems to be more difficult to be a gender-nonconforming child today than it has been for decades. Although, as mentioned earlier in this chapter, current research suggests that the vast majority of children with childhood gender dysphoria outgrow the condition by early adulthood, these studies were mostly carried out prior to the conception of social transition and/or the widespread use of puberty blockers. This generation is the first to be offered the option of social transition in the early years and medical intervention at puberty, and nobody knows the long-term outcomes. Puberty blockers are experimental and have never been tested for large-scale use on children with gender dysphoria. Little is known about the long-term side effects, such as whether or how much hormone blockers can affect the development of the teenage brain or children's bones.[12]

While books, films and other media can be helpful to introduce gender-nonconforming figures, introducing real-life role models is also very important. Becoming familiar with cultures whose perspectives on gender are different – for example the fa'afafine in Samoa or the muxe in Mexico – can further broaden your child's perspective. Learning about places where a third gender has been introduced apparently as a way to cope with homosexuality in patriarchal societies could lead to thought-provoking conversations between parents and children. The general idea would be to bring about a deeper awareness of how society can have an impact on our behaviour.

Although many gender-nonconforming children in previous generations felt lonely and isolated, these kids today seem to be more confused and anxious. Gender-nonconforming young people often report feeling a sense of relief that they finally have a clear path before them when they identify as trans, and in many schools and colleges announcing a trans identity can elevate a child's social status. Teenagers have always had a greater sense of invincibility, one which is often responsible for impulsive decisions and poor risk assessments. The older we get, the more risk-averse we tend to become. It is the role of teenagers to push against boundaries, but it is the role of parents to maintain boundaries in their children's lives.

TREATMENTS FOR GENDER-RELATED DISTRESS

As we have seen, whether we are discussing young children or teens, it is unlikely that their gender-related distress can be attributed to a single, simple explanation. Instead, a complex interplay of factors goes into shaping each person's experience. Gender-related distress manifests a little differently for each person who develops it. An individualised method of treating such distress therefore makes the most sense. Unfortunately, in the last decade or so, a single one-size-fits-all approach to treating it has taken hold.

The affirmative approach to treating children and youth with gender dysphoria was developed in the first part of the century and has since become widespread. It rests on the assumption that children who announce a trans identity have an innate gender identity which is at odds with their biological sex. From this premise comes the conclusion that the most compassionate and effective way to respond is to affirm this child's stated gender and offer support for them to socially and/ or medically transition. If people had an innate, unchangeable gendered essence that could be at odds with their biology, early medical transition would likely make sense. However, as we have seen, there is no evidence that this is the case.

Affirmation is a relatively new approach, without a lot of solid evidence to back it. Gender dysphoria in children was not treated according to the affirmative approach in the past; clinicians usually recommended 'watchful waiting', that is, monitoring a child's gender issues without intervening. We explore this approach further in Appendix 4. The affirmative approach doesn't accord well with treatments for any other mental health issue – therapists don't usually simply agree with a patient's self-diagnosis and green-light whatever treatments the patient wishes. According to the affirmative approach, not only therapists are meant to affirm; everyone in the child's life is meant to validate and even celebrate the child's perception that she is a boy. This includes teachers, friends, family – and parents.

Some affirmative clinicians take their time and assess a young person thoroughly. They may take several sessions and consider factors such as social influence and comorbid conditions in their assessment. In our experience, though, these more careful clinicians are in the minority. In any case, the paradigm of the affirmative model is that some kids are 'truly trans'. We believe this is the wrong framework. We all tell ourselves stories to help us make sense of our distress. Sometimes these stories allow us to find constructive or neutral responses to our distress, and sometimes they lead us to choose destructive ways of coping with it. We believe it is better to address the causes of the distress rather than its symptoms.

A growing body of research has not yet identified the most effective treatments for gender-related distress. Though many studies tout the efficacy of social and medical transition for children and young people with gender dysphoria, lots of these have significant methodological limitations that make it difficult to place much confidence in their conclusions. Social transition appears to set kids on a path to medical intervention, and medical intervention can have significant health consequences. Anecdotally, we often see the mental health of young people who have transitioned getting worse instead of better.

Conventional psychotherapy, on the other hand, has an established history of assisting people in finding lasting solutions to handling their distress. Since the three of us are psychotherapists, it is probably not surprising that we favour therapy as a first-line treatment for gender-related distress. Psychotherapy is an exploratory process that facilitates deeper self-understanding, and the gender-affirmative approach, with its narrow-minded focus upon gender, can deprive individuals of sufficient psychological care. Clinicians who advocate gender-affirming treatment sometimes equate psychotherapeutic approaches with conversion practices. On the other hand, others argue that gender-affirmative therapy is a form of conversion therapy, as an individual who is experiencing internalised homophobia could seek to 'trans away the gay'; a butch lesbian might end up medically transitioning to become a boy who is attracted to girls. This accusation is rooted in the fact that a disproportionate number of gender dysphoric children are same-sex-attracted.[13] We have met enough adolescents with internalised homophobia to know that this is a real issue and must not be discounted.

We have more information about treatment approaches to gender dysphoria in Appendix 4, and we encourage you to familiarise yourself with this material. You need to be aware that many therapists are providing treatment according to the affirmative model, which could foreclose exploration and lead a young person to a medicalised pathway without careful assessment and time for open-ended questioning. If this is the only option available to you, you may be more effective at helping your child through this experience yourself rather than going to a therapist.

So, is your child trans? As you probably realise by now, we don't think that's the right question. Your child may be experiencing utterly real, painful distress. He or she needs your love, support and understanding. But how we conceptualise psychological suffering varies dramatically depending on the lens we bring to the situation. How we understand someone's distress often determines how we respond to it, and responding with medical intervention carries significant risks. We prefer to look at a child's gender distress through a psychological lens that considers the whole person. Through compassionate connection, loving engagement and a holistic, depth-oriented understanding, we believe that parents can support their children's healthy growth and development.

2

SOCIAL CONTAGION AND
RAPID ONSET GENDER DYSPHORIA (ROGD)

During lockdown, thirteen-year-old Becky was allowed free access to her devices – there was little else to do and so she immersed herself in the digital world. Puberty had brought difficult changes, and Becky started to hate her body. Online meanderings led her to take a quiz touted as 'simple and accurate' to find out if she was trans. After answering questions such as 'Do you feel comfortable in your own body?' and 'What is your first memory of learning about gender?', the results declared 'Congratulations, you're trans!' This made Becky feel both thrilled and scared. Finally there was an answer to all her inner turmoil. Naturally risk-averse, she felt worried and intimidated by the road before her, but the knowledge that she was 'truly trans' gave her confidence and courage.

Becky continued to read about LGBTQ+ issues and came to believe that she only needed to transition to feel comfortable in her own body. Internet sources suggested that her parents wouldn't be happy about this and so she began a secret, online life which offered a community of other distressed people who seemed to be feeling just as she did. Most parents wish to only do what is best for their beloved kids, and had Becky confided in her parents she would probably have received a good deal of love and support. But by the time kids like Becky come out as trans to their parents, they have often been led to believe two things: that they have an innate gender identity within them, and that their parents could well be resistant. Parents, on the other hand, are generally blindsided by this unexpected swerve into gender issues and race frantically to catch up with their child while desperately trying to figure out whether their child could be trans.

Often parents have assimilated gender identity theory without thinking about it much, and so they assume 'being trans' is an innate condition affecting a small number of people. They tend to believe this is unlikely to be their child, as the announcement feels bizarre and incongruous. Their children perceive this as transphobia. To complicate matters further, parents often believe their child has been unduly shaped by online influences; their child often reacts with bitter fury, as if this somehow degrades the purity of their trans self.

Social contagion is a concept that social scientists have observed and discussed for over a hundred years. It refers to the spread of ideas, behaviours, emotions and beliefs among networks. Our modern idiom, 'going viral', recognises the potential for the contagion-like spread of ideas. As humans, we have an innate susceptibility to being influenced by those to whom we are connected. Research on social media shows that interpersonal influence can spread happiness, divorce, weight gain, smoking, bulimia, political engagement, cooperation, climate change action, suicidality, depression, and any other number of 'conditions'.[1] Social scientists have recently become concerned about the potential for mental health concerns to spread via social media, particularly among young people. It appears plausible that online networks could help disseminate symptoms and an accompanying belief system about these symptoms that would result in an internet-mediated mass sociogenic illness. 'Mass sociogenic illness' refers to the spread of disease-like symptoms where no infectious agent exists.

A fascinating example was recently chronicled by researchers in Germany, who noticed a spike in the number of young people presenting to Tourette's clinics with functional tic-like behaviours. Many of these young people had a novel presentation of Tourette's syndrome. They were mostly teen girls, when Tourette's most often affects young boys. Many of the young people presenting to the German clinic had the same tics. These turned out to be tics manifested by popular TikTok influencers who claimed to have Tourette's and frequently exhibited their tics on their social media.[2]

SOCIAL CONTAGION AMONG PREPUBERTAL CHILDREN

There has always been a small cohort of young children who, from a very young age, typically three or four, resist their own biological sex and gravitate instead towards the stereotypical play, clothes and behaviour of the opposite sex. Historically society has smiled upon tomboys, and although some strict adults might have admonished them, there tended to be some level of acceptance. Feminine boys, however, have had a difficult time of it – evidenced by the fact that there is no socially acceptable term to describe these boys. Previous generations of feminine boys and masculine girls were typically left to their own devices. They usually went through a difficult puberty, and many emerged to be same-sex-attracted adults. These days, however, these gender-nonconforming children often become acquainted with the internet during their difficult puberty. Their typical interests often lead them into trans-affirmative platforms which encourage them to believe they are trans. Gender-nonconforming children are more vulnerable than others to be convinced they are 'truly trans'. Living as we do in a world where nonconforming children are assumed to be trans, they can feel at odds with the world and find it easier to yield to the general assumption that they should medically transition. This is a new issue, and it emerges as a combination of childhood-onset gender dysphoric children colliding with online social contagion, which entrenches their gender identity. In this context we recommend parents take the time to make concerted efforts to place boundaries upon their child's online engagement and, in the meantime, continue to try to expand the child's world beyond gender.

Peer and internet influence can permeate the culture and affect even its youngest members. Though there is scant information about increasing numbers of prepubertal children identifying as trans, anecdotal evidence suggests that this is happening. Some young children may come to think of themselves as trans because they want to emulate an older cousin or sibling. Other children may believe they are trans because they behave in a gender-nonconforming manner. When schools teach gender identity theory and ask young students about their pronouns, children are exposed to the contagious idea that they could be the other gender. When they see classmates change their hairstyle or gender presentation, they may 'catch' the idea that they could do this too. It is extraordinary how many trans people trace the origin of their bid to transition back to meeting or seeing a person who has transitioned. If you have a prepubertal child who has recently claimed a trans identity or is in an environment with other trans-identified children, there is much you can do to inoculate her against the harmful belief that her body is wrong.

It is your job to help your child orient and adapt to reality. Though we may make special exceptions when it comes to things like Santa Claus or the tooth fairy, we usually try to reflect the reality of things to children in an age-appropriate way. This grounds them, allows them to develop a sense of self in the world, and empowers them to gain more agency.

SOCIAL CONTAGION AMONG TEENS – ROGD

When out of nowhere there was a sharp rise in the number of adolescent girls identifying as various novel genders and seeking medical transition, the physician and scientist Dr Lisa Littman undertook research to figure out what was going on. This cohort had never been seen in the medical literature, there is no solid explanation about why these teenage girls want to transition, and yet it has led to a huge increase in the numbers of those presenting at gender clinics.

On 16 August 2018, *PLOS ONE*, a peer-reviewed scientific journal, published Dr Littman's study of 256 parental reports of adolescents experiencing a phenomenon described by Littman as 'Rapid Onset Gender Dysphoria', and the concept of ROGD was born.[3] Rapid Onset Gender Dysphoria (or late onset gender dysphoria) refers to trans identification that first occurs after puberty in an adolescent or young adult without a childhood experience of gender dysphoria. In Littman's research, many of the teens and young people who announced a transgender identity 'out of the blue' did so after spending time consuming transgender-related media online and/or in conjunction with real-life peers. It is therefore hypothesised that social and peer influence may be at play. ROGD describes a feeling of dissociation a young person experiences from their body and their biological sex, typically following extended periods of time spent online, often socially influenced, and appears to be a maladaptive (inappropriate or inadequate) coping mechanism. Littman noted in her descriptive study that ROGD is 'not a formal mental health diagnosis'. Although there were many scurrilous attempts to undermine Littman's work, the ROGD hypothesis is arguably the only study so far to offer a viable explanation for the extraordinary change in the cohort.

In 2020, Abigail Shrier followed Dr Littman's study with her book *Irreversible Damage: Teenage Girls and the Transgender Craze*. Shrier points out that gender dysphoria historically 'afflicted a tiny sliver of the population (roughly 0.01%) and almost exclusively boys. Before 2012, there was no scientific literature on girls ages 11 to 21 ever having developed gender dysphoria at all… [Now] they constitute the majority.'[4] We recommend that parents of children who seem to match the ROGD description read Shrier's book, as it provides a comprehensive and evocative account of this phenomenon.

Many ROGD teens have not shown signs of gender-nonconformity before they identify as transgender, so you might feel confused by this sudden announcement from your distressed teen. However, you may feel impressed by the breadth of knowledge your child shows on the subject. The conversations following the announcement tend to be startling for parents, as if they are being introduced to a whole new persona in their child. Some teens have offered PowerPoints to back up their online diagnosis, while others may have emailed their parents impressive documents complete with peer-reviewed research. Parents tend to feel way behind, like the train has left the station and they are pedalling furiously on a bicycle, hopelessly trying to catch up.

Although typically cerebral, these are often very vulnerable kids; 62.5% of the parents in Dr Littman's study reported that their children had one or more pre-existing mental health or neurodevelopmental issues. This combination of intelligence and vulnerability can be difficult for parents to handle, as the teen can often outsmart the parent and may lean heavily on her extensive knowledge about trans issues and the long list of associated acronyms and newly coined terms. We believe lack of knowledge about this new jargon can be a serious impediment to connecting with the young person, and so we recommend learning about the underlying concepts outlined in the Appendices and also reading the terminology in the Glossary. Once you have a good working knowledge, the inappropriate power balance in the parent–child relationship can begin to be recalibrated.

SOCIAL CONTAGION AND THE SYMPTOM POOL

The medical historian Edward Shorter proposed that people can exhibit a range of culturally recognised symptoms that signal their distress to others. People draw on the culturally approved 'symptom pool' to elicit a response from their clinicians, and the result is a 'shared diagnosis' between patients and doctors. As Shorter points out in his book *From Paralysis to Fatigue: A History of Psychosomatic Illness in the Modern Era*, patients seek to please their doctors. They don't want the doctor to dismiss their troubles as imaginary and so they strive to describe symptoms that the doctor will recognise and take seriously.[5] For example, prior to the 1970s, anorexia nervosa was seldom seen in medical literature, but once it was more known, especially after the death of the singer Karen Carpenter in the 1980s, anorexia became a common manifestation of mental distress. This condition appeared to elicit a social contagion – especially among teenage girls, who tend to co-ruminate, engage in empathy and seek commonalities among their peers. Equally, bulimia nervosa was seldom seen until it arrived into the 'symptom pool', and then, in a similar manner some years later, self-harming behaviour also spread. Now we appear to have gender dysphoria as the latest way for teenage girls to hate their bodies. As with other social contagions, the teenage girl is the canary in the coal mine, as these conditions then spread to other cohorts.

The Canadian philosopher Ian Hacking coined the term 'semantic contagion' to describe how naming a phenomenon increases its incidence.[6] For example, the arrival of the term 'born in the wrong body' inevitably brought about more people who believed they were 'born in the wrong body'. We saw this previously when the term 'multiple personality disorder' began to be used and, as a result, more doctors diagnosed multiple personality disorder. 'Repressed memory syndrome' became another way for individuals to understand themselves, and this concept proliferated. Hacking wrote about the concept of 'making up people', and 'trans kids' or 'non-binary' are good examples of how we tend to 'make up people' once we come across an underlying concept.[7] A key aspect of semantic contagion is that the description can shape the narrative, and so these new terms to describe people, be it 'genderqueer' or 'agender', are likely to shape the way people act. Given the recent rise in the numbers of people detransitioning and the subsequent increase in the level of discourse about 'detransition' and 'desistance', it seems likely that this will trigger more cases of detransition and desistance.

SOCIAL CONTAGION AND TRANS ACTIVISM

Trans activists believe they are protecting one of the most vulnerable, marginalised groups of people in the world. There has been a huge level of misinformation (and disinformation) disseminated about the trans community, and many youths today genuinely believe febrile hate groups roam the world intent on causing violence to trans people. Thankfully, the data suggests otherwise.[8] Research indicates that gender-nonconforming people are at as much risk of being targeted by bullies as trans people.[9] Bullies tend to target difference, and it doesn't matter what type of different you are.[10] Young people need to know this is not a problem specific to the trans community. Parents can help by educating their child about group dynamics so the child understands how and why bullies operate.

Young people who become trans activists can slip into bullying behaviour online. They might be driven by ideas they have gathered from social media. Pumped up with self-righteousness, they think they are fighting the oppressors. Trans-identified young people appear to be as likely to be perpetrators of bullying as targets of it, and if your child is worryingly aggressive online, it might be time for you to step in.[11] It is up to you to carefully widen your child's bandwidth about the world around them. For example, you might send your teenager a TikTok about some Ukrainian teenagers making sense of war, or a YouTube clip about an oil spill affecting wildlife. You could encourage them to watch *The Social Dilemma* so they can better understand the impact of being in an echo chamber and how it seemed to lead people to march on Capitol Hill without any real idea about what they were going to do there. This takes a great deal of honesty from parents, as many of us prefer to look away when we see our kids behaving badly. It is appropriate to have some control over your younger teens' online life, and then, as they grow older, to loosen the controls accordingly, but many young people still need parental guidance. Just as you once taught them to say please and thank you, you might now have to explain why it is not appropriate to join an online mobbing or operate anonymous accounts that cause distress. If you have an adult child in your household who is behaving in an inappropriate manner online, consider how you would respond if they behaved like this in real life.

Thoughts on ROGD five years after publication of the study

Lisa Littman

When my first research article on the topic was published, just a few pieces of the puzzle were coming to light. Young people who were vulnerable for a variety of reasons (social difficulties, isolation, mental health issues, etc.) seemed to adopt the frame of gender dysphoria and trans identification as a way to interpret their distress. In addition, peer groups were observed to engage in behaviours, both offline and online, that ranged from the mild exploration of identities to hardcore, 'us vs them' behaviours that drove wedges between children and their parents. At the time, I had no idea how common these occurrences might be.

Since publication, I have learned a lot from detransitioners who shed light on the process of how they were exposed to a set of beliefs, embraced those beliefs, then ultimately relinquished them. Reflecting on their experiences, many detransitioners perceived that mental health issues, traumas and difficulties accepting themselves as lesbian, gay and bisexual were the root of their distress that they interpreted as gender dysphoria and the need to transition. I spend a lot of time thinking about what is most important to know next, and I come back to three questions: What happens to these kids over time? How can we best protect their long-term health and well-being? What can we do to provide parents and families with the resources they need to help their children? Although these answers won't be found overnight, I look forward to the day when there will be more public awareness about the complexities that can drive a vulnerable person to identify as trans.

AUTISM, NEURODIVERSITY AND GENDER DYSPHORIA

Current research indicates that a high percentage of young people presenting with gender dysphoria have autism and/or autistic traits. In the UK, between 35% and 48% of children presenting to the Gender Identity Development Service (GIDS) display such traits.[12] While activist clinicians reassure parents that it's possible to be both trans and autistic, our developmental approach invites us to ask why there is such an over-representation of autistic people in gender clinics. We'll touch on a few of many factors that might explain this trend.

Children with autism are more likely to prefer cross-sex friend-ships than neurotypical children.[13] There is a higher likelihood of developing obsessive behaviours and body dysmorphic disorder.[14] In our experience, highly intelligent adolescents with autism also take a keen interest in counterculture topics, sometimes enjoying the prospect of shocking others; while others desperately try to fit in but lack the discernment for subtle social cues that come naturally to other teens. These young people can be delightful to adults, with their in-depth knowledge of particularly offbeat issues, but other teens may find them quirky or strange. Autistic kids are often naturally gender-nonconforming. The feeling of being an outsider is a common driver for young people to seek community within the LGBTQ umbrella of identities. Theory of mind, or the ability to accurately understand the thoughts and experiences of others, is also more limited for autistic teens, making them more likely to take the social affirmation others provide them through names and pronouns as proof they have indeed 'transitioned' to a different gender. They may lack the sophistication to understand that people are simply being polite. Lastly, your child may struggle with emotional regulation, often experiencing outsized emotional reactions and distress which may feel disproportionate to the situation. This makes it difficult to set limits, enforce rules and communicate about gender.

It can be helpful to educate your autistic teen about all the gifts and challenges that come with being neurodivergent. This may build self-awareness and better emotional regulation. Use simple, clear language when explaining the biological realities of the body and help your child to understand the social dynamics involved with changing your identity. We offer further information in Appendix 6 and we recommend the work of several autism experts in the resource list of this book.

COMORBIDITIES

Comorbidities (pre-existing conditions, usually mental health-related) are a significant issue for gender dysphoric young people and challenges such as ADHD, OCD, eating disorders, anxiety, depression and self-harming behaviour often present along with gender dysphoria. Yet the Cass Review, the NHS's commissioned report on gender services for children in the UK, noted a tendency for other mental health issues to be 'overshadowed' by a diagnosis of gender dysphoria.[15] Many parents have described how they attempted to ensure that other issues such as autistic spectrum disorder (ASD), ADHD and anxiety remained central concerns when discussing their child with a clinician, but all too often these concerns were dismissed. Dr Littman's study showed that, according to the parents' reports, 43.1% of their kids had a history of being isolated from their peers, 45% were engaging in self-harm prior to ROGD, 48.4% had experienced a traumatic or stressful event prior to ROGD, and a whopping 69.4% had social anxiety during adolescence. With such a high level of comorbidities, it can be difficult to figure out which challenge is driving any maladaptive behaviour. We recommend you proceed carefully and cautiously and try to keep the more holistic view of your child in the forefront. We offer more information about comorbidities in Appendix 6.

THE TRAITS OF THE ROGD TEEN

ROGD seems to be particularly common among a certain type of young person: they tend to be clever, quirky, socially awkward, sensitive, naive, hypervigilant about trans issues and filled with emotion. They are fond of online self-diagnoses and yet they also tend to be obedient and rule-oriented. ROGD young people are frequently neurodiverse and find the conventions and categories offered by gender identity theory and queer theory (see Appendix 1) attractive. They also tend to find it mentally satisfying to follow a treatment path with strict instructions about how everyone should respond. They may seek – or hope for – total compliance from their loved ones. Typically, they begin the process in a secret manner, with heavy influence from online media. Many first come out as gay, lesbian or bisexual and then, feeling increasingly uncomfortable with this tag, they come out as trans, non-binary and sometimes pansexual (an attraction regardless of sex or gender). Some will have been flirting with their online persona and following trans issues for a long time prior to coming to the belief that they are trans.

A trans identity can feel galactically important. The young person may begin to despise everything their old self represented. Indeed, a trans identity can often appear to consume the child's entire personality. Parents need to be sensitive but at the same time retain their authority, otherwise the ROGD child can lead the parent instead of the other way around. Many ROGD teens create a secret trans identity that they nurture and hold close to their heart. It can sometimes, but not always, be helpful to gently penetrate the wall of secrecy, as secrecy can foster negativity and self-loathing and keep us trapped within a narrative. Once the secret is exposed to the light, its power is often reduced. If the topic of gender is too inflammatory, perhaps you could speak about how burdensome it can be to keep secrets.

Some are eager to identify out of the 'oppressor class' – especially if they are white and come from a relatively privileged background – while others are more bewitched by the idea of becoming another person. There has perhaps never been a more beguiling concept unleashed upon teenagers: to hear, as an uncertain, unhappy adolescent, that you can become someone different, with a new name, a new identity, and nobody will be allowed to refer to your old, loathsome, shame-filled self ever again. Cruel optimism describes a situation where others cheer along a person who is becoming increasingly attached to a future that is impossible or will be a good deal harder than they have been led to expect. ROGD young people are often gullible: although medical transition is possible, it is usually at considerable cost. We can change our bodies, we can forbid anyone to refer to our old self ever again, and yet we can never leave ourselves behind. Or, as the master of mindfulness Jon Kabat-Zinn puts it, 'Wherever you go, there you are.'[16] No matter what medical interventions we experience, we will always be the human who was born at such and such a time, to such and such parents, with various strengths, weaknesses and idiosyncrasies that are part of who we are. This is both the tragedy and the beauty of life.

The ROGD young person can be formidable in an argument. Kate, the mother of Annie, a fourteen-year-old natal female, described at a parents' meeting how she came to be intimidated by her teenager: 'Annie is frighteningly clever, and she argues the points so well that all I can do is put my hands up and say "You win". I've never seen her so impassioned before this. It feels like an almost religious zeal. And she knows so much more about this subject than I ever will. She has always been obedient, and this seems to be the first ever "no" she has uttered in her life.' It is often profoundly difficult for parents to push against the zeal of the ROGD teen, yet this is often what is required.

A majority of ROGD teens are excessively introspective. They think a lot about themselves, who they are and how they present to the world. Yet their thoughts don't necessarily lead to deep insights or self-awareness. Instead they seem to lose themselves down a rabbit hole and often need some help in contextualising themselves to the world. They may also need help in learning how to engage with other people in an authentic and appropriate manner. We have noticed how some ROGD young people can have an inner self that is incongruent with their outer veneer. Perhaps their inner self is seething with rage at the world, bitingly incisive and astute, but then their outer self is mild, effusively positive and bland. If this is the case with your child, it can be valuable to help them to honour their emotions and learn how to be more authentically themselves. If you think your child does not have a very developed self-awareness, be aware they might not realise they are presenting a fake exterior, and so some sensitivity will be required.

IDENTIFYING AS NON-BINARY

While many ROGD teen girls identify as transboys, many also claim new identities such as non-binary. These novel gender identities are a significant aspect of the ROGD phenomenon. These presentations were non-existent prior to the appearance of the new cohort of sufferers that ROGD describes. In the film *Dead Poets Society*, Robin Williams is the inspirational teacher who leads the students to utter their 'barbaric yawp', a phrase taken from Walt Whitman's poem 'Song of Myself, 52', 'I sound my barbaric yawp over the roofs of the world.' A 'yawp' is a loud cry or yell. In many ways a young person who comes out as non-binary is sounding their barbaric yawp. Non-binary is a rejection of the sexed body – they are neither male nor female; they reject this framework. The teen's determination to suddenly say no and perhaps go to war with their parents after having always previously been compliant suggests that some teenagers are sounding their barbaric yawp as a way of rejecting the pressure they feel from the world.

Some young people need to be helped to say no more often. Perhaps you can teach them how to say no in other contexts? Perhaps they *need* to sound their barbaric yawp! Help them to tap into the part of themselves that wants to feel more liberated, less self-conscious, more able to do what they want.

Being a teenager seems to be very difficult today, and many are buckling under the strain. The hypersexualisation of young people has been a source of concern for some years: imposing a sexuality upon a child before they are ready for it is abusive and dreadfully distressing for the child. Yet this regularly happens in a multitude of ways across the Western world. Children who have not yet had a sexual awakening feel a natural sense of revulsion towards sex – this is arguably an evolutionary instinct which serves us well. However, alongside the arrival of the considerable spending power of the tween has come a sexualised expectation that some children can engage in joyfully but which can horrify others. For example, one patient we know, Susie, felt revolted when she was exposed to porn as a nine-year-old. Her peers seemed to be able to handle it and giggled along, but the images seeped into Susie's dreams and gave her nightmares. She wasn't ready for this, and it gave her a horrible introduction to sex. In this context it is perhaps understandable that some young people want to say no and do this by coming out as non-binary.

There are many other reasons for a young person to identify as non-binary. It is often the easiest option, as being non-binary doesn't require a person to present in any specific way. Nor do they feel the need to manifest certain stereotypical behaviours. It's important to note that coming out as non-binary can sometimes, but not always, act as a stepping stone both into and out of a trans presentation. Ali, fifteen, initially came out as lesbian, then identified as non-binary and pansexual, then a year later came out as trans-masc. In terms of identity exploration this is all normative and healthy. The problem comes when these identities are medicalised, and the cultural context today tells young people like Ali that they need medication if they are to feel comfortable with their identity. It is a false premise, and can lead to a lot of emotional pain.

IDENTIFYING AS ANY OTHER GENDER

There are over a hundred gender identities to choose from, and this number is growing all the time. Whether your child is agender, androgyne, neutrois, gender-fluid, two-spirit, omnigender or whatever else takes their fancy, is not the point. The issue at heart is that your teen is perhaps feeling uncomfortable with who they are, they are seeking a solution to their mental pain, and they believe if they can embody a certain gender, and if everyone agrees with this embodiment, then they will feel better. When we are in deep mental anguish and we fix upon a solution, we can hold this solution with the grip of a drowning person. Some young people grasp upon the idea of a gender identity being the solution, and so they might move through a range of increasingly unusual gender identities and become intensely preoccupied about whether they are truly this gender or that one. It is not your role to travel alongside this introspection; instead you can be a sounding board as the young person discovers who they are. Think of it as personality exploration. Many of us became absorbed by personality tests when we were young. For example, the Myers–Briggs Type Indicator (MBTI) is an introspective self-report questionnaire that is perceived by some as pseudoscientific rubbish and by others as a helpful tool to indicate differing psychological presentations in how we view the world and make decisions. It can be valuable to encourage your child to take a personality test, along with other members of the family – you too – as this can lead to further exploration about who they are, and it also contextualises other people.

THE LOUD AND ANGRY ROGD TEEN

There is a notable exception to the obedient, sweet-natured ROGD type who needs to learn how to say no, and this is the more 'fiercely gender-questioning' kid who was described eloquently by the clinical psychologist Lisa Duval in episode 75 of the podcast *Gender: A Wider Lens*.[17] In this episode, Duval puts forward her fascinating theory about how kids with traits of borderline personality disorder are more vulnerable to ROGD, and how aspects of gender identity ideology inadvertently bring about dynamics in dysphoric kids that are reminiscent of borderline personality disorder. Parenting the loud and angry ROGD kid is an utterly exhausting roller coaster, and we recommend that you ensure you have adequate support for this challenge by creating a network of friends and family who understand the issues. If you feel your child is exhibiting borderline traits, you might also take a look at the book *Stop Walking on Eggshells for Parents* by Randi Kreger et al.

ROGD BOYS

This landscape is changing quickly. Although 82.8% of the children involved in Dr Littman's study were natal females, we have noticed a recent increase of boys showing signs of ROGD.[18] In our meetings among the online network of parent groups across the world, we have noted stark similarities among these boys, who share some of the traits of ROGD girls.[19] Like the girls, they're typically intelligent, quirky and socially awkward, but there are also notable differences: they seem to engage with gender in a more secretive way, they are less likely to seek validation among their friends, and many of them maintain a private transgender persona online while not seeking social transition in the real world. This may be because they are gay or bisexual but unwilling to declare this. It may also be because they have mixed up wanting to have sex with girls with wanting to *be* a girl. From our clinical work we have noticed that these boys seem even more likely to have neurodevelopmental conditions such as ASD or ADHD. They are often more intent about hormonal and surgical procedures and may view the social aspect of transition as a frippery. Many parents report an apparent body hair phobia, as ROGD boys can spend hours in the bathroom removing every hair. This intense focus on body hair removal can have a compulsive quality to it and may be an expression of obsessive–compulsive traits. Parents of ROGD boys seem to find it even more difficult to connect with their child than parents of ROGD girls.

We have noticed that ROGD boys find it very challenging to speak about what's going on for them, and can become utterly absorbed by their trans persona. All they want is to stay in their bedrooms, living their lives online, cultivating their identity and aiming to access medical treatment as soon as they can. As testosterone rages through the teenage male body, some of these boys may become influenced by trans porn and seem especially vulnerable to grooming from online predators, who flatter them about how girlish they look and can offer them special attention or even money to engage in sexual acts. Though the literature is scant, we have seen this numerous times in our practices. Often the attention can feel more valuable than the money – many trans-identified teens report feeling very lonely. Groomers are aware of this, and are often able to zero in on the child's vulnerabilities. The child who is being groomed often becomes confused: both disgusted with themselves and compelled to seek out more. This grooming might bring about the first sexual awakening of the child, and it can create a heavy burden of shame around sex. Grooming can also lead a young person to become hypersexualised, as they learn to view sex as a transactional affair without any intimacy, warmth or potential for bonding. Being groomed can also bring about a sense of self-loathing in the individual and feelings of alienation from other people. The impact of grooming is severe, and we recommend that parents maintain a close connection with their child's online life, as it is much easier to prevent than to withdraw once it has started.

Parenting the ROGD boy

I am a mother of an ROGD son who has become lost in the world of gender – and unfortunately there are thousands of other mothers just like me. My son was a sweet, gentle boy who had autistic traits, although we didn't have him tested. He was a loved and appreciated child, adored by me and his father. He was the centre of our universe.

We were very close, at least until high school. We first noticed something was amiss when his grades started to slip. Around the same time, he became disrespectful and secretive. I assumed it was normal teenage rebellion at play. I soon learned what was going on when he said the most inconceivable and confusing words: 'I'm trans.'

My gut knew something wasn't right, since he had previously shown no distress about being a boy. After a few phone calls we ended up meeting with a gender doctor who, we figured, would sort this out. But that's not what happened, and you've heard all the stories of the doctors saying, 'Would you rather have an alive daughter or a dead son?' That's exactly what this doctor said to us in front of our son, in addition to quoting unproven suicide statistics. My son gave us a look of *I told you so*. We did not believe this doctor. After this appointment my son became very depressed, and later he started making name and pronoun demands.

In my ROGD world, if you don't affirm the trans delusion you are considered a hateful bigot and treated like the worst parent in the world, even by family. Your parenting is undermined at every turn by the school, doctors and even good friends.

I spent three years trying to repair a relationship that had always been good. But my son stopped trusting us. He stopped believing in us, in our family. He started to hate us. Unimaginably, coming from my loving boy. After years of us believing he'd grow out of it and him showing signs of desistance, things changed when he turned eighteen. He suddenly felt emboldened by a teacher who advised him on how to find housing, medical and legal resources.

Today, I find myself estranged from my sweet boy. He came to believe that we were abusive parents because we did not affirm, and society told him to get rid of us, so he did.

Rejection from your child is incredibly painful. There is no professional help you can trust or count on to help your child, and you feel alone in this awful sci-fi dystopian novel waiting for the next step your child takes.

I feel like a failure because I couldn't stop him when all I was trying to do was keep him safe and away from medical harm. This is something my son does not understand today. I hold out hope that someday he will. I do not blame him nor am I angry with him, because he was indoctrinated by the professionals you are supposed to trust.

There are many reasons for boys to become absorbed by medical transition – a boy who is small for his age or unhappy around rough play may be fearful of being picked on, so it may seem safer to be a girl. Other boys become disturbed by their sexual impulses and wish to unshackle themselves from what they perceive as the beast of testosterone. Magical thinking can often play a large role in these boys' lives, especially if the boy has some neurological difference like ADHD or ASD. A trans identity often evolves in young people when they are lonely and spending too much time online. An improved social life, with friends and a girlfriend or a boyfriend, is often helpful for these young people to move beyond their self-obsession.

PARENTING THE ROGD TEEN

It is notable that many parents of ROGD kids seem to be kind, diffident and have a fear of conflict with their children. These parents are often in awe of their children and have difficulty holding their authority. If the teenager holds all the power, then they will be calling the shots, and this is often too big a burden for their young shoulders. Although they might try to convince you they can handle it, parents should be careful not to allow this to happen. Retain your power by leaning into the situation, saying little but noting everything. Some parents of ROGD kids report that they too are neurodiverse and so they find it difficult to manage the big emotions at play, and they might also have difficulty communicating effectively with their child. We recommend that parents consider learning how to carefully attend to all ways of communicating – verbal, non-verbal, behavioural, tone of voice and mannerisms. There are a multitude of ways for your child to communicate, and 'active listening' requires you to gently ask questions and respond and reflect on their answers. It can be an exhausting but also a heartening experience if parents can begin to understand their child more accurately during this complicated process.

In Dr Littman's study, 86.7% of the sample came out as trans following an intensive period of social media usage and/or had one or more friends who came out as trans at the same time. Detransitioner

Helena Kerschner wrote in 2019 about how online 'call-out culture' and Tumblr had considerable influence on her own gender identity.[20] If your teen meets the ROGD descriptor, you might consider bringing in some rules around tech use, as transition vloggers may have a tangible impact on your child.[21] Many ROGD teens seem to be unduly influenced by social media influencers who have medically transitioned. In addition, sexual exploitation through online grooming is a real threat – our work with detransitioners has brought about a deeper understanding of the impact online grooming has played in trans identification. You might also re-evaluate the school you have chosen for your child or the activities they attend, as these might be intensifying a preoccupation with gender. Although many parents can feel compelled, often by their teen, to find a therapist, this is not always the most appropriate path to take. ROGD teens often view therapists as specialists who will provide them with the confirmation that they are really trans. We believe it can sometimes be more beneficial for parents to lean in, fully embracing your child with love and boundaries, than to presume a therapist will have the keys to unlock the young person's distress.

It is important that parents don't allow online self-diagnoses to become acceptable ways for teenagers to understand themselves. Dr David Bell, consultant psychiatrist, psychoanalyst and ex-governor of the Tavistock Clinic, has spoken about 'the collapse of gender medicine into customership' and expressed concern about the new trend for clients to self-diagnose through online resources and dictate their treatment path to the clinician.[22] There is a worrying trend among this generation of young people to focus their identity on whatever diagnosis they might have, be it gender dysphoria, ASD, ADHD or anxiety. Parents can encourage the young person to become more deeply self-aware of their complexities. This might entail gently pushing back when the young person ascribes the majority of their personality to their trans identity or ASD traits.

Some parents choose to take their child away from the environment that is deepening this distress – this might be their online life, their school or another cultural context – and only then allow the watchful waiting approach to unfold.

Love, sacrifice and strategy

A parent of an ROGD teen

Our daughter was gender-conforming until she was sixteen. Then, during Covid, after a friend had committed suicide and when she was struggling with depression and anxiety, she suddenly came out as transgender and a few months later requested a double mastectomy. Our daughter is on the autism spectrum and fit the Rapid Onset Gender Dysphoria mould perfectly.

We did the research to figure out where we stood as a family. We let her know we would not support her doing anything that could cause permanent damage to her body until she was financially independent, living on her own and twenty-five years old.

We had incredibly difficult conversations with our daughter. We set firm boundaries – exploration, NOT affirmation – and then completely dropped gender as a topic of conversation in our household. We spent the next nine months laying the groundwork to help our daughter find her way back.

We told her daily, 'First and foremost: we love you no matter what – there is nothing you could do that could ever change that. Nothing.' We lived in a very liberal city where there is zero diversity of thought. We decided to leave the liberal echo chamber, and our daughter's social circle, by renting our home, quitting our jobs and moving abroad, where our girls would go to another school in another country.

Building critical thinking skills, introducing the concept of free thought and the importance of diversity of thought were imperative to open her perspective not just on gender ideology but as a necessary lifelong skill. This was a long, slow process that lasted the better part of a year and did not have anything to do with gender until the very end, when we knew she was open to other perspectives.

Our daughter has now rejected that she is trans. We believe that love, compassion, boundaries, sacrifice and strategy were critical.

LEANING IN WITH AUTHENTICITY

The issue of walking on eggshells around ROGD kids is a common theme. Many parents are intimidated by their teenagers' intensity and the fear that if they say the wrong thing their teenager will punish them for days, if not years, or even cut off ties. An understandable resentment can build. If possible, try to be authentic so your teen can start to renegotiate their relationship with you. You will need infinite patience and a lot of emotional support. You may also need to develop your skills in managing conflict and holding authority.

Parents of ROGD kids need to think about penetrating the wall and becoming more used to entering their teen's bedroom. These kids have often created a vibe whereby parents feel so unwelcome that gradually this becomes forbidden territory. It can be helpful if you begin to visit your kid's room respectfully but regularly, maybe with a drink or something you want to share on your phone – regular, short visits that help you re-engage in a gentle, non-threatening way. Knock first, but also try to create a warm, light-hearted atmosphere. Seek out content your child might be interested in. Tolerate the rolled eyes, the coldness and the lack of engagement. But it is important you don't deplore the mess when you visit. If you begin tidying up, you will ruin the mood and probably unconsciously become more irritable with your child – this is not the time to give speeches about how they need to clean their room. Teenagers typically respond to authentic offers of a deeper connection, although it might take a considerable amount of time. Parents might view these small attempts to bond as pebbles in a barrel. Insignificant at first, these interactions might eventually fill the barrel and strengthen the bond.

3

SEXUALITY

Understanding the sexuality of your gender-questioning child is among the most confusing aspects of this parenting experience. Maybe you tried talking about how they define their sexuality and were left with more questions than answers. Parents of some teens say their child is a 'late bloomer' who is sexually innocent, with little or no real-life intimate experiences, but maybe your child can rattle off a dizzying array of labels for her own sexuality, giving the false impression of sexual maturity. Beneath the sophisticated language, however, the identity proclamations can feel scripted. Some children who have experienced trauma or harassment may withdraw into depression, trying to minimise parts of their body associated with the negative experience. Others discover online pornography that simultaneously stimulates and disgusts. For children coming to terms with their same-sex attraction, today's concept of same-gender attraction can confuse this process. The self-concept of older teens and adult children can be profoundly affected by romantic relationships with other trans-identified young people. And still other children, both young and adult, are struggling with the plight of being average: being a 'straight cis' kid is not always a favourable identity in many youth circles. Here we'll explore such constellations, and the strategies to support healthy development of sexuality in teens and young adults.

EVEN HEALTHY PUBERTY AND
SEXUALITY DEVELOPMENT ARE DIFFICULT

Physical changes during puberty, typically between the ages of ten and fourteen for girls and ages twelve and sixteen for boys, are tremendous. Met with excitement, dread, and often both, puberty ushers in disruptions and opportunities. While we try to prepare our children, we can't completely protect them from the struggle. Quickly developing new and conspicuous body parts is a profound transformation managed differently by each young person – some with more success than others. Many decades removed from that period of our lives, adults often forget how confusing puberty can be. In the vulnerability of youth, we spend many hours obsessively checking and rechecking our body as it changes. We may be convinced our breasts are 'growing in wrong', and that something medically anomalous makes us an outlier. Nonetheless, most of us move through this period relatively intact, even if it's not easy, quick or without a great deal of struggle along the way. Adolescent confusion about one's body and sexuality, and even some self-destructive behaviour, is developmentally normal, but a transgender identity can further complicate this already messy process.

ESCAPING THE PROJECT OF SEXUALITY

Children who feel intimidated or explicitly harmed by intimacy may choose to opt out of the whole project. For some who have experienced an assault, whether verbal or physical, a non-binary, trans or asexual identity may be seen as self-protection from vulnerability. A shame-inducing and aversive experience, coupled with the normal bodily discomfort of puberty, can further incentivise a young woman to demand, 'No, I refuse to be a girl!' Even hypersexualised social media images and unappealing pop culture depictions of boys and girls can contribute to a child's desire to withdraw. Here it's important to validate the fear and anxiety that can come with girlhood. Targeted trauma therapies may be appropriate to help heal the wounds of a sexual assault or a scary experience, giving back a feeling of safety in the body. Instilling in your child a sense of resilience, strength and confidence offers an important counterpoint to the feelings of helplessness and fear that accompany trauma.

SEXUAL IDENTITY LABELS: PUTTING THE CART BEFORE THE HORSE

Adolescence is a time when young people begin to experience romantic infatuation and sexual attraction. They ask, 'Who am I attracted to?' Young people today are conscious of sexual identity and all its variations. Children may become familiar with terms like bi, gay or queer even before they develop any sexual feelings at all. Eleven-year-old Taylor, for example, 'came out' as a lesbian to her mum before entering secondary school. When Sheila asked her daughter if she had ever wanted to kiss a girl, Taylor responded with horror: 'Gross, Mum! I don't want to kiss anyone!' Whenever Sheila tried to talk with her about sex, Taylor ran away with her fingers in her ears. For Taylor, and many other kids like her, experimenting with labels seems more important than sexuality itself. We'll check in with Sheila and Taylor later in this chapter.

GENDER-NONCONFORMITY AND SEXUAL ORIENTATION

For decades, it's been clear that some children, regardless of their parents' rearing practices, don't conform to stereotypical gender roles. Many ROGD children, however, only begin playing with gender explicitly in adolescence. We'll consider these two groups of kids.

You might have noticed your child was 'different' from other same-sex peers even as young as four or five. As well as gender-nonconforming behaviour, your child might have explicitly claimed to be the other sex. Such children often grow up to be gay, lesbian, or at least highly nonconforming and creative in gender expression. Particularly for boys who exhibit typically feminine behaviour, researchers once suspected these kids would grow up to be transsexuals, but studies have shown that almost all of these males identified as gay in adolescence or early adulthood.[1] This research has since been subverted by gender identity theory beginning in the early 2000s, especially after the airing of the show *I Am Jazz*, which featured a gender-nonconforming male child who was socially transitioned and raised as a girl. Subsequently, Jazz took puberty blockers, cross-sex hormones and had vaginoplasty surgery which resulted in significant complications. This popular TV show gave the world a new concept for understanding the feminine male child: no longer considered a potential future homosexual, the feminine boy could, in fact, be a girl. As discussed in Chapter 5, which focuses on social transition, this powerful intervention may 'lock in' the cross-sex identification instead of giving the child space and time to come to terms with his sexuality, body and natal sex.

Boyhood femininity

Paul Vasey

Developmental research shows that boys and girls differ, on average, in their behaviour and preferences. Typically, boys enjoy rough-and-tumble play more than they enjoy nurturing play with dolls, whereas the reverse is true for girls. These childhood sex differences occur across many different cultures, and even emerge in monkeys and apes.[2]

That said, exceptions to these general patterns do exist. For example, when asked, the average gay man recalls childhood behaviours and preferences that are shifted in a female-typical direction, that is, more feminine than what straight men recollect but not as feminine as what straight women remember about themselves. In addition, many gay men remember that as children they sometimes enjoyed fantasising or pretending that they were someone of the opposite sex, such as Wonder Woman. This sort of boyhood femininity can vary in intensity and manifest in even more extreme ways. For example, a minority of gay men recollect levels of childhood femininity that are similar to, or even surpass, those of straight women. Some remember cross-sex feelings involving the desire to be a girl, or even the belief that they really were a girl.

Boyhood femininity is a normative aspect of gay men's childhood development and one that has been documented in many different cultures. Feeling one was born the wrong sex is not the exclusive experiential domain of transgender individuals. Such feelings can, and do, characterise feminine boys, most of whom grow up to be well-adjusted gay men. Parents of feminine boys would do well to remember this underappreciated developmental reality.

If your child is gender-nonconforming and prepubertal, we recommend giving him or her the freedom to explore natural interests and preferences. You can acknowledge that it's challenging to feel different from others, but we must learn to be proud of our quirks and unique qualities. If the child expresses gender confusion, affirm reality to help your child stay grounded in truth. Sex constancy, the cognitive ability to discern that biological sex cannot be changed, should be reinforced by parents. Toys, haircuts, play preferences and the like are open and available to both boys and girls, but their bodies cannot fundamentally change. You can use age-appropriate books or discussions to help explain what changes will come along with puberty. You'll find a list of such resources at the end of this book.

INTERNALISED HOMOPHOBIA AMIDST THE PRIDE

Many older gay adults recall that their adolescence was marked by feelings of deep confusion and shame about their attractions. They may not have had a positive way to understand their homosexuality or it may even have been explicitly derided or shamed. In these cases, coming to terms with sexuality was an incredibly difficult process. But young people today who are lucky to live in more tolerant, accepting environments may still feel ambivalent about their own same-sex attraction. After all, it's one thing to intellectually hold progressive views, and it's another to successfully integrate private sexual thoughts and feelings. The fear of being rejected or perceived as sexually intimidating or 'creepy' is a mortifying prospect to many lesbian, gay or bisexual teens. And unfortunately, homophobic bullying and teasing is rampant in many schools. Many detransitioners, in hindsight, believe internalised homophobia played a role in their transgender identification.[3]

If your teen has always been gender-nonconforming, or you suspect he or she is gay, try to normalise any questions about identity and gender. Internalised homophobia can be difficult to heal, and is likely operating on a subconscious level. It's worth noting that within LGBT youth culture today, the term 'gay' seems to hold higher status than the word 'lesbian'. Young women with same-sex attraction who are questioning their identity may cringe at the word. We suspect that their exposure to 'lesbian pornography', with its sensibilities and aesthetics geared towards a male viewer, plays some role in their reactions, and if people calling themselves 'lesbian' in online forums or dating apps are biologically male, girls who like girls may prefer the term 'non-binary'. Furthermore, clients have indicated to us that 'lesbian' conjures up images of older, 'uncool' women who are less interested in sex and more interested in politics. Most young adult gender-nonconforming females who are same-sex-attracted today identify with modern edgy labels like 'non-binary' or 'trans-masc'. Like 'non-binary', 'queer' seems to have more social cachet than 'gay', even though 'queer' no longer only means same-sex-attracted.

Rather than arguing about gender, we invite you to focus on aspirational values. Consider saying something like 'I love you very much and just want you to accept yourself with all your unique qualities and differences. It seems like trying to change genders might be an attempt to run away from yourself because it's hard to be different.' Also, exposing your teen to positive gay and lesbian role models who are relatable, interesting and cool can be an important counterpoint to the confusing messages about lesbian, gay and bisexual people that dominate transgender activist beliefs.

With an adult child, you might consider sharing your concerns, with the understanding that your son or daughter has full autonomy and could make decisions about transition regardless of how you feel. While this is a challenging aspect of parenting a gender dysphoric adult, staying connected, asking open-ended questions and lovingly sharing your perspective can help you to remain truthful and genuine during your child's individuation process. If gender is the elephant in the room in your home, do all you can to keep the lines of communication open.

A SEXUAL COMPONENT OF GENDER DYSPHORIA

Before the recent dramatic increase in young people identifying as trans, adolescent and adult males with childhood-onset gender dysphoria have been typically sexually attracted to men (androphilic). Meanwhile, males who developed gender dysphoria in adolescence or adulthood were typically motivated by transvestic behaviour with sexual excitement.[4]

Some of the current cohort of teen and young adult boys seeking transition may fall into this category, although the picture is likely to be much more complicated. Anxious or autistic boys who have retreated into the world of online porn may develop symptoms that mimic these earlier manifestations, but which potentially have different root causes.

Autogynephilia is a term coined by Dr Ray Blanchard that describes a condition whereby the male is sexually aroused by the thought or image of himself as a woman.[5] A proportion of male teenagers who identify as trans will be consumed by this fetishistic drive and can become utterly absorbed by their mental image of themselves as a girl. Paraphilia is characterised by persistent, recurrent and intense sexual interests, urges, fantasies or behaviours that involves objects, activities or even situations that are atypical in nature.[6] It can be dreadfully challenging for parents to discover that their innocent teenager, who has never shown any prior interest in sex, has acquired a disturbing paraphilia that could take over his life.

Many males with autogynephilia may feel a sense of shame about their sexual fantasies and forcefully assert that they are female in order to counteract this shame. Parents may feel entirely at sea when they learn that their adolescent or adult child is erotically motivated to seek medical transition. We recommend that parents who suspect their child is autogynephilic spend some time learning about this difficult condition. *Men Trapped in Men's Bodies* by the transwoman Anne A. Lawrence is a good place to start. *The Man Who Would Be Queen* by J. Michael Bailey and Sasha and Stella's podcast *Gender: A Wider Lens* are further good resources that discuss this subject.

ROGD AND SEXUALITY

Sexuality can be an especially confusing experience for children who only began identifying with a different gender around adolescence. You might not understand why your historically feminine daughter now thinks of herself as a 'gay transman'. Or perhaps your son, who has always been fixated on trains, computers and studying the history of war is now insisting he's a woman and claiming to be a lesbian. Exploring some of these contemporary labels for sexuality will help orient you in this disorienting world.

Gay female-to-male (FTM) boys (girls who like boys)

This identity can completely baffle the mind. 'FTM gay trans boys' are girls who have typically been quite feminine. Around adolescence, they begin dressing more androgynously, question their identity, and eventually claim to be gay boys. This often happens in the context of in-person groups, like LGBT affinity clubs at school, or online forums full of anime fans and fan fiction writing on the same theme. These groups are chock-full of girls claiming to be boys. And these girls are busy developing fictional gay male characters. They have created an unrealistic female fantasy version of the gay relationship, expressed through story, narrative and elaborate digital art. The gay male protagonists are fabrications of the teenage girl's imagination, and as a young girl reads more of these stories, she comes to believe the fantasy – not only about the gay relationships of her favourite characters, but also about what's possible for her own identity trans-formation. Emerging from the world of online fandom, the 'gay trans boy' is taking on a life of its own. Helena, a detransitioned young woman in her mid twenties, recalls her adolescence and the intense infatuation she had with boys:

> I had a one-track mind and I craved an intense fantasy element. This led me to the world of fanfiction, mostly male/male pairings. What could be better than boys? Double boys! But they're written by girls so they make sense and feel familiar instead of different and intimidating. I loved the unlimited amount of creative and exciting content other girls were writing about my favorite characters. I wasn't super into erotic fanfiction, and if I did read it, it was always within the context of a longer, more relationship-oriented story, but pure erotica was popular too (often carrying heavy kinky themes…). I began to identify with

these representations of boys written by other young females, and the themes within male/male fanfiction were so much more titillating than anything in mainstream, professionally produced media, or even heterosexual fanfiction for that matter. The pairing being same sex seemed to give writers and readers the freedom to explore these characters and their relationships without being constricted by the norms that come with heterosexual dynamics. It became this liminal space where I could explore what interested me about boys and fantasies about relationships, connecting it to whatever my media obsession was at the time, without the pressure of interacting with real boys, as real boys made me painfully bashful.[7]

This gay FTM boy character holds many parallels to the 'pretty-boy' heart-throbs in a boy band and other dreamy male figures who have captured the adoration of girls throughout modern history. These characters are male, but not too masculine. They are sexy without being sexually aggressive, offering girls a safe way to dip their toes into the world of adult sexuality without the risk of being drowned in it.

If you've discovered such online material in your daughter's browser history, you might have tried explaining that becoming a gay boy would severely decrease her dating pool for future relationships. But as we've seen, in *her* world, these relationships are abundant, rich and satisfying, at least in fantasy. It might be helpful instead to remind your daughter that it's normal and healthy to experiment with fantasies about attraction and romance. As Helena did, adolescents often leave fantasies behind, because while they play an important role in the consolidation of a sexual identity, fantasies have a limited shelf life and must eventually be replaced by real-life human relationships.

Boys pining after the feminine

Boys' sexuality also gets confused in this new landscape of fantasy and contemporary identity labels. Some parents might have discovered women's lingerie in their son's room, or found photos on his computer of him in suggestive poses or wearing make-up. There might have been a coming-out letter accompanied by a demand for immediate intervention with puberty blockers or cross-sex hormones. Meanwhile, he has likely made little effort to look feminine. 'Medication first, appearance later,' say many of the ROGD boys we've worked with. At this stage of discovery, parents feel that there's a looming mystery and secrecy standing between them and their son. This can be confusing and distressing, particularly when there seems to be a dark sexual element behind their son's new fixation. Let's examine some of the pathways into a trans identity that are common among straight ROGD boys, particularly as they relate to the development of their sexuality.

There are often two main vectors for this new fixation: the computer, and an influential but troubled female friend. Unlike the highly gender-nonconforming would-be gay male we discussed earlier, this boy is quite heterosexual. He is not the popular, charming, athletic type. He's also not interested in machismo, bravado or becoming a womanising Casanova. Instead, this is a sensitive boy who is savvy with computers, a history buff, train-obsessed in his childhood, or maybe one with a reputation as a maths or science whizz. He may also be brilliant academically, perhaps corroborated by an off-the-charts IQ test, and could be on the autism spectrum.

Online life can be a powerful draw for such young men. Gaming can become an important social outlet, and many games feature user communities. Trans-related material can feature prominently on some of these. On social media platforms such as Reddit or Discord, they find others who share their interests. Through an interest in anime or certain belief systems or gaming subcultures, these boys can be introduced to online trans communities. They may also find online porn or other sexual content that exposes them to the concept of trans. (Trans-related porn is a very popular genre even on mainstream porn sites such as Pornhub.) The online world can be a place to experiment with a female identity. Boys may make female gaming avatars for themselves or use an anime girl as their profile picture. As for girls, a life lived substantially online can begin to feel more compelling and salient than the real world. Relationships there can be profoundly influential.

This boy can be socially challenged, struggling to make and maintain friendships despite a strong desire to do so. When the intriguing female friend enters the picture, she seems to be the answer to his social problems. Perhaps she is charismatic, with a magnetic personality, despite being a bit troubled. This girl may identify as non-binary or as a transman. She may also be a 'cis ally' who gets deeply involved in various gender and sexuality issues as part of her social justice ambitions. She is smart, knows a lot of the trans lingo and makes it her project to help a gender-questioning boy become his 'authentic self'. The boy in this story might be shy, somewhat passive and people-pleasing, and usually socially immature. He is vulnerable in other ways too, due to his extremely exceptional intelligence and corresponding social naivety. We have a recipe for a complex, deeply interdependent and powerful relationship that could shape the development of both children's identities and sexualities, especially the boy's.

The details of what could happen in these friendships will vary. One pull factor may be that inching towards a feminine presentation, clothing, hair and identity gives this young man a sort of backstage pass into the world of girls. A new kind of intimacy is established when the male-to-female (MTF) 'transgirl' becomes a mannequin for the female friends in his life. The girlfriend may help him sneak behind his parents' backs to order make-up and women's clothes. This new secrecy bonds them in ways that feel private and exhilarating. Now being invited to attend girls' sleepovers, this boy, who might have struggled with social awkwardness for years, has become the centre of attention. How seductive and intoxicating! Martha, mother of Jason, a seventeen-year-old ROGD boy, described how a group of 'female cheerleaders' in his class seemed to view him as a fun project: 'They loaned him clothes and enjoyed dressing him up and doing his make-up. Jason revelled in the girls' attention. They played with him like a doll. They were vapid and he was enthralled. It was horrible to watch. Then, at the end of the year, they headed off to college while my kid stayed at home, discarded and morbidly obsessed with medical transition.'

In a different version of this story, the boy is triggered to question his identity when his love object confesses that she is bi or a lesbian.

She's not interested in dating boys, sorry. But they can still be good friends! This kind of heartbreak leads to creative problem-solving and a renewal of hope: *Maybe I can be exactly what she wants and needs.* After all, this wouldn't be the first time an infatuated, swooning boy tries to bend over backwards to regain the affections of his crush. In another scenario, the young man may feel somewhat pressured against his will to begin adopting a feminine persona. Cases like these often involve a friend who is forceful and manipulative, imposing her will on others in her circle.

If you're watching your son wade into choppy waters with a risky relationship, what is the best way to respond? In the case of the pushy female friend, consider something along these lines: 'We've noticed that Emily is pushy with you and gets to make all the decisions in your friendship. Have you noticed this? We don't feel this is a healthy way to build a relationship. Let's talk about this.' Conversations like these may even lead to a sense of relief in your son if he felt pushed around by Emily and didn't know how to assert himself. Gentle and passive boys often struggle with this sort of self-advocacy. Pointing this out could also strike a nerve if your son recognises some truth in your observation. He might then immediately deny the unhealthy dynamic and defend his friend. That's OK too. You can validate how much this friendship seems to mean to him.

With an older teen boy or adult child, it may be ill-advised for parents to try to get between their son and the woman who has become important to him, especially if a romantic relationship has developed. Still, given his lack of social sophistication, even an older child may need some support in managing his powerful feelings and navigating the complex dynamic developing with a partner. Start the conversation and listen intently. Avoid shaming or ridiculing him. You can let a teen boy know that experimenting with how you present yourself is normal, and that it is even common to change aspects of yourself in your teenage years to fit in or to keep the attention of someone you like a lot. Adult children in committed long-term relationships can be pushed towards alienation if they feel they must choose between their partner and family. Ultimately, each family must decide how much guidance and direction is appropriate.

Social justice, reinterpreted

The ROGD boy, in addition to being sensitive, can also have a passion for justice and ethics. He may be highly attuned to the suffering of others and subsequently get involved in causes, whether in real life or online social justice spaces. He may be horrified to learn about injustices, crimes or other abhorrent behaviour carried out by males. If he has a propensity for obsessive thinking and self-scrutiny, he may question if his own male privilege makes him 'toxic' or 'an oppressor'. As he develops sexual feelings for girls, he begins to face a dilemma about his own role or complicity in women's suffering: 'Am I objectifying women? What does that say about me?' Furthermore, in online social justice spaces, anyone considered to have privilege is expected to be quiet, put his opinions aside and defer to anyone with less privilege.

Twenty-year-old John was very lonely when he first attended university a long way from home. He found it difficult to make friends and instead immersed himself in an online world. Trying to make sense of his life, John eventually found queer theory and social justice activism. Through YouTube videos, John learned that the current structure of society needed to be subverted and that the family bond should be dismantled. He started to feel a powerful sense of belonging with the LGBTQ+ community and reckoned they were the only people who could understand what was going on for him. It's a heady experience for the young person to feel as though he has the keys to the universe; teenagers and young adults are particularly susceptible to theories which promise to bring about utopia. John joined the LGBTQ+ society on his campus and engaged in the many deep discussions on this subject found in colleges and universities across the world. When John returned home for the Christmas break he was distant and argumentative with his parents. Sarah, John's mother, took the time to engage and commented, 'Although his ideas were not practical, I found it more helpful to ask thought-provoking questions that led John to think on a deeper level, rather than criticising these new concepts and creating a wider gulf between us.'

Things can get even darker as ideological bubbles tip into more extreme rhetoric. One male detransitioner writes about his shift from online social justice to MTF trans forums. He explains a popular concept there – 'testosterone poisoning':

> The idea is that, for male-to-female trans people, the testosterone naturally produced by their bodies is toxic. It makes them grow hair, causes their bodies to develop in a masculine direction during puberty, deepens their voices, changes how they smell, increases their libido, and often makes them more aggressive and prone to anger… These changes are upsetting and confusing to many young boys as they enter puberty.[8]

Parents can directly address these ideas with their son. What do these ideas mean to him? Where does this leave boys who want to develop a healthy sexuality? What does he think of belief systems that tell certain people to take a back seat based on their immutable characteristics (unchangeable physical attributes)? Assure him that experimenting with values and morality is a normal part of growing up, but that *you* don't have to share the same perspectives. Older teens and adults may be engaged with open-ended questions and the invitation to think for themselves.

Pornography

A survey of college-aged males found that the average age of first exposure to pornography is around thirteen.[9] Animated cartoon pornography often serves as a seemingly innocent stepping stone for children. Far from the *Playboy* magazines of previous generations, young people today are watching easily accessible porn that routinely features degradation, torture and humiliation.[10] Boys report that looking at porn for years leads them to compulsively seek out genres they find disgusting. The pull is irresistible despite a conscious aversion to the imagery.

Autogynephilia – or something that very much looks like it – can develop in some boys, and this can become an all-consuming fixation. Another genre, called 'sissy porn' or 'forced feminisation porn', is often referenced by MTFs who claim to have 'discovered' their trans identity through such imagery. In these clips, cross-dressing males wearing lingerie are depicted in submissive positions while being degraded and 'feminised'. In the 'hypno' version of this genre, visual elements such as repetitive swirling graphics and subliminal messages flashing across the screen make it even more enticing and addictive. Users of NoFap.com, a porn recovery website, indicate that this genre warped and twisted their sexuality and gender identity.[11]

It would be unlikely for you to know for sure if your son is viewing such disturbing material. After all, few of us voluntarily shared our pornography viewing habits with our parents as teens. But it's still important to consider internet safety and digital hygiene, just as you might deliberate carefully over what healthy foods you feed your kids, what schools you send them to, or what neighbourhood you live in. Communication is important, but talking to kids about porn can be incredibly challenging and scary. Fightthenewdrug.org is a helpful resource with information and step-by-step suggestions on how parents can begin a conversation. Whether you have a son or daughter who has been exposed to porn, they suggest the following:

- Emotionally and mentally prepare yourself
- Set a loving, supportive tone that doesn't shame or criticise
- Learn the science behind the harms of pornography
- Pick the right time and place where you can be calm and undistracted
- Have open discussions frequently, show compassion, and honour his or her privacy and discretion.[12]

FACING SEPARATION

Let's revisit Sheila and Taylor. Sheila felt hesitant to take her daughter's self-proclaimed label too seriously, given her lack of maturity. Then again, Taylor was doing exactly what she was supposed to be doing at this age – experimenting with identity and separating from her mum. The feeling here might be, 'Mum, you think you know who I am, but I'm not that innocent, childish girl you thought you knew.' The truth is, even the most deeply attuned parent can't understand EXACTLY what her child is going through. Sheila focused on honouring her daughter's differentiation while maintaining her own beliefs as a mother: 'As you are growing up, I am discovering aspects of your personality and identity that surprise me. Of course I don't know exactly what you're going through! I may not always see you the same way you see yourself, however, and that's OK.'

Teens and older adolescents will begin to learn about relationships through trial and error. You can reinforce basic principles about respect and trust. Especially if your child sometimes struggles to understand social dynamics, they might benefit from guidance through specific examples and gentle observations. Be someone she or he can bounce ideas off regarding their relationships and friendships. If your older teen or adult child is in a relationship, welcoming the partner into your home may ease tensions and give you further insight into their relationship. For example, if you suspect the partner doesn't like you because of your stance on 'affirmation', why not humanise yourself by being warm and embracing your child and her partner. You might even encourage your child to discuss the relationship with you.

Puberty and sexuality have always been confusing and thrilling aspects of adolescent life. It takes courage and honesty for parents to address these issues head-on. With some experimentation and guidance from families, young people stumble towards healthy relationships with their bodies and with others. And even if a great deal of awkwardness, shame or secrecy remains around the topic, acknowledging this outright can facilitate conversation and your child's move towards maturation.

4

PARENTING ALTERNATIVES TO AFFIRMATION

Proponents of affirmation claim that parents of gender-questioning kids ought to agree with their children's declaration that they are trans, and readily facilitate a social and even medical transition. Parents who immediately affirm their daughter's chosen gender and buy her a breast binder or boys' clothing and allow her to cut her hair are often held up as 'brave, supportive parents'. It is easy to find blogs or Facebook posts of parents announcing the 'happy' news that their child is trans. If your son or daughter has shared with you that they are trans, you may feel pressured to respond in an affirming or even celebratory manner, even though you feel that something is not right and believe a deeper exploration is warranted.

Psychologists have been studying child and adolescent development for over a century, and there is a rich literature on this topic. In Appendix 5, we have summarised the most important knowledge on this subject as it relates to sex and gender. We encourage you to read this material as it can help you know what to expect as your children grow. It is helpful to remember that children are not small adults. Their bodies, brains and personalities are growing and developing, and they need different things from us at different stages. While it is always important to support our children and communicate our unconditional love for them, this does not have to include agreeing to hasty social or medical transition. In this chapter, we will provide a framework for loving and connected parenting which supports your child's whole self and considers all aspects of her development.

There exists a dizzying number of competing and complementary theories about what makes 'good parenting.' The last thing you need is a rigid prescription telling you how to behave and alienating you from your parental instincts. We strongly believe you know what's best for your child and encourage you to trust yourself. Nevertheless, it can help to learn a bit about parenting styles so you can reflect a bit on what works for you and what doesn't.

In the 1960s the clinical psychologist Diana Baumrind developed and refined a theory of parenting styles that has been strongly supported by research from around the world. She identified four broad parenting models: authoritative, authoritarian, permissive and uninvolved.

Diana Baumrind's parenting styles

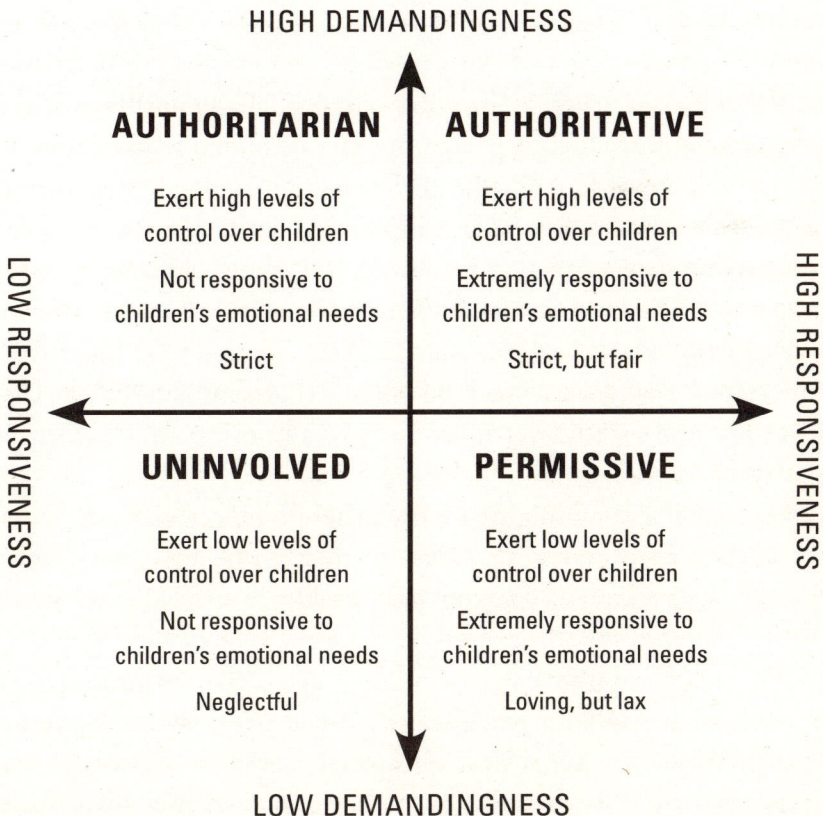

HIGH DEMANDINGNESS

AUTHORITARIAN	AUTHORITATIVE
Exert high levels of control over children	Exert high levels of control over children
Not responsive to children's emotional needs	Extremely responsive to children's emotional needs
Strict	Strict, but fair
UNINVOLVED	**PERMISSIVE**
Exert low levels of control over children	Exert low levels of control over children
Not responsive to children's emotional needs	Extremely responsive to children's emotional needs
Neglectful	Loving, but lax

LOW RESPONSIVENESS — HIGH RESPONSIVENESS

LOW DEMANDINGNESS

These reflect varying degrees of responsiveness and 'demanding-ness'. Responsiveness refers to the parents' sensitivity towards the child's needs, and demandingness to the expectations they place on the child's behaviour. We think of these as warmth and structure, respectively. Parents who demonstrate both would be called authoritative parents, Baumrind's ideal. Their children tend to feel cherished in the family, and grow up to become independent, happy and confident people with good mental health.

The other three parenting styles were associated with less ideal outcomes. Permissive parents are indulgent, warm, emotionally sensitive and attuned to their children's needs, but struggle to set boundaries and enforce rules. They are high on warmth, low on structure. Their children have a hard time following rules and regulating their emotions. They have poor self-control, can be egocentric and selfish, and therefore experience more relational difficulties.

Authoritarian parents exhibit a high level of control, but lack connection and empathy. They rarely compromise. They are low on warmth, high on structure. They may be domineering or dismissive of their child's perspective. They may employ harsh punishments and coercion to enforce their expectations. Their children tend to be more insecure and dependent on others. They may also struggle with mental health or behavioural issues, or exhibit lower academic performance.

Lastly, uninvolved parents are low on both dimensions: they expect little of their children by way of achievement, and they are less attuned to their emotional or physical needs. Their children tend to struggle with mental health issues, exhibit more delinquent behaviour, experience low self-esteem, act more impulsively, and have a hard time regulating emotions.

Baumrind later highlighted individual differences in children that may elicit certain parenting styles. So this can be a two-way street. Perhaps, for example, with your 'easy' child you naturally fall into a balanced and healthy authoritative style, while your more 'challenging' child brings out authoritarian dynamics when you try to keep him on track, or permissive dynamics when you try to avoid triggering his aggression. If parents have completely different styles, this can create havoc, and is exacerbated by two single-parent households where a usually authoritative parent may struggle to connect with the children after they have spent time with the mainly permissive ex-partner.

What can we deduce about the gender-affirming approach in light of these parenting styles? We believe that when clinicians, therapists and activists recommend affirming a child's gender, most of the time they do so with a genuine desire to help. When parents are told to agree with their child's stated identity, this recommendation appears warm and responsive on the surface, as it takes into account the child's desires and requests. However, if a child seeks to change his identity or medically alter his body because he is stuck in a pattern of self-loathing, is it an act of compassion to affirm his identity and thereby confirm there is indeed something wrong with him as he is now? The affirmative approach acknowledges that gender-questioning youth are extremely fragile in some ways. Instead of using time-honoured support systems to stabilise and strengthen them, affirmative clinicians often collude with the youth's self-sabotaging behaviours, attitudes and relational patterns. They often recommend that parents lessen their expectations or allow their child to withdraw from life's demands. They fail to exemplify the role adults *should* play when a child, in full distress, is pining after irreversible and poorly researched interventions. For example, advocates of 'gender affirmation' in the US have surgically removed the breasts of thirteen-year-old girls and continue to push for earlier and earlier intervention.[1] The direction and course of interventions are based on the desires of the child, not the wisdom and guidance of adults.

PARENTING THE GENDER DYSPHORIC CHILD

If parents discover that the recommendations from medical professionals are irresponsible, they also realise no one else is going to take responsibility for helping their child. How then can you, the mother or father of a gender-questioning child, develop an authoritative, loving stance that prioritises the bigger picture of your child's whole life and long-term well-being?

1. Clear the noise and tune inwards

Trust yourself. Trust your parental instincts built over the last twelve, sixteen, twenty-two years. Remain vigilant and cautious about whom you recruit for help. If you hear advice or hypotheses from professionals that simply feel wrong, inaccurate or grossly incomplete, don't discount your own take. Nobody knows or loves your child more than you do, and thinking for yourself is crucial.

2. Mind your own mental health

Maybe you fell into a 'rabbit hole' of online research about childhood gender dysphoria. Connecting with parents who have similar experiences can be incredibly grounding and relieving: you're not alone, and you're not crazy! On the other hand, maybe you feel overwhelmed, destabilised or depressed, getting totally consumed by this research while watching your child deteriorate. There are sleepless nights, uncontrollable crying or an indescribable numbness. Relationships are strained and you become disoriented. You need to take excellent care of yourself and try your best to find balance. Attend the support group. Avoid the support group. Figure out what helps you stay grounded and allows you to lean in wholeheartedly to this parenting challenge in a sustainable way. Build a routine of getting outdoors, eating well, exercising, reading, seeing trusted friends or enjoying hobbies to fulfil and restore your spirit. Do not lose yourself in the process.

3. Set firm, compassionate limits with your prepubertal child

If your prepubertal child is gender dysphoric or is saying he or she is trans, consider the potential root cause of the child's gender discomfort. Decades ago, most of the paediatric cases of gender dysphoria occurred in early childhood. Multiple studies documented that the majority – upwards of 80% – of these cases resolved by early adulthood as long as no steps were taken towards social transition.[2]

As a parent, you can do much to help your child come to terms with his sex. We advise against trying to enforce rigid gender norms. Many young children with cross-sex play and presentation preferences will grow up to be same-sex-attracted.[3] Accepting a little boy's preferences to dress up as a princess, while clearly stating that he is a boy and that he will grow up to be a man, will help him accept himself and the immutability of sex. You can affirm your child's creativity, uniqueness and his gender-nonconformity while clearly communicating to him the truth about our sexed bodies. It's OK to communicate in language appropriate to your child's age that the world can be a cruel place for those who don't abide by gender norms. Offer him love and unqualified acceptance while also preparing him to be resilient to what he might meet beyond your door.

Consider the fact that puberty for gender-distressed children is often necessarily difficult as it involves a challenge towards self-acceptance. Encourage your child to become proud of what their body can do – such as rowing, running, climbing or other activities that don't necessarily highlight sex differences but do challenge the body – not what their body looks like. Spend some time seeking out role models in real life or online that might resonate with your child. Most of all, be careful with online influences – gender-nonconforming children are a good deal less likely to accept their bodies if they are told from a very young age that they are trans.[4]

Decide on some household rules about presentation that you can implement, and stick to them. Some families allow gender-nonconforming boys to wear skirts and dresses at home but require them to dress in more gender-neutral clothing for school. Unfortunately, if you allow your young child to present as the opposite sex in today's environment, others will likely assume she is trans. Your child may be continually asked for her pronouns, or placed in groups with opposite-sex children. It's a sad state of affairs that our society has become so rigid in its expectations for young children, but that is the reality. It may be easier to help a young child stay in touch with his sex by ensuring that his presentation when outside the home doesn't signal unequivocally that he is a girl.

If your son wants to experiment with make-up, it's OK to explain that make-up is for grown-ups. Though it can be great fun for children of either sex to get dressed up and play with make-up, nail polish and high-heeled shoes, it should be acknowledged that these are accoutrements of adult dress.

If your child first asserts a trans identification when he or she is slightly older, you might wonder whether there is peer or social media influence afoot. This might especially be the case if your child is in a school with other trans-identified kids, or where gender identity ideology is taught. Does your pre-teen have access to the internet? If so, you should know what sites they are visiting and what they are doing there. You should limit internet use and use parental controls to wall off access to inappropriate sites.

As with younger children, it is important to meet your child's gender-nonconformity with acceptance while affirming the reality of biological sex. Beware of giving gender issues too much oxygen or allowing them to become a battleground. If your child is struggling with social, school or emotional concerns, offer lots of loving support and explore ways to ameliorate his difficulties. Take the focus off gender and address the underlying issues. Find ways to connect with your child and let him know you value him for who he is. You might make space to talk about what is hard about being a boy, as well as what's great about it. Affirm that there is no right way to be a girl or a boy. Our bodies just are, and we don't get a say in them. But they don't dictate what we do, how we behave, what we're interested in, or whom we love.

4. Communicate with your teen in heartfelt, calm and respectful dialogue

If you have a trans-identifying teen or young adult, there may be a great deal of conflict in the relationship and the feeling of walking on eggshells. Genuine, honest dialogue is needed to break this tension. Start by directly calling out the dynamics: 'I know it's been really hard for our family to talk about your identity exploration.' You and your child are coming at the topic from different perspectives, and this makes it difficult to be open. You can explicitly acknowledge this with your child. Apologise for the times when you lost your temper, and take responsibility for things you regret saying. But don't lie to them.

Communicate truthfully about your perspective: 'I know you really want us to use different pronouns. This is something I've reflected on a lot, and it just feels inauthentic for me. We have always been honest with each other, and I can't refer to you in a way that feels like I'm lying to you or being fake.'

Try using open-ended questions, avoid political debates, listen intently. Thank your child for the moments when he's willing to talk despite how difficult it feels. Acknowledge the positive impetus behind the identity: 'I know you're just trying to feel better/find your people/ feel comfortable in your body/carve out a unique identity.' Articulate your position in a simple statement that reflects your beliefs and values or make an observation in a kind, compassionate manner. You can also make tentative observations. For example, 'I don't believe changing your body is the best way to deal with your difficulties' or 'I could be wrong, but it seems you're trying to run away from yourself and become a new person.' Or, 'It's completely normal for people to change parts of themselves a bit to fit in. I could be wrong, but it seems to me that identifying as trans helps you to be a part of your friend group.' Or, 'It's great that you're exploring some new ideas on gender and sex, but no matter what surgeries someone has or hormones someone takes, they cannot change their biological sex: it's in every single cell of their body.'

Sprinkle in conversations like this every now and then. As much as possible, we recommend that parents speak truthfully about their views. For example, older teens and young adults should know exactly where you stand on medical transition, and may benefit from hearing what you believe more generally. If your adult child is no longer living at home, acknowledge and respect their need for some autonomy and independence, but make room to share what you believe: it's risky to change one's identity and medically transition before resolving other difficulties, developing financial stability, getting some life experience and having some healthy romantic relationships. Some parents find that their child is so resistant to any dialogue on this subject that it is easier to avoid it completely. You may be fearful that your child will cut all ties. The 'glitter family' or 'queer house' can become an alluring alternative to a family home where challenge has become the norm.

Parents must carefully weigh the potential risk of estrangement and proceed accordingly. Offering a happy space that will always be a sanctuary for your child will help to maintain your relationship.

5. Treat gender as a distraction and maintain high expectations

When ROGD teens are expressing distress through gender, that can become a smokescreen, distracting them and their loved ones from addressing a different, and more pressing, core problem. Take some time to reflect on what you think those core issues may be. Is your child looking for a way to rebel and carve out her own identity? Is your child afraid of growing up and subconsciously using gender to avoid life's future demands? Is your child deeply enmeshed in a peer group where being distressed about gender is the most potent form of social currency? There can be a myriad of reasons why gender identity has strong appeal at this point in your child's life. Once you've figured out what some of these are, consider healthier ways you can help your child meet her needs. Keep her engaged and broaden her day-to-day experiences. When a young person is in self-sabotage mode, respecting their autonomy can be at odds with helping them to mature. Here is where using your loving, assertive parental authority becomes crucial.

Here's one mum's approach to her son's gender fixation. This level of intervention may not work for older children, but suggesting alternative interests can be useful at all ages:

We minimised his exposure to trans ideas and deliberately reinforced positive and healthy behaviours, ideas, people – and risks. Our message was 'Yes, you feel lonely and weird, because you are lonely and weird (Unique! Beautiful! One of a kind!). It is going to take time to find your people. You've got to put the effort in, but we promise it gets better. We believe in you. You can do this!'

Step by step, we helped him stretch. We started with individual activities (chess and composing lessons). Then group things: philosophy camp, chess club, wilderness camp. We were 'unavailable' for get-togethers with the 'trans' friend/s. I snuck in and removed the pro-trans channels from his Reddit feed. We watched *The Social Dilemma*, and read *The Hidden Brain, Useful Delusions* and *The Coddling of the American Mind*. We encouraged risk (Try out for the play! Ask the girl to prom! Set up game night!) and helped him survive the inevitable failures.

After six months his trans behaviour started breaking up. After nine months it was very inconsistent. Around fourteen months he stopped shaving his legs. Finally, at around eighteen months, he cut his hair. Had we made it through? Around twenty-two months in, I gently asked where he was 'with the whole gender identity thing'. He responded, 'Mom, I never want to talk about it again.'

Maintain high expectations for how your teen treats others – yourself included. Some young people spend a lot of time online arguing with strangers about their perceived transgressions. This can lead to a feeling of superiority and even invincibility as they believe they can crush all their opponents with their clever arguments. These arguments can easily spill over into the dinner hour as every tiny instance of misspeaking is pounced upon as an opportunity to pontificate about how everyone else needs to 'do better'. If your child fervently believes in a cause, we recommend you learn all about it. Ask any questions you might have, protect your right to disagree and, perhaps most importantly, protect your right to make a mistake. The well-being of the family can quickly unravel if the children in the household are allowed to dictate the rules of conversation, and so it is essential that you retain your sense of authority. Maintain a focus on appropriate behaviour rather than allowing intense emotion to be a justification for bad behaviour.

Young people may benefit from a broad exploration of the many issues involved in social justice, such as advocacy for the disabled, support for migrants, prisoners and other vulnerable groups, efforts for the environment, exploration of women's rights, ethnicity, social equality, and re-examination of historical figures. They are searching for a better world, a fairer way of living.

With some guidance and thoughtful conversation, parents can gently nudge open the door so that the narrow focus on gender and social justice is broadened out. This can be a way of connecting with your child on subjects close to her heart. You can also encourage an in-depth understanding of concepts and ensure she is not relying on superficial knowledge that depends on slogans instead of real comprehension.

6. Have fun with your child

This might be a difficult prospect if your child has become withdrawn, moody, rude or sarcastic. Maybe his behaviour seems like an attempt to push you away while he gets further enmeshed in gender-focused online discussions or further involved with gender-focused school peers – these are competing attachments. Perhaps you enjoy baking, hiking or watching your favourite show together. Try to carve out light, low-pressure, easy moments. Go for a weekend road trip without the pressure of regular life. Consider the 80/20 rule: the majority of your interactions with your child should have *nothing* to do with difficult gender talks.

7. Expand outside of the bubble or routine

When possible, facilitate expansive opportunities to help buy some time and give your kids more life experience. New experiences outside our comfort zone help us expand our sense of self. We can be proud of doing something a bit challenging, or see ourselves in a new light. If you have concerns about your child's self-esteem, challenging but manageable experiences are a great way to build confidence. Structured, age-appropriate travel opportunities offer a fantastic way to develop a new perspective, though you should be careful that these are not with other trans-identified kids or the experience might reinforce this identity. When the destination is different from 'regular' life at home, the experience can be even more transformative and meet the need for autonomy. Can you look for a foreign exchange programme where your son can live with another family and become immersed in the language and culture? Is there a way for your daughter to travel abroad in a structured programme? Are there volunteering opportunities that give your kid a chance to contribute in a meaningful way, far from home? Could you travel together and use the time to build positive memories and share new experiences? On a smaller scale, do you have any like-minded family in another part of the country who might host your child for the spring or summer break? What local activities could your child participate in that might connect her with a new friendship group or new interests? Working with animals, being outdoors in nature or learning a new skill are all great ways to help develop your child's character and capacity.

8. Mitigate unhelpful influences

If you're actively engaged in all the ways we've discussed so far but your child's school, therapist or unhealthy social media habit is driving a wedge between you, much of your hard work will be compromised. Especially for younger teens, it's crucial to implement some healthy digital practices. It's become widely recognised that isolated teens during the Covid lockdowns became transfixed by social media content that encourages self-diagnosis and an obsession with mental disorders like Tourette's, dissociative identity disorder, bipolar disorder and of course gender dysphoria, to name a few. Programmes that specialise in treating high-risk behaviour advocate for abstinence from screens as part of the healing process.[5] Abstinence may not be feasible for many families, but some intervention is still important.

You might start by educating yourself and your children about the vitality of digital wellness. *The Social Dilemma* discusses the way social media algorithms capture and warp our attention. Watch it together and have a discussion with your kids. Share some of the ways you are also drawn in by this technology. Cutting down screen time, restricting apps or implementing some parental controls can be useful. Perhaps you'll start doing 'phone checks' with your younger teen's technology. Maybe you can bring the computer into a common area and limit time alone in the bedroom with the devices, set up downtime and insist her phone is outside her bedroom overnight. To connect with friends, encourage your child to use text messaging or, best of all, encourage her to spend more time in person.

9. If necessary, minimise contact with those who aren't supportive of your position

Especially if you have younger children who still live at home, it will be up to you to make decisions about how your family handles various aspects of your child's identity questions. Once you have a plan, we recommend communicating your strategy to close family members, friends and loved ones. If other adults in your child's life cannot co-operate with you or insist on contradicting your parenting, you may find yourself working at cross purposes. This can be draining. Some families find it necessary to maintain some distance with other adults who are unable to lean in with the same kind of love and structure.

In conclusion, adolescents are on a roller coaster journey of self-exploration, angst and change. Parenting at this stage can feel just as chaotic, especially with gender identity in the picture. Now is the time to be fully present, with a lot of love and structure, because your dis-oriented younger child needs some guard rails while they grope around in the dark, trying to figure out who they are.

5

SOCIAL TRANSITION

Social transition is the term used to describe a process whereby a person changes their identity socially. This generally includes a change of name, a change of pronouns (for example, she/her, he/him or they/them) and a change of gender expression. Gender expression can include clothes, style, hair, grooming and even mannerisms that are believed to represent the gender grouping that the individual feels better matches their inner sense of self. Social transition can also involve the person coming out as transgender to their school, family, friends and/or community, requiring the participation of others. Many educational institutions now have policies that allow the socially transitioned individual to use the toilets and dressing rooms and to play on the sports teams of the opposite sex.

Until recently it was only adults, having already gone through a therapeutic process, who would embark on social transition before taking the final step of genital surgery. Some critics of social transition believe that this process relies wholly on language and gendered stereotypes. It would arguably be more helpful to expand our concept of what it means to 'live like a girl' or 'live like a boy'.

We don't yet know whether living as the opposite sex can have an impact on a person's self-perception, although the preliminary data suggests that social transition can concretise children's desire to medically transition.[1] Social transition of prepubertal children has been shown to increase persistence of a transgender identity.[2] Never before have children changed pronouns and identities en masse, and it will be years before we have a body of research to properly inform us about the long-term impact of social transition. We cannot fully understand this new psychosocial intervention until we acquire the data.

Although this can often be the first step on the road to medical transition, many young people never go beyond social transition. Some feel liberated by the freedom to use a different name, pronouns and style; they embody the identity, try it on fully, and, when satisfied, are free to move on. Their social transition is one element of a larger exploration of identity and, having explored this fully, they focus on other aspects of their self. Others have the same experience and become locked in by their social transition. Perhaps some of these kids find their gender exploration difficult to come to terms with – for example they cannot fully engage in a process of exploration as they close down any thoughtful analysis. This might make them less likely to resolve their identity crisis and so they could become more reluctant to move beyond it. On the other hand, there have been reports that intense and immediate affirmation from peers can encourage gratified children to fixate upon their gender identity as the most important aspect of their identity. We humans are complex creatures, and it is difficult to discern why one child moves beyond social transition while another doesn't. No matter what the reason, it can be challenging for parents to know how to navigate the various challenges associated with social transition, and so we recommend meeting other parents who can share similar experiences.

Some young people who have socially transitioned feel stuck in a corner they can't get out of. Desistance seems like a dirty word, as they are often transfixed by the concept of their 'true self' manifested in their trans identity. Desistance may attract accusations of having lied about a new gender identity in the first place, and negatively affect a child's social status at school or college. Much like those who leave a cult and its values behind, some desisters have felt ostracised and excluded from the tribe that once welcomed them. Desisters often feel ashamed, as if they have been fake, and so it can be a long and difficult process. We discuss this further in Chapter 12.

THE COMING-OUT ANNOUNCEMENT

A quick Google search elucidates nearly four hundred million hits for young people to choose from if they seek information about 'coming out as trans'. It is all very exciting. There are letter templates to download and YouTube videos with compelling accounts of coming-out announcements. The way the individual chooses to come out as trans can be a big deal for them. During the course of our work, we've heard of these announcements happening in many different ways – a letter on the parents' pillow, in Christmas cards or birthday cards, icing on a cake, at a wedding and, popularly, by email or text. Some young people are heightened in the build-up to the announcement. Although they feel this is a huge moment, they are also keen to say that they were always trans, that nothing essentially has changed except that they now have a specific path before them. This can seem disingenuous to parents, like everything has changed.

The highly charged announcement reveals the way the teenager is absorbed by the idea that their trans identification is everything. They may have learned online that their new identity will fix all their problems but will also expose them to omnipresent transphobia. They may have been led to expect that their parents will be an obstacle to their progress and are therefore poised to see any reaction other than enthusiastic celebration as proof that their parents are transphobic. Even though the child may come from a progressive, educated and loving family, the online view is that parents need to be re-educated by teenagers. Many teens accept this narrative and are very sensitive to any resistance or flickers of doubt or questioning from their parents. The hypervigilance associated with the socially transitioned young person can be exhausting for everyone else, as all subjects seem to centre on the new trans identity.

Although the horse might have already bolted, it should help if you can be reasonably quiet during the announcement and the aftermath. This is the child's moment, and she is probably bubbling with emotion – even if she seems muted, it is a major event in her mind. *It is, after all, the first day of her new life.* In the initial stages, you should try to listen to everything the child has to say on the subject. If you tend to speak over your child, we recommend you keep the acronym WAIT (Why Am I Talking?) central in your interactions. Active listening means paying careful attention to everything she tells you. It involves asking questions and attending patiently to the answers so that you can more fully understand. You may want to ask for more information. For example, you might ask your child where she got her information and what her preferred online platforms are. If you do so, be sure that your tone expresses authentic curiosity. Your child will likely become defensive if she senses that you are interrogating her.

It is best if no decisions are made at this stage. It can be enough for you to listen intently and say, 'Thank you for sharing all this with me. I've a lot to catch up on and I will certainly embark on that with full vigour. You will need to have patience as I catch up on this subject. I'm your parent, I care about you more than you can ever imagine, and I will endeavour to become an absolute expert on this. But I'm not there yet, and so I need you to be patient.' The teen might not be happy with this at all. They might believe it is essential for parents to act immediately. However, pleasing teenagers in the moment can be reckless and not necessarily good for the young person in the long term.

At this emotionally charged time, it can be useful to remember that a big emotion does not have to be met with a big emotion: it is your role to sit tight when your teenager is filled with passion and certainty. If your partner or co-parent is completely thrown by the announcement and ready to agree to your child's demands, request that you both listen and learn before making any big statements. It is also important to note that certainty is not a sign of great mental health – the human condition is filled with uncertainty. This is one of the reasons the child's zeal should not be a justification for you to go against your parental instincts. It can be terrifying if your darling child rails against your apparent inaction. *Wu wei* is an ancient Chinese concept that means 'effortless action', or 'inaction', and it highlights the wisdom of knowing when it is important not to act. Knowing when to act and when not to act is often difficult: we suggest that when emotions are running high, you should probably offer compassion, love and tenderness but resist making any decisions until you know what they're doing.

It is worth pointing out that when a younger child's trans identity is very new, parents may be able to arrest any further commitment to the identification with a straightforward show of parental authority. Some parents have been fortunate enough to anticipate a child's announcement. For example, Shelly was friends with the parents of her daughter's friends. They tipped her off that their daughters had recently come out as trans. Twelve-year-old Lela had not spent a lot of time consuming trans-related social media and had only recently been swept along on this heady current when her friends began experimenting. Shelly and her husband were able to nip Lela's trans identification in the bud, so to speak. When she came out to them, they were prepared. They lovingly but firmly explained that she was female and always would be, and that they would be open to her experimenting with clothing and hairstyles but not with identity. Note that such a strategy is unlikely to work with an older child or one who has become deeply committed to the new identity as a result of spending a lot of time ruminating about it online or with friends.

NAMES AND PRONOUNS

Some parents are deeply connected with their child's name – one loving father described how his child's name was the first word he said to his daughter when she was born and placed in his arms. It was a treasured memory, as he called his child after his mother, whom he lost when he was a little boy. This opens a much wider discussion about who owns a name.

Some believe that parents hold authority over the child's legal name until they are eighteen or until the child is fully independent (for example, no longer relying on their parents' financial support). Others believe that the child's name is the child's, theirs to change as often as they wish, whether they are four or fourteen. The name a trans-identified person chooses often has a purpose – to signify that they are leaving behind their old self and embracing a new identity. It can suggest a rejection of their deepest self. There are manifold unintended consequences and risks with a name change and it is not necessarily the benign act that it may seem to be. Having worked in this arena for some time, we have come to believe that legal changes feel premature when an individual's identity and their brain continues to develop until they are in their early twenties. However, the use of an informal nickname can be a compromise worth considering. We're aware that compromise does not come easily to people who believe that names and pronouns represent everything, and this can become a source of major conflict: none of this is easy.

It's valuable to separate a name change from a pronoun change: these are very different events. Many parents believe that using a different pronoun, especially a cross-sex pronoun, feels like colluding in a false reality, whereas they can accept that their child hates their birth name and wants to change it. Perhaps you might give permission for your child to informally change their name – not permanently on the school register, but as a nickname to be used in class – but maintain the same pronouns as you feel it inappropriate to deny biological reality. If teachers address a boy as 'she/her', that sends a powerful message that all the adults in the building believe he's now a girl. You could remind your child that your job as a parent is to consider his long-term needs, not just his short-term wishes. Non-binary pronouns may be a workable compromise for some; others find them even more egregious.

Some families feel that changing names and pronouns is a minor concession. Doing so feels like a low-stakes intervention that can signal that parents are listening and taking the young person's distress seriously. We have seen it happen where families changed names and pronouns and this seemed to strengthen the parent–child bond, avoided an unnecessary power struggle, and created some space for the young person to explore and experiment. In some of these cases, the young person eventually moved through their stage of trans identification. The parental strategy of adopting the new name and pronouns apparently succeeded in helping to minimise conflict and allowed the child to work through their gender exploration without medicalisation.

However, we have also known cases where parents made the same decision for the same reasons. Even though these parents were firmly against medicalisation and were hoping to avoid it at all costs, they wanted to be sensitive to their child's growing need for autonomy and hoped to express respect for their process of exploration. They acceded to the request to call their child by a new name and to use new pronouns in the hope that such a move would build more trust, reduce distress and allow the child to move through a trans identification without hormones or surgery. Yet, years later, these parents have come back to us and told us that their child's gender issues didn't resolve and that their young adult is now on hormones or is pursuing surgery.

We have seen both scenarios happen many times, and it would be difficult for us to say what factors lead to one outcome and what to another. Agreeing to the change has certainly worked for some families, but we've also seen considerable fallout and regret about having done so. Arguably, changing names and pronouns signals supportiveness and a willingness to listen. Equally arguably, changing names and pronouns may help to cement a young person's commitment to their new identity. Given that the stakes involve the potential for medicalisation, it may be better to err on the side of caution and not agree to change name and pronouns, but there are many individual variables and we do not have straightforward answers.

As with all decisions, the burden is on your shoulders. It is up to you to figure out how you wish to deal with this issue. We don't believe that it's appropriate for therapists or anyone else to provide diktats. We have noticed how parental authority has been undermined over the last couple of decades. We can't tell you what to do, but we hope we have provided thought-provoking information so you can harness your thoughts and come to the conclusion that makes the most sense for your family.

You may find it helpful – although this can be incendiary – to initiate discussion about compelled speech: who owns the pronouns? Is it the speaker, or is it the person they are referring to? Can we force other people to speak about us in the way we want? Considering that not everyone feels they have a gender identity, should those people be made to use the language of a belief system they don't subscribe to? If a person can dictate the pronouns, can they also dictate the adjectives and the nouns? Should it be 'they are' or 'they is'? Is there room for a polite request to use pronouns to be equally politely refused?

The following suggested script shows how a conversation could unfold:

YOUNG PERSON: Mum, I've been thinking long and hard about this and I've decided I need to change my name and pronouns. This means everything to me. It's hard to explain because you're not non-binary, but when someone calls me by my dead name it hurts me very deeply. I just can't handle it any more.

PARENT: I can see you're dreadfully upset. Why don't we sit down and have a good chat?

YOUNG PERSON: You don't understand. I don't need to chat. I just need you to go into the school and explain to the staff that they can't dead-name me any more.

PARENT: I hear you. However, it's not my role to take this on. My role as a parent is to slow things down when you want to speed things up. I know it's really distressing for you, but you matter to me more than anything. I know I sometimes do things that might be wrong, but trying my best is all I can do. I'm simply too terrified to allow you to officially change your name. It's going too fast, and I can't allow this pace of change. I'm happy to support an informal change, though.

YOUNG PERSON: What good is that? I need it to be a proper name change, otherwise nobody will take me seriously.

PARENT: Your name is one of the most precious words in my life. I think we'll need some further reflection on this so we can both come to some compromise. You can change your name among your friends if you wish, but adults need to offer guidance and so we need to hasten slowly.

YOUNG PERSON: You don't understand. This means everything to me. I can't live with the name Isabelle any more. I hate it.

PARENT: I'm so sorry you're upset. I really am.

Sometimes it's important, especially when the conversation is going around in circles, that you take charge of the situation and leave the room. Conversations like this can descend into an emotional and messy brawl, with the child trying to play off one parent against the other or making wild threats about leaving home and never coming back unless you do what he wants, and you need to be sensitive to this. You may wish to stay there until you have cheered up your child, but this is not necessarily possible, nor is it always the right thing to do. Every adolescent needs to overcome certain challenges so that they one day become a mature and reflective adult. These challenges can be difficult, such as learning to accept our limitations and develop our coping skills. Just as when your little boy was small and learning to walk, you can't do it for him – you need to let him stumble and fall until one day he can walk without falling over. Back then, you bit your lip as he laboriously overcame other challenges in childhood such as learning to ride a bike, or learning to read and write. Today, you might need to bite your lip and leave the conversation, knowing that your child is upset but needs to confront reality and that you can't do it for them.

HAIR, CLOTHES AND STYLE

Many kids who identify as trans may adopt a new voice, a new accent and an entirely new persona. Calling it 'fake', although it may seem so, isn't a true representation of what's going on: identity exploration requires the person to fully embody the identity so they can properly try it on. It's like trying on a dress in a clothes shop – you can't do it by halves, you need to put on the shoes, the tights, and only then can you see if it suits you.

Some kids, during their process of social transition, make huge changes to their look. Although it may be tempting to become over-invested in what clothes your child wears, it can be helpful to allow them the freedom to express themselves, even if you don't personally like it, as long as it is not endangering their health. Teenagers undergo a process of identity exploration during which they try on different styles and personas. This is a serious business – as serious as make-believe play was when they were younger – and so we believe that allowing your children the freedom to wear whatever they want is an important aspect of loosening your control over them. If there is a certain dress code in school or other places, you might ask your child to adhere to these rules, but otherwise teenagers need to be free to express themselves however they wish, so long as they're not harming anyone. Some parents take the view that dressing in a certain way can be provocative and dangerous, and it might be valuable to say this to your child; however, the process of emotional maturity requires the adolescent to begin to take charge of her body and how she presents it. It could be very important for the child to feel a sense of power over their gender expression, and we believe it is vital to honour this.

Parents might find an opportunity to bond with their child when discussing appearance. Looking at different people's styles, especially famous musicians such as David Bowie, Boy George, Grace Jones, Annie Lennox and Lady Gaga can lead to interesting conversations about whether the clothes maketh the person. As always, if parents can move the conversation from their child's own gender expression to a more generalised philosophical discussion, the young person's mind will inevitably benefit from some lateral thinking.

The grooming habits of gender-distressed children can be intense. Some girls might stop shaving their legs and underarms, or they may actively want to be smelly if they believe this makes them more boyish. Marie, a forty-three-year-old mother, reported feeling disgusted by her daughter's hairy legs and her facial hair, while her daughter, Ella, was equally disgusted by her mother's shaved legs and her obsession with removing all traces of the hair on her upper lip. These can be generational choices that we can learn to live alongside if we try hard enough. Over time both Marie and Ella learned to smile at the other's habits and a deeper liaison was formed. Other gender-distressed young people can develop an aversion to the shower or to mirrors. This can be because their dysphoria is causing them so much distress that they want to avoid the truth of their bodies; however, it can also be because they believe in the stereotype that boys are smelly and don't shower and so, in their bid to act like a 'real boy', a trans-identified girl might adopt these behaviours. While we think it's important to be compassionate and understanding, you need to be aware that these kids are often very vulnerable and need a deeper level of care.

MUM: I've been thinking. I reckon you need to spend less time in the bathroom.

YOUNG PERSON: Is this about me being trans?

MUM: Well, kind of, but it's also about you becoming fixated, and I want to make sure your hair removal doesn't become harmful.

YOUNG PERSON: Just leave me alone. I need to be who I really am.

MUM: I'm afraid it's my role to intervene over matters of safety, and I think this is causing you harm. I love you very much and I need to protect you. While I understand you might want to spend some time in the bathroom, I don't think we can allow you to spend hour after hour in there any more.

BREAST BINDERS AND TUCKING

Breast binding and tucking are dangerous aspects of social transition that parents need to know about. Breast (or 'chest') binding is a strategy some girls use in a bid to flatten their breasts. Using constrictive materials such as cloth strips or purpose-built undergarments bought online, the binder can be extremely tight and uncomfortable. Some people create their own by using a number of tops layered from tight to loose.

On a psychological level, binding can exacerbate any fixation the teen has with her breasts. To focus on the most despised aspect of your body so much that it causes you pain and restricts your breathing is not healthy; building self-acceptance and using distraction and mindfulness techniques probably work a lot more effectively. On a physical level, peer-reviewed evidence shows that breast binding is damaging for bodies in the short and long term. Binders have a negative impact on skeletal growth, skin health and more. One study showed that the most common symptoms were back pain (65%), shortness of breath (48.6%), bad posture (32%), chest pain (30%) and light-headedness (30%).[3] Another study found that those who use breast binders have abnormal lung function.[4] When children wear binders for too many hours in a row, binders become a good deal more dangerous.[5] There is also an insidious element to breast binding: a survey of 1,800 people showed that sometimes it can take years for the negative health effects of binding to be fully seen.[6]

Some parents compromise with binders that are several sizes larger or allow the teen to bind or tuck on special occasions, while other parents allow their teen to use a sports bra or compression shirt in a certain context as this minimises the breasts and also acts as a comfort for those with sensory issues. Many others refuse, and endure the conflict that follows. Your teenager may decide to order one online anyway, or threaten to self-harm or leave home if her needs are not met. Some girls hate the male attention they receive from having large breasts, so binding seems the logical solution. You could suggest getting her professionally fitted for a sports or compression bra. In these contexts, parents often need to weigh up whether the young person's concern about their appearance should override serious health concerns.

The term 'packing' refers to the process of adding some material to your crotch to create a bulge that looks like you have a penis. Like binding (and tucking), these garments tend to exacerbate gender-related distress in the long term, although they certainly provide what feels like short-term relief to the individual. While a trans-identified girl who wears a binder and a packer can feel a sense of pride that she looks like a boy, she may also aggravate a deeper, niggling feeling that she is dressing up as a boy – and become more defensive as a result. And so the surface feeling of satisfaction might suppress the unconscious and more disturbing emotions that she is creating a fake persona.

Tucking is a technique where the crotch bulge of the penis and testicles is hidden by using materials such as bandages or masking tape. This creates a smooth shape around the groin but comes with serious health consequences, such as oligospermia (low sperm count) and testicular torsion. The reported symptoms of one study included itching (28%), rash (21%), testicular pain (17%), penile pain (14%) and skin infections (12%).[7] While the psychological impact of tucking is insufficiently studied, the ceremonial aspect of tucking and the associated pain and discomfort suggests that, like breast binding, this can be a form of self-harm. As for binding, it is psychologically harmful for your child to engage in a painful activity that leads them to focus on the part of the body they most abhor.

SOCIAL TRANSITION: AN ACTIVE INTERVENTION

Social transition is a powerful psychosocial intervention that we believe should not be undertaken without considerable forethought and clinical supervision. According to Dr Hilary Cass, social transition is an 'active intervention' and 'not a neutral act'.[8] Many misinformed but well-meaning adults can inadvertently engage in a process of socially transitioning your child by going along with requests for certain facilities, exemptions and preferred pronouns. For this reason, parents need to be prepared for meetings with other adults who are involved in their child's life. This might be a teacher, doctor, dentist or therapist. They might choose to use your child's preferred name and pronoun, and you need to figure out your position on this. Some parents choose to ring ahead and tell the adult that their child is a gender-diverse child who presents as a boy but goes by this name and that pronoun. For example, Liz, a parent of a nonconforming thirteen-year-old, rang ahead before a visit to a hairdresser and asked the hairstylist to refrain from commenting on boy/girl issues and instead focus on the hairstyle.

Well-meaning adults may unintentionally impose their views on parents of gender-questioning children and attempt to convince parents that social transition is of no consequence, allowing the child to 'work it out for themselves'. Many parents describe how they lost friendships, fell out with their siblings and spent many sleepless nights tossing and turning about the devastating conflicts that have erupted in their lives. You might need to learn how to draw a hard boundary when your child is becoming unduly influenced by adults who should have more respect for your parental authority, your love for your child and your ability to research and evaluate the most appropriate pathway. It might be helpful to do some journalling and even consider writing your 'elevator pitch' so that you can explain in three sentences how your child is vulnerable to external influences right now, and that while you are happy for them to explore their identity, it is also your role as a parent to ensure they don't prematurely come to any decisions they may later regret. You might follow this up, if the concerned adult is particularly pushy, with a clear request that they respect your role as a loving parent and remind them that they do not know or love your child more than you do. This can be hard to get right the first few times. With practice, it might become a concise way of explaining your position without getting drawn into lengthy debates about gender ideology.

Your friends and family may not be as well informed as you are, but they must respect your role. Your priority is to guide your child and nurture your attachment relationship. It can be extremely important to become aware of what sets you off and devise a plan to make sure you don't go off the deep end. If you can work out your triggers, and how you are going to avoid getting upset by well-meaning or interfering adults who feel free to express their opinions about your parenting decisions, then you will be better able to put forward your position in the most effective way.

A PSYCHOSOCIAL MORATORIUM

Many people believe that social transition is a minor event. We are unconvinced that children should be allowed to reject their body when, developmentally speaking, they should be learning how to handle reality. Parents might consider proposing a psychosocial moratorium (a period of time, as outlined by the developmental psychologist Erik Erikson, in which decision-making is suspended in order to provide the young person with the time to consider who they are and what they want) on all major decisions concerning their unfolding identity. This could mean that the child can wear whatever she wants, explore her gender identity with style and creativity, and ask her friends to call her by her chosen name. But there is a freeze on any significant decisions that could foreclose future options. It would be great for young people if society engaged with the concept of a psychosocial moratorium in general. Then young people could fully leap into whatever identity they wanted to try out without commitment. Unfortunately, society does the opposite and encourages children and teens to look to the future and get ahead by mapping out their college and future career before they have reached adulthood.

Proposing a moratorium on big decisions does not mean the family should avoid the subject of sex or gender. Some parents might ask their child if they feel that their social transition will further promote gendered stereotypes, and how this will affect gender-nonconforming children in the future. Gender-distressed young people are typically socially aware, and so long as the parent is gentle and exploratory, rich conversations can unfold. Why is blue for boys? Why can't boys wear dresses? Where did we get the idea that boys have short hair and girls have long hair? (You might want to spend a little time googling these subjects before you begin to speak about them in a meaningful way.) The general idea is to lead your child to a more expansive understanding, so their brains become accustomed to thoughtful and challenging conversation. Agreeing with your child all the time might help them in the short term, but learning to disagree and yet still maintain a good relationship is a stronger basis in the long term.

WHAT CAN PARENTS DO TO HELP?

We have noted that a change of environment can often help dysphoric young people – maybe a change of school or an extended visit abroad could give the young person the opportunity to expand their sense of self. If your child is at college or university, you might consider offering to pay for a mind-expanding holiday. Sometimes it is more helpful to take your child to a different culture than to bring them to a therapy session every week – and we say this as three therapists who believe in the value of good therapy. While outsourcing the issue to a professional can feel reassuring, your child might benefit more from interventions that support the parent–child relationship.

Try to give your child the space to explore their identity, while ensuring they are kept safe from harm. This is difficult to manage, as it is easy to see threats everywhere. For the process of emotional maturity to begin to take place, parents need to communicate with their children that they will one day be the captain of their own ship. It is the role of parents to keep them safe until adulthood, when it will be time for the young adult to be responsible for their own decisions. Although many parents are fearful of bestowing this power on their children, it is important that these adolescents begin to feel both the power and the burden involved. Many ROGD teens in particular do not want to take responsibility for their life – preferring instead that their parents take on this role – yet this can be essential for their recovery and encourage much-needed emotional maturity.

There are endless ways to deepen our understanding of what it is to be human. Exploring the family tree can complexify the young person's understanding of themselves, and parents might point out that their child is similar to other relatives. Also, the cultural background of both parents can encourage the child to come to a deeper understanding of how they have come to be this person. Some parents believe it is only when their offspring are fully functioning adults that they should be free to make their own decisions. As the cliché goes, time is a great healer. Adolescents often engage in power struggles with their parents and as adults find to their surprise that many of their beliefs correspond with their parents'. If parents can ride this tumultuous wave and help their child press the pause button as the chaos reigns, everything might change with time.

6

MEDICAL INTERVENTIONS

Millie was a delightfully quirky kid with idiosyncratic interests. When she announced to her parents at twelve that she was bisexual, her parents weren't at all surprised. When she told them she was transgender a few months later, they were a bit taken aback, but they wanted to be supportive. They allowed her to change her name and pronouns and cut her hair. Her mum even took her shopping to purchase a typically male wardrobe. At first, Millie was elated, but as time passed, her mental health started to deteriorate. She began hating her growing breasts and started wearing a binder. Within a few months, she was demanding access to testosterone – she was certain she needed it to be happy.

As discussed, social transition is often presented as a low-stakes, fully reversible intervention that relieves distress and invites self-acceptance. Some parents may view requests to change name and pronouns as a harmless fad, a social craze, or just part of being a teenager today. However, there is significant concern that social transition leads to medical transition. Further, one medical intervention tends to pave the way towards the next one. Transition – whether social or medical – is a high-stakes endeavour.

Initially, medical transition was focused solely on genital surgeries until the 1990s, when there was a move towards hormonal treatment.[1] As we write, the context around minors accessing medical interventions is changing rapidly. The Gender Identity Development Service

(GIDS) of the Tavistock Clinic in London has come under increasing scrutiny. Hannah Barnes's *Time To Think*, the inside story of the collapse of the Tavistock, noted that 'The clinical team had never discussed as a group what it even understood by the word "transgender"… Differential diagnoses – ones that suggested other factors at play – were discouraged.'[2] The disproportionate number of young people on the autism spectrum who are referred to GIDS at the Tavistock needs to be addressed, especially considering how both Barnes's book and the interim Cass Review highlighted the issue of diagnostic overshadowing where other conditions such as ASD, ADHD, OCD and eating disorders are often given little attention once gender-related distress is mentioned. As GIDS is due to close, it is likely that minors in the UK will have an increasingly difficult time accessing medical intervention.[3] However, some private doctors and online operators continue to offer puberty blockers and hormones to minors.

Medical transition is also available to adults from a wide range of private physicians, and many parents are concerned that vulnerable young adults, especially those between eighteen and twenty-five, will be fast-tracked into medical transition as soon as they reach their eighteenth birthday, without being offered routine psychological interventions.

There is little consensus across the world about how to tackle gender-related distress. In the Nordic countries, there have been recent policy changes curtailing access to medical interventions. In Sweden, hormones for youth are recommended only in exceptional cases; psychotherapeutic care is emphasised instead.[4] In 2020, Finland recommended that psychotherapy should be the first-line treatment, not puberty blockers and hormones.[5]

Meanwhile, gender-affirming medical care for minors is big business in the US, and has become a political and legal battlefield. At the time of writing, some twenty-six states have attempted to enact legislation that will make this illegal, while California's laws will make the state a sanctuary for those seeking to medically transition their child.[6] Gender clinics and private doctors in the US routinely prescribe blockers and hormones to minors, and double mastectomies are performed on under-eighteens.[7] In extreme cases, some clinicians have removed the breasts of thirteen-year-old girls, and continue to push for earlier intervention.[8] In 2015 the US National Institutes of Health awarded a $5.7m grant to study 'the impact of early medical treatment in transgender youth'. Robert Garofalo, one of four principal investigators, told a podcast interviewer in May 2022: 'There is universal support for gender-affirming care from every mainstream US-based medical society that I can think of.'[9]

In September 2022, the World Professional Association of Transgender Health (WPATH) released the eighth version of their Standards of Care, known as SOC8. Although these guidelines originally included minimum ages – fourteen for hormones, fifteen for mastectomy, seventeen for vaginoplasty – they released a correction removing these, effectively leaving the decision to individual doctors.[10] The same document contained a new chapter on eunuchs as a legitimate new gender identity, and did not include one on detransitioners. Consequently Genspect, an international organisation that promotes a healthy approach to sex and gender, questions WPATH's reliability and now offers an alternative vision to WPATH for gender-distressed people.

Some countries have deviated from WPATH guidelines, including the UK, Ireland, Sweden and Finland. These countries have conducted their own evidence reviews and determined that a more cautious course is required. Other practitioners in the US and Canada see the WPATH guidelines as overly restrictive. It is not unusual for interventions to be offered to adults based on informed consent, meaning the patient must only sign a form stating he has been made aware of the treatment's potential risks. No mental health assessment is required.

What kind of interventions your child has access to will depend on where you live and how old she is. It may depend on the individual practitioner. Young adults can generally access most medical interventions without significant assessment, evaluation or exploration. This can be a huge source of distress and worry for parents with young adult children, given that the brain is still developing. It is well established that the brain undergoes a 'rewiring' process that is not complete until approximately twenty-five years of age.[11]

PUBERTY BLOCKERS

Puberty blockers are usually the first medical intervention offered to children entering adolescence. WPATH's SOC8 recommends that these be prescribed as soon as puberty begins. These gonadotropin-releasing hormone (GnRH) agonists work by decreasing gonado-tropin, thereby decreasing oestrogen and testosterone. The two most prescribed are Leuprorelin or Lupron, and Triptorelin. These drugs are used for various purposes, including the treatment of breast cancer, endometriosis, prostate cancer, precocious puberty and the chemical castration of violent sex offenders.

In the early 2000s, Dutch clinicians began offering puberty blockers to gender dysphoric youth in early puberty. A cohort of seventy young people were studied. They had all suffered from gender dysphoria since early childhood. It is significant that the vast majority (sixty-two) were lesbian, gay and bisexual children. After being carefully screened to ensure that there were no significant mental health issues, they were offered puberty blockers, followed a few years later by cross-sex hormones. From age eighteen onwards, they all had surgery (one of the participants of the study died as a result of complications following this surgery). This series of treatments became known as the Dutch Protocol.[12] A modified version of the Protocol was adopted in the US by paediatric endocrinologist Norman Spack, who opened the first clinic to treat trans-identified children in 2007. In the UK, GIDS at the Tavistock launched an Early Intervention Study between 2011 and 2014, offering puberty blockers to forty-four adolescents aged twelve to fifteen. However, it is important to note that there have been many critiques of the Dutch research, and in *Time to Think* Hannah Barnes reported that 'GIDS appeared to have data that showed there was no impact on psychological well-being, when using more objective measures rather than self-reported satisfaction.'[13] Today, in gender clinics around the world, puberty blockers are usually offered to children who identify as the opposite sex at the beginning of puberty (Tanner stage 2) irrespective of their age. This is an off-label use, meaning that these drugs were originally intended to treat different conditions and have never been tested for large-scale use on gender dysphoric children.

THE CASE FOR PUBERTY BLOCKERS

Puberty blockers halt the progress of normal puberty. This means that boys will not develop facial hair, an Adam's apple or a deep voice. Their genitals will not mature. Girls will not develop breasts and will not menstruate. This makes it easier to 'pass' as the other sex as an adult. Male-to-female patients who transition post-puberty will often have a difficult time passing convincingly as a woman because of the effects of male puberty. For female-to-male patients, the effects of female puberty are less likely to affect one's ability to pass later in life. However, because blockers prevent breast growth, an FTM patient may not need to undergo a double mastectomy later. These are benefits for gender dysphoric children if we are absolutely certain that it will be right for them to always present as the opposite sex throughout their entire life, and if they continue to value passing over other considerations such as fertility and/or sexual functioning.

These drugs are touted as a neutral 'pause button' that allows a young person to 'buy time': the delay was meant to allow a child to evaluate whether they want cross-sex hormones. It has been claimed that blockers are fully reversible, that puberty will resume without incident if the drugs are stopped, but studies repeatedly find that close to 100% of those on blockers progress to irreversible cross-sex hormones.[14] The Tavistock Clinic's own nine-year study found that 98% of patients chose cross-sex hormones.[15] This leads us to believe that being on blockers hugely increases the chances that someone will go on to hormones. We believe that the second possibility is far more likely. It seems plausible that part of what reconciles gender dysphoric youth with their bodies is the enormously complex changes that happen to us during adolescence. The hormones of puberty don't just change the body, they change the brain in important ways that we don't fully understand. Interrupting this process will likely have unforeseen consequences.

Puberty blockers are part of a cascade of interventions. Let's imagine a twelve-year-old MTF child who was socially transitioned at five or six. Since early childhood, he has been dressing like a girl, called by a girl's name, and treated in every way as if he were a girl. As he nears puberty, the thought of his genitals getting larger, his voice getting deeper and his facial hair appearing would most likely seem alarming. Social transition then creates a situation in which puberty is seen as a potential trauma and an emergency. Parents may feel that getting such a child on puberty blockers is a matter of great urgency. If such a child remains on blockers for years, he will see the boys and girls around him begin to develop while he stays in a childlike state. This will likely increase his desire to begin puberty along with his peers, thus creating pressure to begin cross-sex hormones.

RISKS OF PUBERTY BLOCKERS

As explained above, being on blockers appears to inhibit the normal reconciliation with one's natal sex that happens in most trans-identifying young children. As the British Society of Paediatric Endocrinology and Diabetes (BSPED) recommended in 2005, puberty was 'the most likely time for change and reversibility of the Gender Dysphoria'.[16]

Puberty blockers have been associated with significant bone health issues when prescribed for precocious (early) puberty.[17] Reports of serious bone fractures and osteoporosis have been noted among teens who have been on blockers.[18] It is possible that such bone health effects are widespread and that we don't know the size of the problem because there has not been good follow-up on many of these cases. In animal studies with sheep, for example, puberty blockers appear to affect spatial reasoning.[19] For natal males, puberty blockers will make subsequent vaginoplasty surgery more difficult and riskier because the penis remains child-sized (traditional vaginoplasty technique involves the inversion of the penile sheath to form the neovagina). There is some evidence that blockers may worsen mental health. In one study, they were found to increase anxiety and depression among female-to-male adolescents.[20] The US Food and Drug Administration (FDA) introduced a warning on the labelling of puberty blockers in 2022 regarding an increased risk of vision loss.[21]

A child who begins blockers in early puberty and progresses directly to cross-sex hormones – as most children do – will be permanently infertile.[22] What is more, it appears that male children may never develop orgasmic capacity in adulthood. According to Marci Bowers, surgeon and current president of WPATH, 'If you've never had an orgasm pre-surgery, and then your puberty's blocked, it's very difficult to achieve that afterwards.'[23] To state things plainly, puberty blockers, when followed by cross-sex hormones, render children infertile and may leave male children without normal sexual function.

DIFFICULTIES WITH CONSENT

In December 2020, the British High Court ruled that it was unlikely a child under the age of sixteen could consent to the use of puberty blockers.[24] Although the case, brought by ex-Tavistock patient Keira Bell and the mother of a fifteen-year-old girl on the GIDS waiting list at the Tavistock Clinic, 'Mrs A', was later overturned on appeal, it highlighted the difficulties with a child making an informed decision about the loss of future choices she may not be able to imagine.

Because of this case and subsequent focus on the safety and efficacy of puberty blockers, the NHS has ensured that GIDS is much more careful about prescribing puberty blockers, and currently must justify this recommendation to a panel. GIDS is shortly due to close permanently, with a new system of regional clinics that focus on a more multidisciplinary approach, and require mandatory psychological assessments.

IF YOUR CHILD IS REQUESTING PUBERTY BLOCKERS

Puberty blockers are an intervention with a high potential for negative side effects and/or potential regret, and their benefits have not been proven. For these reasons, we do not recommend puberty blockers as a treatment option for gender dysphoric children; as we have seen, they are not a reversible neutral 'pause button', and the risks appear to outweigh the benefits.

Luckily, because of the age at which blockers are usually prescribed, parents will usually have considerable input. If a child in early puberty asks for blockers, saying no may require a short, definitive statement, such as 'Your mum and I are not OK with you taking this medicine. We have learned a lot about it, and we don't feel it's safe.' Parents can let doctors and therapists know that the family is not open to considering blockers and set boundaries around any adults who may be encouraging children to ask for them. If you are unhappy about the way your GP is handling your child's case, consider changing your doctor.

CROSS-SEX HORMONES

Hormones are offered after puberty blockers, or on their own if puberty is well under way. Some of the effects are permanent, some are reversible. Natal females are offered testosterone, and natal males are offered oestrogen. These can either be taken via injection, or as a patch or cream. People of either sex taking hormone replacements as part of gender-affirmation therapy face a substantially increased risk of serious cardiac events, including stroke, heart attack and pulmonary embolism.[25]

In females, testosterone will eventually result in fat redistribution, facial hair and the deepening of the voice. The last two are permanent. These are often alterations that the young person herself wants, but there are other common effects that are not so desirable. Testosterone may cause acne, and eventually male-pattern baldness. It will likely cause the clitoris to grow. Vaginal atrophy is another common side effect. After several years on the hormone, vaginal atrophy can become such a problem that a hysterectomy is needed. Other complications include polycythaemia (a high concentration of red blood cells), weight gain, hypertension (high blood pressure) and changes in one's lipid profile (the amount of fat molecules in the blood). Females on testosterone seem to have a higher incidence of problems with urinary tract and bladder infections.

In males, oestrogen will cause skin to soften, fat to redistribute and breasts to grow. In addition to these desired effects, oestrogen may also increase the likelihood of developing Type 2 diabetes, deep-vein thrombosis, weight gain and infertility.[26]

SURGERIES

Gender-affirmation surgery is a growth industry in the US. There were approximately 11,000 such surgeries performed in 2019, an increase of 10–15% over the previous year. The market is expected to expand by around 14% per year, with most of that growth from female patients.[27]

Surgeries are irreversible and, in many cases, destroy healthy tissue and impair physiological function. In our experience, regret tends to be more severe among detransitioners who have had surgeries, and the more surgeries one has had, the more regret one tends to feel.

Mastectomy

Natal females often seek double mastectomies, or 'top surgery'. Young people can access this without parental consent once they have reached the age of medical majority. This is usually eighteen, although in some jurisdictions such as the US state of Oregon, young people are able to make most of their own medical decisions at fifteen. If surgery costs are not part of a covered healthcare expense, young people can fundraise online. GoFundMe.com has an entire section of their site devoted to transition-related fundraising.[28] Much of this is for double mastectomies. As stated above, WPATH SOC8 posits no minimum age for this surgery, and no recommendation for a mental health evaluation, even among adolescents.[29]

Hysterectomy

Some trans-identified women seek a hysterectomy, with or without an oophorectomy (which removes one or both ovaries), as part of their transition. Some may seek a hysterectomy after being on testosterone because of the possible increased risk of cancer.[30] Hysterectomies significantly increase one's risk of developing Parkinson's disease and dementia.[31] There is an association between hysterectomies and an increased incidence of heart disease, certain kinds of cancer, metabolic conditions and stroke.[32] If a young woman also gets her ovaries removed, she will be dependent on hormones for the rest of her life.

Metoidioplasty and phalloplasty

Metoidioplasty is a procedure in which ligaments around the clitoris are cut, releasing it from the pubis. Since testosterone causes clitoral growth in females, metoidioplasty can create something that approximates a penis. A separate procedure offered with metoidioplasty is urethral lengthening, which allows the patient to stand to urinate. Testicular implants are another possible surgery that may accompany metoidioplasty. Many patients elect to undergo a hysterectomy. In general, it is not possible to have penetrative intercourse with a neophallus created through metoidioplasty. Complications of metoidioplasty include the development of urethral fistulas (unwanted openings) and stricture (scarring).

Phalloplasty is the creation of a neophallus, often using skin harvested from the arm or the thigh. Patients may have urethral lengthening to allow them to urinate from the new phallus. This may require multiple surgeries and will usually necessitate a hysterectomy. Testicular implants are also an option. A patient can choose to have a prosthesis placed in the new phallus which will allow the penis to harden for penetrative sex.

Phalloplasty comes with a high rate of complications, some of which can be serious and even life-threatening. These include urethral fistulas, urethral strictures, death of the transferred tissue, and bladder or rectal injury. There can be complications at the site of the donated tissue, including scarring, decreased sensation and pain.[33]

Breast augmentation

Trans-identified males may choose to get breast augmentation surgery. If oestrogen has not created enough breast growth to make room for the implants, patients may need tissue expander inserted in order to stretch the skin. These patients will then require a second procedure to remove the expanders and put in the breast implants. Complication rates for breast augmentation in trans-identified males are similar for the same procedure in natal females.[34]

Vaginoplasty

The penis and scrotum are partially removed and reconfigured to create labia and a vaginal canal. The most common procedure for adult transitioners is called penile inversion vaginoplasty and involves removing the skin from the penis sheath and inverting it to create the neovagina. Patients must undergo laser hair removal beforehand to avoid hair growing inside the neovagina. It appears that the majority of vaginoplasty patients do retain some ability to orgasm, but recent studies have noted that 'up to 29% of patients may be diagnosed with a sexual dysfunction due to associated distress'.[35] Another reported 'an overall 24% post-surgery rate of inability to achieve orgasm'.[36]

We note that even affirmative clinicians such as well-known transgender doctors like clinical psychologist Erica Anderson and reconstructive surgeon Marci Bowers are now expressing concerns about performing medical interventions on children. If a young person never went through male puberty, there may be insufficient tissue for the penile inversion technique. In these cases, a neovagina may be constructed using a piece of colon or by using the abdominal lining. Both procedures have higher complication rates than the inversion technique. Some of these complications can be deadly. Of the original cohort of seventy young people involved in the Dutch Protocol study, one died from tissue necrosis as a result of undergoing vaginoplasty.[37]

Other potential complications for all types of vaginoplasty include fistulas, infections and suture line dehiscence (where cuts made during the surgery reopen). All forms of vaginoplasty require regular dilation to keep the neovagina from closing up. For the first three months after surgery, it is recommended that the patient use a dilator three times per day for ten minutes at a time. Dilation can be painful and unpleasant. After nine months, the recommendation is for the patient to dilate once or twice per week. This is a lifelong requirement.

Other MTF surgeries

Male-to-female transitioners may also seek facial feminisation surgery, tracheal shaving (to reduce the size of the Adam's apple) and voice feminisation surgery. We often hear reports of dissatisfaction with many of these surgeries when the reality doesn't live up to the promise.

A WORD ABOUT NON-BINARY-IDENTIFIED YOUNG PEOPLE

An increasing number of young people are identifying as non-binary, genderqueer, gender-fluid or some other variation, rather than the opposite sex. Sometimes a non-binary identification is a stepping stone towards a cross-sex identification, or it may be a step towards desistance or detransition. Many young people will identify as non-binary and perhaps alter their hairstyle or clothing but not have any desire to undergo medical interventions. However, a non-binary identity does not rule out medicalisation. Many young women who identify as non-binary will seek out a double mastectomy, for example.

Some surgeons are offering interventions specifically for people who identify as non-binary. These include phallus-preserving vaginoplasty and vagina-preserving phalloplasty, which would allow a patient to have both their own genitals and a surgically created version of opposite-sex genitals. Non-binary top surgery might include the option to remove the nipples altogether, or to reduce the size of the breasts. Non-binary procedures for natal males could include penectomy (removal of the penis), scrotectomy (removal of the scrotal skin), orchiectomy (removal of one or both testicles) and nullification. According to one website, 'Genital nullification, Nullo, or Eunuch procedures involve removing all external genitalia to create a smooth transition from the abdomen to the groin. In some cases, this involves shortening the urethra. For patients born with a uterus, a hysterectomy is required prior to any genital nullification procedure. Your specific goals can be discussed with one of our surgeons to develop a plan that works for you.'[38]

WHAT CAN PARENTS DO?

If kids are seeking medical interventions, it makes sense to focus on strengthening the parent–child relationship first. We believe that most gender-questioning kids are recruiting gender to manage other problems, including developmental challenges, relational conflicts and distressing emotions. Declaring a new gender identity serves to draw attention and care from others, often making the child the centre of attention in the family and giving them tremendous power. In short, if a child is asking for hormones, it's likely that there is something else going on that is not just about gender. So responding with compassion and warmth while maintaining firm limits can help a young person through a difficult period.

Make a point of spending time with your child doing what he enjoys. If she likes video games, sit down and watch her play. Let her tell you about the game. If he has always enjoyed baking, make brownies together every Saturday. Invite him to walk the dog with you. Make plans to visit a favourite family member. By the time our kids are teens, we may have dropped the family routines we had when they were younger. Now would be a good time to reinstate those or start some new ones. Bring back family movie night with a takeaway. Go for a hike on Sundays. There are only three rules – the activity should be one you do together; it should be fun for everyone, but especially for your child; and the conversation should avoid the topic of gender. There is a time and place to have discussions about gender (more on that soon). The emphasis should be on getting connected, offering love and warmth. If it's difficult to persuade your teenager to do anything as a family, tap into whatever they're interested in doing, however brief or small-scale an activity this may be. Getting connected will help set the stage for important conversations about medical interventions.

TALKING ABOUT HORMONES AND SURGERY WITH YOUNGER CHILDREN AND ADOLESCENTS

As discussed above, hormones are powerful drugs that can cause permanent changes and may compromise health. Their effects tend to be more pronounced the earlier they are started. For example, a natal female who begins testosterone at age fourteen will likely end up having a much deeper voice than one who begins testosterone at twenty-one. If this patient decides to detransition, she will have greater difficulty presenting as a woman if her voice is a deep baritone instead of just a little low-pitched.

When a young teen announces a trans identity, many parents assume there are many years ahead before medical transition may be on the table. If your young teen asks for hormones or surgery, you may have an instinct to say something like, 'There will be no medical intervention while you're living under my roof, but once you're eighteen, you can make your own decisions.' We would caution against this. When a child is thirteen or fourteen, eighteen can seem like a long way off. In our experience, children who are affirmed in early adolescence or who reap social rewards from their trans status can easily become entrenched in the new identity. Eighteen can sneak up on families surprisingly quickly. If you have promised your child that medicalisation will be exclusively his decision when he's legally an adult, you will have left yourself without a leg to stand on. Instead, we prefer, 'There won't be any medicalisation while you are growing and developing. Once you are on your own and supporting yourself financially and you've had romantic relationships and a job, if you still want to take hormones at that point, it will be your decision.'

It is important for kids to know you have done your homework on these treatments. It's OK to set a clear limit around what is not acceptable in your family. Part of the job of parenting when our kids are young is to assess risks on their behalf. Our kids may be consuming online content that tells them hormones and surgeries are life-saving and they need to access them right away, that not going on hormones will make them suicidal, and that parents who refuse are transphobic and motivated by bigotry. These messages undermine your position. While sharing your views is crucial, arguing will probably make your relationship worse. In extreme cases, kids may recruit other family members or adult authority figures to help them access interventions, or even purchase hormones off the black market. It is best to avoid the matter becoming a power struggle. This can be done by explaining your limits around medicalisation firmly and clearly, while also making efforts to listen to your child.

Many parents of trans-identified teens have told us: 'My child is so bright, and she's always loved science. If I could just get the right information in front of her, I'm sure she would see that it doesn't make sense to take testosterone or have surgery.' Parents often provide their kids with research or links to detransitioner vlogs. They believe that their daughter will change her mind if they can just provide the right information.

In general, we do not recommend sharing lots of research, links and articles with your trans-identified teen. We are all susceptible to confirmation bias, a tendency to seek out and preferentially value information that strengthens the views we already hold. We as parents are susceptible to this – and so are our teens. Psychologists studying cognitive dissonance have found that when we are confronted by facts that go against our deeply held beliefs, we are adept at dismissing these and doubling down on our belief. Teens who are deeply committed to their trans identity will easily dismiss 'proof' provided by parents.

As in any other relationship, it is more important to pay attention to the music than the lyrics. That is, our focus should be on attending to the quality of the emotional connection with our child, not getting certain information across. Are we connected? Are we enjoying each other at least some of the time? If you have a highly defiant or troubled child, enjoyable moments may be few and far between. The more difficult the relationship, the more important it is that we try to listen and connect.

We recommend providing your child with access to information only very occasionally. In general, do more listening than talking. If your child is demanding hormones and surgery, you might ask in a calm and genuinely curious manner what they imagine these interventions will do for them. As discussed earlier, be prepared to really listen: reflect back to your child what they have said and ask careful follow-up questions that open up the topic further. This will undoubtedly be difficult, as your child may repeat things he has heard from the internet that you know are not true, and yet at this point listening is more important than trying to convey accurate information. The goal is to express love, support and genuine concern for the suffering your child is undergoing while maintaining clear boundaries about what you will allow. You can let your child know that hormones and surgery are categorically off the table and still express curiosity about your child's desire for them.

WHAT IF YOUR YOUNG ADULT WANTS TO MEDICALISE?

Young adults of eighteen and older can legally access medical interventions without parental permission. Although recent events in the UK and elsewhere are making medical transition much harder to access among minors, the reverse seems to be true for young adults. Adult gender identity clinics in the NHS are generally affirmative in their approach and offer hormones and surgery – therapeutic interventions are not mandatory.[39] Long waiting times may be a hurdle to speedy medicalisation, but the young person is unlikely to be encouraged to examine his or her motivations, and private clinics offer interventions without the wait.

In the US, informed consent clinics (meaning that no mental health screening is required), including those at most Planned Parenthood offices, will offer hormone prescriptions, usually after a single visit. Hormones are generally not expensive, so cost is rarely a barrier. In the US, many health insurance programmes will cover trans surgeries. If your young adult is in college in the US, the campus health centre may provide hormones for your child or direct her to an informed consent clinic. Many college health insurance programmes will cover hormones and surgeries.

Parents of young adults who are intent on medicalising often feel desperate, distraught and overwhelmed. It is terrifying to think of your child hurtling towards irreversible surgery that he may one day regret and to know that you are powerless to stop it.

SLOWING DOWN

You may be powerless to stop her, but you can offer her some guidance. You might start by asking if she would like to hear your thoughts. If she says yes, you might share something like the following: 'You are at a time of real transition in your life right now, and many pieces are up in the air. When we are in the midst of a lot of change, it isn't necessarily a good time to make big decisions. This is a forever intervention that you won't be able to take back, so it makes sense to take as much time as you need. I know you feel you want to do this right away, but when we feel urgent about something, that's usually a sign that we might need to slow down and think about things more. The option to take hormones [or get surgery] isn't going to go away. In fact, it will probably be easier to do when you are a little older. We recognise that this is your decision, and we will love and support you no matter what, but we think it would be a good idea for you to wait another year [or whatever time period makes sense].'

This can be a powerful way to frame the conversation, since you are not opposing her wish or trying to talk her out of it. You are simply asking her to wait. You are sidestepping a power struggle and making it possible for her to say yes to your request. If your child does agree, though, she may still go through with medicalisation at the end of the stated period. Even if she does, you will have bought her more time to grow and mature before undertaking these irreversible steps.

HELPING A YOUNG ADULT ASSESS THE RISKS OF SURGERIES

The email Alison had been dreading had arrived. Her daughter Leila had written to let her know she had scheduled a mastectomy consultation appointment with a surgeon. Alison was shocked and distraught. She gave herself several days to process her feelings before responding. When she did write back, she conveyed that she and her husband did not think this surgery would be helpful, but they wanted to attend the appointment with her. Leila assented.

Before the appointment, Alison and her husband wrote a respectful letter to the surgeon in which they outlined Leila's significant history of mental health struggles, and asked that this background be considered as the doctor made treatment recommendations. They wanted the surgeon to have this history and to know how much they loved their daughter, and for the surgeon to know they did not feel surgery was in Leila's best interest. Alison shared that it made them feel better to know that they had done everything that they could.

During the appointment, Alison and her husband listened and took notes. They also came with a list of questions to ask the surgeon. To Alison, it was clear that twenty-one-year-old Leila had only thought about the surgery superficially. She had few questions and hadn't considered the risks of major surgery. Alison and her husband were hopeful that hearing a more realistic discussion might help her daughter slow down. Some of the questions Alison's parents asked were as follows:

- What does the research say about long-term outcomes for patients? (This is a bit of a leading question. At this point, there is no such research.)
- What percentage of patients lose sensation in the nipples?
- What percentage lose their nipples?
- What percentage are unhappy with the results and need a revision surgery?
- What are the chances that a patient will experience nerve damage?
- What percentage experience a worsening of gender dysphoria after mastectomy? (Some patients become even unhappier with their hips after they no longer have breasts, since being flat-chested tends to accentuate wide hips.)
- What can patients expect in terms of scarring?
- How long is the recovery?
- Do we know how many regret the surgery?
- What are the risks associated with the anaesthesia?
- What are the risks of bleeding or infection?
- What are the other possible surgical complications?
- How do you assess the psychological readiness of the patient for this major surgery?
- Have you ever declined performing this surgery on a patient?
- Will some breast tissue remain? How do you monitor for breast cancer? Will routine screening need to occur after forty?
- How many mastectomies have you performed on women of twenty-five and under for gender dysphoria? Or how many in a year?
- If there is regret and a change of mind later in life, is breast reconstruction possible?
- What is the percentage chance that the chest area will remain without sensation (i.e. numb) after surgery? We have seen one statistic that shows that 20% of mastectomy patients have chest wall numbness.
- Will breastfeeding be an option after a double mastectomy?

There is no guarantee that having such discussions with your child and his or her surgeon will result in an about-face. However, whenever we undergo any major medical procedure, it makes sense to be prepared and to have realistic expectations about outcomes. For parents whose children are considering other surgeries, you can generate a list of questions, or even request that your child do such research himself. In general, many gender surgeons are cavalier about these procedures, although surgeries come with many risks. Meanwhile, their benefits are for the most part unproven. Getting involved with your child and their surgeon allows you the opportunity to help your child think through what they propose to do.

A BOLD INTERVENTION

We have known a few parents of young adults who took their child out of the country or engaged them in work or study away from the internet and from peers for several months. Time away from pressure to think about gender seems to have allowed these young people to step away from transitioning even though they were on the threshold of medicalising. We encourage families to explore what is possible for them.

With a little creativity, there may be many options that do not require a lot of money. You might be able to send your child to spend time with a family member in a different town. Some families may have ties to another country or culture and could send their young adult to live with relatives abroad for several months. There are opportunities, for example, for young people to volunteer on farms or take part in immersive language exchanges of up to three months or even longer. Some of these opportunities can be found in the Resources section at the back of this book. We have known parents who quit jobs to spend an extended period travelling with their teen or young adult. Obviously, such choices will not be available to every family, but if you allow yourself to think expansively, you may be able to find opportunities that didn't occur to you at first. Structured gap year and travel programmes should be considered with caution, however, as many have cohorts of trans-identified kids who may serve to reinforce your child's identity.

An experience of getting away from the familiar is likely to be helpful as long as it meets the following criteria:

1 It lasts at least three months. Six months or a year are even better. A few weeks are not going to do it. Your child needs time and space to get a break from gender.
2 Your child will be productively and enjoyably engaged and will not be spending large amounts of time online.
3 Your child will not be surrounded by other trans-identifying peers and older adults who are invested in your child being trans.
4 It's best of all if your child will spend time being challenged, getting out of their comfort zone and gaining new skills and confidence. Doing something that requires them to be outdoors and to use their body in new ways is even better.

You might have to be creative, bold and resourceful to find an appropriate opportunity for your child.

Camille's son Mike was on the threshold of turning eighteen and was requesting an appointment at the gender clinic. He had already decided to take a gap year before going to college but had not yet developed a firm plan. Camille had cousins who lived on a farm in rural France. Mike had grown up visiting these relatives. Camille offered Mike the chance to spend nine months living there. At first, Mike expressed some hesitation. Camille suggested that he go for three months before deciding if he wanted to stay longer. Mike had a wonderful time in France and chose to stay the full nine months. His relatives kept him busy working on the farm. Internet access was available, but his free time was limited. Within a few months, gender ceased to be a preoccupation. When he returned home, he matter-of-factly announced that he wanted to go back to his birth name and he/him pronouns.

Denise from 4thWaveNow sent her child to stay on a horse farm, with limited access to the internet.[40] Her child flourished away from the online world. On the podcast *Gender: A Wider Lens*, Maggie described an extended visit to her teen's ancestral country of origin.[41] Among people who looked like her, the teenager finally felt like she belonged, widened her perspective of her identity, and ultimately desisted.

We recognise that many families will not have the resources to find such an opportunity. Even if you can, there are significant caveats. First, your child must agree to go. In our experience, many young people will, provided their relationship with their parents is basically solid and the plan is of genuine interest to the child. Often, young people feel ambivalent about medicalising and are secretly relieved to be offered an alternative solution. Such an opportunity should not be forced or framed as a punishment. You may offer it with love and authority, clearly indicating that the experience would be beneficial, but if your child is strongly opposed, there is nothing you can do.

ACCEPTANCE

If you are a parent of a young adult who is medicalising, the only influence you now have is born of your relationship and connection. Many parents have asked whether we recommend refusing to pay for college or, in the case of US parents, removing the child from your health insurance. We do not recommend such approaches. Young adults are good at finding other sources of funding. Plus, this further sets you and your child at odds, both of you fighting on different sides in a bloody battle. Such a dynamic tends to perpetuate a trans identification, because both parties get locked into their respective positions. It's not advisable to try to browbeat, cajole or argue your child out of his wish to transition. Efforts to influence your child to avoid medicalisation – except for the extended time away intervention mentioned above – usually make things worse and can lead to a child estranging herself from her parents. Though it is incredibly difficult, you may need to work on detaching from outcomes and releasing your child to her fate. More on acceptance later.

Christine's daughter Evelyn announced at eighteen that she was trans. When Christine wasn't immediately affirming, Evelyn left in a fury, stating that she would never speak to her mother again. She moved across the country to attend school and started on testosterone. Christine had minimal contact with her daughter but worked hard to re-establish a connection, and within a year they were communicating regularly. She was devastated when Evelyn sent an email to say she had scheduled top surgery. Christine did a lot of her own work to process her feelings about her daughter's upcoming mastectomy. Eventually, she recognised that she wanted to be there for her daughter while also doing everything she possibly could to help her reconsider. She created the space to have a thoughtful conversation with Evelyn. She wanted her daughter to know that it's OK to change your mind on big decisions, even right up until the last minute. As the date drew closer and Evelyn didn't alter her course, Christine offered to fly out to be with her daughter after the surgery. In many ways it was the last thing she wanted to do, but she also knew she would regret not offering this support. Evelyn accepted her mother's offer of help. The time they spent together was difficult for Christine, but she also knew she had done the right thing in the long term. Evelyn may or may not detransition someday. Either way, she will know that she can count on her mother for support, and Christine knows that she found the strength to show up as the parent she wants to be.

We recognise that reconciling yourself to your child's medicalisation may seem impossible. For many parents, the grief, powerlessness and rage at unethical doctors and therapists are overwhelming. Focusing on trying to prevent medicalisation may mean we lose focus on our overall relationship with our child, who may be vulnerable and suffering from complex mental health issues. Continuing to be a source of support even while watching them make terrible mistakes is a difficult thing to do, but we believe it is something to strive for.

STABILISATION

If you have a young adult determined to transition, you may not be able to prevent her from doing so. However, if you follow the advice in this book, you will likely be able to reach what we call stabilisation. We use this term to refer to a trans-identified young person who functions reasonably well, maintains contact with family and doesn't rush into medicalisation. This might look like a twenty-year-old trans-identified male who takes oestrogen but doesn't have any immediate intention of pursuing vaginoplasty, or a twenty-three-year-old trans-identified female who has been on testosterone for several years but is not pursuing a mastectomy or a legal name change. Stabilisation creates space for the young person to attend to other things in his life outside of gender. He might be doing well in school or making professional strides. It offers the young person some room to consider whether to proceed down the road to further medicalisation while she continues to mature. It may be hard to see these scenarios as 'wins', but we believe they are, and we encourage you to see them that way.

7

DEALING WITH THERAPISTS, SCHOOLS, UNIVERSITIES AND OTHER PROFESSIONALS

THE PROBLEM

You may already know how difficult it can be to curate a team of therapists, school administrators and thoughtful adults who will support your parental decisions about how to best help your child. Children's clinics, hospitals and schools across the world, though tasked with supporting the well-being of youth, have adopted contemporary gender beliefs that only confuse kids and exacerbate their vulnerabilities. This institutional capture is destructive, not only because it can create further deterioration in the mental well-being of young people, but especially because it can push children and families apart. We've heard hundreds of stories in which schools, behavioural and mental health centres, therapists, counsellors and recreational summer school staff undermine parental decisions – and in some extreme cases actively conspire to keep secrets from parents and encourage children to regard their own mother or father with suspicion. Or perhaps an external provider delivers part of your school's curriculum, teaching contested ideas about gender ideology and instructing children that LGBT phobia must be reported (which could mean that a child is disciplined for not using the preferred pronouns of a student or teacher). You might have been treated with hostility by an authority figure who implied that your hesitancy about transition means you don't 'support' your child. Or maybe a therapist suggested (in front of your child) that your refusal to give in to your son's demands makes him more likely to take his own life (more on suicide statistics later).

Not only are many therapists quickly affirming children's transgender identities and encouraging medicalisation, but some are the first to suggest that the child's eating disorder, body image problems, OCD, autism or other challenges may be caused by an undiscovered 'transgender identity'.

We believe that clinicians are likely well-meaning, but they can be just as caught up in the social contagion as any young gender-questioning person. And a look back through the strange history of our field indicates that this parallel contagion has happened before. In the 1980s and 1990s, a bizarre theory swept through America that had originated among mental health professionals: a wave of horrific Satanic abuse rituals was taking place and children subjected to this abuse could completely 'repress' the memories. Therapists saw it as their job to help 'uncover' these memories. These ideas were intriguing and captured the attention of therapists, patients and the mainstream media. The 'extracted memories' were often flamboyant, easily disproved, and coaxed from the imagination using hypnosis, sedative drugs and relaxation techniques.

The implausibility of these recollections didn't stop the public from subscribing to the repressed memories theory. Innocent people were convicted of shocking crimes and punished on the flimsy imagined memories of abuse that were extracted in therapy. Journalist Ethan Watters has studied the recovered memory trend extensively, and he theorises how it's possible that intelligent, educated and competent therapists contributed to its growth: 'This was a group of healers who believed that they not only had discovered the key to their patients' suffering but also were exposing a hidden evil across society. The therapists, in short, were as caught up in the cultural currents as their patients.'[1] Similarly, if a clinician truly believes that they can save a closeted 'transgender child' from unsupportive parents, this powerful motivation serves as the precursor for bizarre and unethical behaviour not seen in other realms of youth mental health services.

Even when clinicians promise parents that therapy will be a slow, careful process, sometimes the therapist comes to see gender exploration as the primary goal and inadvertently leads a child into a ruminative process around identity. We suspect that many clinicians are not well versed in the social drivers of mental health conditions and the ever-present pull of culture-bound syndromes (symptoms found only in certain cultures). Mental health diagnoses tend to be culturally shaped and often cannot be traced to tangible biological factors.

BAD THERAPY CAN BE WORSE THAN NO THERAPY

We often say, 'Bad therapy can be worse than no therapy.' This is precisely why we wrote this book for you. We hope to give you the tools and framework you need to navigate your child's gender-identity distress within the family context. We would like to give you the freedom to think for yourself, trust your parental intuition and act with more loving authority. You may be pursuing all these aspirational parenting goals and still need professional help for your child. Here we'll lay out some considerations and suggestions to help you connect with a mental health practitioner who treats your child as an individual rather than a walking gender identity.

WHAT DOES GOOD THERAPY LOOK LIKE?

The most meaningful therapeutic processes are based on a positive relationship between client and therapist. Clients should feel respected, heard, understood and cared for. The therapist regards their client as a complex, whole person, and considers the client's development and growth. Therapists must also avoid co-rumination with patients, helping them instead to understand their problems in new ways and ultimately grow beyond their distress.

The therapist should honour regular appointment times and behave in a professional manner. The informed consent process gives the client an idea of the therapist's theoretical foundations and how therapy will go. Therapists should not make outsized promises about the outcome of therapy, and clients should feel free to end the relationship at any time. Additionally, therapy should also commit to the injunction 'do no harm'. The therapeutic relationship is a powerful force in a client's life, and therapists should humbly appreciate this fact, being cautious and mindful about how their work may affect the client. When working with youths and families, therapists should be aware of the risk of exacerbating rifts in the parent–child dynamic. Helping increase healthy communication and improving family dynamics is a laudable goal.

THE PARTICULARS OF GENDER IN THERAPY

Now that we've examined general principles of good therapy, let's turn our attention to some qualities that might make a therapist more adept at working with gender in an exploratory (rather than an affirmative) manner. With younger children, we strongly advocate for family over individual therapy. You may even want to consider counselling for yourself. Whoever enters therapy, and for what purpose, the following characteristics in a therapist can be helpful.

Knowledge about ROGD and detransition

Therapists who already recognise and have concerns regarding the social influence of gender dysphoria are more likely to be sceptical about a young person's surface story, rewritten history and claims of certainty about wanting to transition. They will also be more likely to understand the harms and risks associated with medical interventions if they are familiar with the detransition experience. Explicitly rejecting the current 'affirmation model' of therapy can be a good indicator of more nuance in the treatment of gender dysphoria. The Global Exploratory Therapy Association (formerly the Gender Exploratory Therapy Association), which we founded in 2021, is a resource for clinicians with this perspective, and also provides a directory for individuals looking for an exploratory therapist. That being said, we've met many wonderful therapists who were unfamiliar with ROGD and detransition initially, but who took an active interest in learning more about these phenomena and subsequently worked effectively with young gender-questioning clients.

Supports family cohesion

With the exception of rare cases of severe dysfunction and abuse, keeping families together should be a priority for the therapist. While some distancing and differentiation (being able to have different opinions and values while remaining connected) is normal and healthy for adolescence, estrangement can be a real concern for families raising a gender-questioning child. A good therapist should encourage, when possible, intact relationships, improved communication and healthy dynamics.

Offers touchpoints for parents of younger children

We believe that therapists who treat young clients and minors should work in collaboration with parents and ensure that mothers and fathers have touchpoints of communication, such as regular meetings where the therapist speaks to the parents or has a meeting with the client and their parents. Many parents give away their power and have no idea how the therapy is proceeding. We recommend seeking regular feedback about your child's treatment. This should ideally be a collaborative arrangement where everyone acknowledges the benefit for family dynamics to keep parents in the loop; however, as the child matures, they might prefer to focus on a more individualised therapy that allows them to begin to move beyond the household. This can be worked out within a staged process.

If you've identified a therapist who seems to espouse the ideas we've described, it is still important to carefully interview them and assess if you feel comfortable with your child or family entering a therapeutic relationship. Keep in mind that your approach matters: you cannot demand that the therapist address specific issues or respond in certain ways to your child's gender-questioning. When you engage in a conversation with the therapist, try not to coax out a verbal contract about how they will handle names, pronouns or social transition right away. Instead, discuss potential issues before they start seeing your child. The interview should give you a feeling about who the therapist is, how they approach gender in general, and help you figure out if they're a good fit. Here are some questions you may want to ask:

- How do you work with gender-questioning clients?
- What is your stance on the medicalisation of young and vulnerable people?
- Have you heard of ROGD? What do you think of this term?
- Have you ever worked with a detransitioner? Are you familiar with this term?
- Are you open to learning more about ROGD or detransition?

WHAT TO AVOID WITH GENDER IN THERAPY

For reasons we've expounded, we recommend avoiding the following characteristics and interventions when seeking therapy for a gender-questioning young person:

- Gender-affirmative therapists
- Gender clinics
- Narrowly focused social justice therapists
- Reference to the WPATH Standards of Care
- Suggestions to 'try on' various gender identities to see what fits
- Therapists who completely ignore gender or refuse to address it, claiming it's outside their scope
- Any influenced by queer theory – this may be indicated by the term 'kink-allied' in their pitch. These therapists often place too much emphasis on validating identity categories and not enough on exploring the psyche.

Opportunistic clinicians

With the rising number of families desperate to find help for their child, and the small number of qualified therapists available, some families will inevitably be willing to stretch their budgets and tolerate behaviour from therapists that would otherwise be unacceptable. We encourage you to be careful about hiring a therapist if anything about their practice, professionalism or fees feels 'off'. For example, we are wary of 'concierge' services that ask families to pay upfront for a long block of therapy. Unrealistic promises of guaranteed desistance are also red flags, as no therapist can predict the future or impose their will on a therapy client. Some mercenary therapists focus on affirming parents, as they know these parents pay the bills; however, as we know, affirmation tends to feel immediately satisfying but seldom leads to long-term satisfaction. Be mindful of your own fears, hopes and emotional drivers so that you can make decisions with clarity.

DEALING WITH SCHOOLS

Multiple short-term studies suggest that social transition can increase the likelihood of the persistence of a young person's gender-related distress, and that it can interfere with children's natural identity development.[2] Nevertheless, there is no qualitative long-term peer-reviewed evidence about the impact of social transition on the current cohort of ROGD adolescents, and so it is imperative that parents make sure that involved adults – be they teachers, school counsellors, therapists, parents or others – are sensitive to the needs of the individual child.

Depending on the geographical region, many parents have experienced schools choosing to carry out social transition on their child. One parent, Jean, described how, at a meeting, she highlighted her problems with the school's decision to socially transition her young and vulnerable child. The school didn't understand what she meant by 'social transition'. Jean became very distressed. 'They socially transitioned my child, but they didn't even know what social transition was. How could I feel confident that they knew what they were doing?' For this reason, it can be valuable for parents to emphasise that this is a child safeguarding issue, so that schools can avoid causing further, more complicated challenges for the child. Jean believes that the social transition of her fifteen-year-old daughter was a significant step on the road to medical transition. 'The school cast me as the mean, transphobic parent who didn't understand her child. But they were wrong. I actually cared much more deeply for my child than they did. My daughter became further entrenched in her identity and very hostile towards me after she had socially transitioned at school. She started cross-sex hormones at eighteen, and had a mastectomy at nineteen. But she has since detransitioned and lives back at home with me now. She's twenty-two years old and the school have no doubt long since forgotten all about her.'

Historically, young people often change their names and use nicknames during their process of identity exploration in adolescence. These days there is a good deal less formality between teachers and students, and so many teachers might employ the student's preferred name without thinking about it. Yet teachers are holding a position of responsibility; they are *in loco parentis*. If they begin to see themselves as saviours, they can set up what is known as a drama triangle, which can significantly undermine parental authority. The drama triangle is an unhealthy scenario where one person is the victim, another the persecutor and another the saviour. When teachers take on the role of saviour of the poor helpless child victim against the evil, persecuting parent, they are setting the stage for destructive conflict. It is important that you feel empowered to call out any triangulation system developing – especially in the context of overeager school staff who are keen to socially transition your child without considering the impact on their life.

We have worked with schools who, by their own admission, 'made a mess of gender'. These schools, in a bid to be kind, had overcelebrated children who came out as trans and later become concerned as they observed social contagion sweeping through the school. Following some workshops provided by Genspect, the schools re-evaluated their approach to sex and gender and reported a 'culture of desistance' in the school: a reversal of the initial trans identification contagion.

Parents in the UK, Ireland and Europe appear to have more authority over their kids than parents in certain states in the USA, Canada or Australia. It is essential that you know your legal position and your school's guidelines, and also the approach your child's therapist might take. Regular face-to-face meetings where you show that you are a well-informed and loving parent are typically more productive than long emails filled with evidence and science. Many of us who have been in the trenches of the gender world for some time suffer from what we often call 'the splutters' when talking to somebody about gender, especially when that person doesn't know much about the subject and you do. It is important that you are well prepared, with just a few well-chosen points to make. You might have a good think beforehand and consider the most important issues. You might write down some bullet points in order of importance. It is recommended that you suggest another meeting to discuss things further if this is what you need. Some parents will have to be a 'polite nuisance' in the school, or with the therapist. This might mean that you insist upon a phone call, and another one and another one, to ensure that the involved adult fully understands the situation. This can be exhausting and intimidating for parents, but then, as Winston Churchill advised, 'It is not enough that we do our best; sometimes we must do what is required.'

MUM AND DAD: Hi there, we're here to discuss the need for the school to respect our parental authority.

SCHOOL PRINCIPAL: We've had many trans kids go through our school, and we follow best practice.

MUM AND DAD: I'm not sure that you do. You seem to follow WPATH guidelines; however, there are many other professional bodies that disagree with WPATH.

SCHOOL PRINCIPAL: With due respect, we are fully up to date with the science of trans kids.

MUM AND DAD: We need to retain our parental authority. By keeping secrets from us about our child you are undermining us and going against best practice. You are also inadvertently creating a triangulation that will not help our child. We are providing extensive professional support to our child, and you are not aware of how this might be affecting it. We follow Genspect's guidance on this, and we don't agree with WPATH. We need you to work with us, work alongside us, rather than presume you know more than us. Could you please agree to refrain from keeping secrets from us and to proceed more slowly, as you are hurrying our child and this is not going well?

SCHOOL PRINCIPAL: We are following the guidelines.

MUM AND DAD: You are following certain guidelines, and others strongly disagree with them. I will send you some information from Genspect, as they show an alternative view to WPATH. Also, I will put you in touch with our child's therapist. Finally, I will need to meet you again next week so that you can get to know that I am a loving and engaged parent and that it is profoundly inappropriate for the school to keep secrets from me about anything that might have a significant impact on my child's well-being.

We recommend that parents make regular appointments to speak with involved school staff. Visit the school. Show your love and concern for your child. Demonstrate your awareness of the issues and make sure you retain your authority. Too many parents have spoken about feeling dismissed, and so if you feel waved away, point this out immediately. Stay calm, retreat when necessary, but always make it clear that you will return again and again to make sure that the relevant adults are aware of the impact of complicating factors such as ASD or anxiety, and that social transition is the first step on the road to medical transition. Speak authoritatively about 'diagnostic overshadowing' and make sure those involved are aware of the issues highlighted in the Cass Review. You may want to request to see the PSHE (personal, social, health and economic) curriculum, and ask which external agencies are invited to deliver workshops on the subject of gender identity. If this feels beyond you, try to enlist the help of an advocate, perhaps from a supportive organisation such as Genspect, who offer a parent advocacy service. Lastly, make sure you access some support for yourself – meet other parents who are going through similar experiences. If you believe that the school are unapologetically dismissive or are actively damaging your child, seriously consider changing schools.

Holiday camps and after-school and extracurricular activities

Activities outside school are often an important part of a young person's development. Camps – especially residential – can play a key role in helping our children separate from us in healthy ways and gain greater confidence.

If you are hoping to provide your child with an enriching experience where he will not be enthusiastically affirmed in his trans identity, you must choose an activity carefully. Some opportunities will attract a variety of young people and will offer a wholesome experience relatively unaffected by trans ideology. Others will tend to attract trans-identified kids and be run by staff committed to this ideology.

In general, look for camps or extracurricular activities that meet the following criteria:

1 Your child is interested in the activity or focus of the camp.
2 It doesn't attract a large cohort of trans-identifying kids.
3 The camp encourages kids to be out in nature.
4 The camp rules require that kids minimise their phone use.
5 The camp seems amenable to parent requests regarding social transition.
6 The camp has a same-sex (not 'same-gender') sleeping accommodation policy.

You will generally have more influence on how your child is treated than you will at an institution like a school. We have known parents who have approached administrators sympathetic to parental concerns who were willing to work with the family.

When communicating with staff, we recommend using language like the following: 'Sarah has been going through some identity struggles recently. We are supporting her while she goes through this, and she is working with a therapist who recommends that we don't use new names and pronouns at this time. We want to help her keep her options open. Can you please ask staff at the camp to call her "Sarah"? We recognise that her peers may use another name for her, but we would like to know that the adults she comes in contact with will use her birth name.' We have found that when parents use such language, camps and other activities are often surprisingly helpful and happy to comply. If the staff do not seem amenable, you may want to find another opportunity.

You may be able to get a sense of the camp culture by examining their online presence. If it's a residential camp, do they have a gender-neutral or a 'same-gender' dorm? Karen's daughter Olivia had requested a gender-neutral dorm at a prestigious arts camp. As the date for her departure drew near, Karen asked if there were going to be any male-bodied people sleeping in the dorm with her fourteen-year-old-daughter. She was told that staff could not offer that information. Olivia ended up spending time elsewhere that summer.

As mentioned earlier, opportunities to spend time abroad can help a child achieve a reset. Having to negotiate the world in a new language can be all-consuming, leaving little mental space for gender rumination. Wilderness experiences in the US can be of value, although several make a point of their commitment to house students in tents according to gender identity. Both travel and wilderness experiences can build self-confidence, which seems to play a key role in helping kids step away from a trans identification. Any activity that helps your child develop their self-esteem should also guide them away from an intense focus on gender, since the trans identification often arises to shore up shaky self-esteem.

ACTIVITIES

One of the patterns we commonly see is that kids who become trans-identified drop their other interests and become exclusively preoccupied with gender. The kid who has always been an avid swimmer wants to leave the team. The maths whizz doesn't want to participate in competitions any more. The talented flautist wants to stop taking lessons. Kids who have a strong interest in an activity and continue to pursue it through adolescence often have a slight advantage when it comes to withstanding the pull of gender ideology. If your trans-identified teen desires to quit the team or the orchestra, there is little you can do to stop her. However, being active and engaged in the world is necessary for mental health. You can let your child know that you support him choosing an activity that suits him better but insist that he spend several hours per week doing something that gets him out into the world. If he doesn't want to be on the robotics team any more, that's OK, but he needs to try something else – perhaps a volunteer job at the animal shelter or a paid job at the shopping centre.

Art and theatre used to be places where quirky misfit kids could feel at home. Sadly, these days, vulnerable kids who find their way to these activities may fall under the influence of gender ideology. Volunteering is almost always a good choice. Helping others can put our own difficulties in perspective and allow us to take the focus off ourselves. Anything that involves being outside and off screens is helpful. Hiking and rock climbing can be appealing to kids who are more physically oriented, but even regular walks or bike rides can be very good for mental health. Minimum-wage jobs introduce kids to the real world. If your child will not agree to an activity of which you approve, harness your parental authority to make your expectations clear. It is not healthy to spend all day in one's room. All members of the house need to be productively engaged.

UNIVERSITY MATTERS

Parents of gender dysphoric children dread the arrival of their eighteenth birthday, as they believe the adult child will charge on to hormones and surgery. Equally, many parents view college or university in the same way. But this is not a predictable scenario. Some parents have described how their child went to college or university without any interest in gender and came back a couple of months later fully enraptured with LGBTQ+ identities and determined to transition. On the other hand, we have known other young people who have thrived once they went to college and expanded their horizons far beyond gender.

It can be useful for you to consider which colleges or universities are most appropriate for your child, especially if you have input in the decision-making process. There are best (and worst) lists of colleges in the US on websites such as Campus Pride, highlighting which colleges will pay for the student's medical transition. Equally, in the

US, the choice of dorm can make a huge difference. We have noticed that students who elect to live in the trans dorm can become more entrenched in their trans identification and their belief that they need to transition medically. Of course, as always, there are exceptions. One college student found herself turned off by the excessive focus on all things identity when she lived in the queer dorms for her first year. This was the beginning of her eventual desistance. Meanwhile, in the UK, some university campuses are extremely ideological, while others are less so. It can be valuable to seek out universities who are more focused on education than social justice. This is often discernible by going online and running searches on their websites.

Parents often believe that university is important, but this is not always the reality. There are many ways to be a young adult – going to university is but one of them. Higher education courses are hotbeds for the cultural zeitgeist, and the current zeitgeist is leading thousands of young people to medically transition.

THE GAP YEAR

Seventeen is often the most frightening age for parents of trans-identified young people. Once these young people reach eighteen, their parents have significantly reduced input on any decisions and may need to begin the process of accepting that things have not turned out as they would have wanted. In the preceding years you may feel increasingly tense as you believe, often wrongly, that the child's eighteenth birthday is the cut-off date to effect change. This isn't true. Many gender-distressed young people do absolutely nothing when they reach eighteen. Some, however, begin their medical transition.

We recommend a structured educational travel-related gap year if your child is roughly sixteen or seventeen, so that they can experience some life-expanding opportunities before they decide to undergo medical transition. Heading straight to university can further entrench a young person in their trans identification. We believe that a gap year is generally good for young people who are mentally stuck, as travel can expand the mind of the individual who has a narrow-minded conceptualisation of life. It can sometimes be more beneficial for a young person to go on a gap year instead of intensive psychotherapy where they remain in situ without meeting anyone different or doing anything different. This does not mean the gap year is always a success. Parents have reported sending their children on interesting programmes and the child returning doubled down and no happier. There is no 'one-size-fits-all'.

THE NEED FOR SELF-COMPASSION

The term 'emerging adult' was coined by Professor Jeffrey Arnett to describe how young adults today may remain dependent on their parents until well into their twenties.[3] This can create a complicated dilemma, as many parents realise they are inadvertently funding a medical transition they do not agree with. Some parents choose not to fund the transition or allow their child to use their health insurance, but this can backfire as the young person can rack up debts and the power struggle can become further entrenched. Other parents allow their adult child to medically transition – and many help by taking on the role of nurse in the recovery. But this can lead to dark nights of the soul where the parent wonders if they did the right thing.

Parents need to give themselves a break. This is an unfolding medical scandal that has treated loving parents cruelly. The devastation that parents have experienced can be indescribable. A certain type of person is more liable than others to become fixated upon a trans identity. A certain type of naive, socially awkward, cerebral, gullible child is vulnerable to this issue, and it's important that parents don't weaken themselves at this crucial time by trawling over the previous twenty or so years worrying about what they did wrong. Self-compassion is required, not endless post-mortems about whatever school you sent them to, whatever friendship group they had (or didn't have), whatever hobbies drew them to other gender-non-conformers. Some children are statistically more likely to be drawn to gender ideology than others. If this was your child, then honour the fact that you did your best with the knowledge you had at the time, and, most importantly, give yourself a break.

8

FAMILY STYLES AND DYNAMICS

COMING OUT CHANGES EVERYTHING

Laura had always been such a joy to parent. She was creative, joyful and funny. She wasn't as socially engaged with peers as her older brother, Josh, but she was thriving nonetheless. Until about the age of twelve. Laura found the move to secondary education difficult. Her new school was larger than her primary school and she only knew one or two other kids. She ate lunch alone, occasionally crossing paths with Josh throughout the day. But he was two school years above her and had his own friends. When the Covid lockdowns started, Laura began spending most of her day behind a computer screen in her bedroom. Between online Zoom classes and leisure time on Discord, anime forums and YouTube, she wandered down the trans rabbit hole. She became withdrawn and moody. She started wearing baggy, dark clothes that lacked the colourful patterns she had loved her whole life. When she asked for a haircut, Jennifer happily took her to the best stylist in town, thinking a new do might help her regain some confidence, but this made no difference. Greg and Jennifer worried about the amount of time Laura was spending online, but comforted themselves with the knowledge that a desire for privacy is a normal part of adolescence. Everything changed one night when Laura came downstairs, solemn as ever, holding a handwritten letter. She confessed that she was a 'transboy', that she was feeling depressed and suicidal, and that she wanted to start binding her breasts and was considering medical interventions to transition.

Greg and Jennifer's world came crashing down upon this announcement. This scenario marks the start of a new chapter in the lives of many families. Whether your child makes this announcement at thirteen or at twenty-three, most parents feel blindsided and unsure how to move forward.

THE AFTERMATH – COMMON REACTION STYLES IN THE FAMILY

You may recognise yourself in one or more of the following broad categories of how parents may respond to their child's trans announcement. Please know that it's completely normal, and ever so human to have any (or all) of these reactions. And in certain contexts, these responses may be precisely the right ones. For parents who are married or partnered, it may be that one of you has one reaction while the other has another. Sometimes these different styles are complimentary, but sometimes spouses can undermine each other.

Paralysis and avoidance

Maybe you had one or two conversations with your child and set some boundaries: no medical intervention, no puberty blockers, no gender therapist. Now three months have gone by and you haven't talked about it again since. Your child might be using a different name with friends or teachers, but at home it's like nothing has happened.

You may feel extremely uncomfortable or too shocked to even begin formulating another discussion with your child. Perhaps you've tried but each time it has turned into a fight. Maybe you feel intimidated and confused by the jargon your child is using to assert his perspective. Or perhaps you're secretly immersed in accumulating research, and the more you find out, the less you want to confront your child in case he stops talking to you.

Maybe your spouse or partner is the one who always brings it up and you feel a little guilty about your reticence but also relieved that you don't have to be the bad guy and your relationship with your child can be relatively conflict free. Or perhaps neither one of you dares mention it. In this case, gender has gone underground and it's not spoken of at home.

Waffling, negotiation, being worn out by your child

You're trying to use the pronouns and stumbling over your words – this doesn't feel congruent with who your child is, but you want her to feel supported. You oscillate between performing some aspect of social transition and reverting to the birth sex identity once you feel burned out. You negotiate: 'You can't have hormones until you do a lot of therapy first.' Your child has promised she'll stop badgering you about hormones if only you'll use her boy name. After a few months of forcing yourself to call her 'Max', she has started begging for hormones again.

Or maybe your son insists that he needs to medically transition right away, reminding you daily that even one more month of puberty means he'll be too far along to 'pass' when he is older. Is the door closing on his future happiness? You offered to buy him female clothes so he could experiment at home. Surprisingly, he was not interested, stating that medical transition must come first and that he'll socially transition once he's 'further along'.

You feel like you're walking on thin ice and getting worn down. The risk of explosive conflict is always brewing beneath the surface. If you and your partner are on the same page, you can provide support and an essential sounding board for one another. Substantial disagreements can undermine your resolve and lead to more indecision and waffling.

Hypervigilance: every decision feels crucial

When your child came out, you jumped into detective mode. Where was this coming from, and how could you stop this in its tracks? You discovered online relationships with ambiguous characters pushing your son to 'come out' and later telling him how awful you are for not 'affirming'. You brought his computer into the living room, started restricting phone access, and regularly delivered monologues as your son stared blankly at the floor. You produced old family photos and pointed out that your son's never been interested in feminine things: 'Look, here you are building a train set and refusing to touch your sister's toys when she begs you to play with her.'

You became hypervigilant about your fifteen-year-old daughter's appearance. What does it mean that she wore a boy's button-down shirt? What if it has a floral pattern? Reading deep layers of meaning into an item of clothing or a solitary statement can lead to future disappointment. She ordered a trans flag from Amazon and you waged war: you took it down, she put it back up. When you finally threw it away, she put a 'he/they' pronouns pin on her backpack. Discussions get heated and may sound like an interrogation: how do you know what it feels like to be a boy, if you aren't one? You've shown her transition-regret horror stories but she insists, 'Well, they're not me! They're nothing like me!'

Perhaps you feel so overwhelmed, terrified and fragile that your emotions are the biggest in the room. You can't have a conversation with your daughter without bursting into tears, begging her not to harm her body. She may now be comforting you: 'Please don't cry, Mum, I promise I won't do anything, I didn't mean to hurt you.'

Perhaps your partner is the hypervigilant one and you find his or her preoccupation draining. Isn't she overreacting? Why can't she just relax a little and trust that this will work itself out? Or maybe you are the worried one. You wish your partner shared the extent of your concern. Sometimes it feels like you are shouldering the burden of fear alone.

Aversion, withdrawal, loss of connection

You no longer know how to connect with your child. Your daughter is so dark and brooding now that you barely recognise her. Or your older son suddenly estranged himself while at university. This happened along with a 'coming-out' letter full of demands and ultimatums. How can you possibly lean in with love when it feels like he is threatening you? Not to mention that this is *nothing* like him!

It may be that you feel disgust or aversion at seeing your child in cross-gender clothing, shaving or not shaving, or presenting themselves in a radical new way. When a boy's gender dysphoria contains an obvious sexual element or he has stolen undergarments from the women in the house, this can be viscerally distressing, a truly disconcerting experience. Furthermore, if your child has begun medically transitioning, you may feel unable to tolerate the physical changes taking place. A sense of embarrassment, self-doubt or disgust is ever-present. What will people think of us? How did things go wrong? What kind of horrible parent am I that this has happened to my child?

Maybe you feel visceral feelings of disgust or painful waves of disappointment while the other parent seems to experience neither of these things. Does this make you a terrible person for feeling this way?

CRISIS MANAGEMENT AND 'GENDER-AFFIRMING' RECOMMENDATIONS

Perhaps you've been told that your child is likely to commit suicide if you don't affirm. Your body has been marinating in stress hormones ever since you heard this terrifying information and you are gutted to see your child's mental health worsening in the weeks after her coming-out announcement. Your son is begging for puberty blockers or hormones and explaining that every week that passes will make it harder for him to pass and live as his true self. In the heat of the moment, you may feel that something must be done. Parents may understandably feel compelled to take action and agree to social or medical transition in such a case. Parents who fear that their teen may be particularly vulnerable could understandably feel more inclined to do anything in their power to pacify them. Some families in 'crisis mode' may comply wholeheartedly with the affirmative recommendations for social and even medical interventions. Often these parents feel they are drowning in fear, and only come up for air once the immediate crisis seems stabilised. If partners are not on the same page, conflict can become intense as terror dominates the emotional landscape.

THE IDENTIFIED PATIENT AND
THE BROADER FAMILY SYSTEM

In psychotherapy, the term 'identified patient' describes the individual with the 'problem'. This is often a child who is exhibiting concerning behaviour and has been brought to a professional for treatment, and yet her troubles are an expression of other issues within the family. We might say this young person is psychologically manifesting the family's dysfunctions. Do you sweep things under the rug, are you conflict-avoidant, or is your family locked into constant bickering, fights or disagreements? Are there unaddressed marital conflicts, communication issues, substance abuse, attachment problems? A child's announcement can be an opportunity to take a look at dynamics in the family and engage in some self-reflection. What unhelpful patterns have evolved? Maybe Mum has been over-invested in her daughter and the trans identification signals that it is time for some psychological separation. Maybe Dad has been uninvolved or has had a hard time connecting with an autistic son who doesn't share his love of sports. Now is the time to find appropriate ways to address these core issues. Parents often describe their child's distress as a 'wake-up call' about the difficulties within the family that they had put on the back burner. Whether you decide to work through these as a family or enlist the help of a skilled therapist, you might start with an honest conversation with your child that recognises the work to be done: 'Our family really struggles with _____. I know this is really hard on everyone, including you. We plan to work on this by doing _____.'

POWER DYNAMICS

One of the pre-existing issues that often surfaces is power distribution in the family. Earlier, we touched upon power struggles between a hypervigilant parent and a child grasping for little tokens of autonomy. But another common issue occurs when a child holds an outsized amount of power. Parents feel they are being controlled by their child's tantrums or outbursts, always walking a tightrope, and may even feel intimidated by an exceptionally bright or forceful child. A parent may be afraid that establishing boundaries or saying no to their child's demand will harm the child or their relationship. These mums and dads do everything they can to make sure their children feel constantly supported and validated, and may believe that conflict or friction is a sign of family dysfunction.

As we discussed in Chapter 4, children need a combination of warmth and structure (responsiveness and demandingness). Inevitably, there will be many times you will have to erect guard rails to protect your child against immature or risky decisions. Even if your child is a young adult, it's worth sharing your opinion. There is a great need for counter-perspectives or even a few speed bumps on the road to irreversible medical changes. If you have a young child at home and you feel you have been too lenient in capitulating to his or her gender demands, we address this in Chapter 14. If a child has begun transitioning against your advice, you may feel powerless. These situations are incredibly difficult, and it is crucial to invest in your own self-care, something we explore in Chapter 10.

Power dynamics with prepubertal children

When parents adhere to the activists' dictum to 'let the child lead', even a very young child can gain too much power in the family. Prepubertal children need their parents to offer structure, guidance and boundaries. They benefit when we have clear behavioural expectations and they know they can count on us to manage their world. Small children are too young to decide their bedtime, manage food choices on their own – or decide their gender. Giving them more power than they can handle is destabilising for them and the entire family.

Children also take their cues from us about how to make sense of the wider world. Social referencing refers to a process whereby a young child looks to her parent to gauge how she should respond to a novel stimulus. When your toddler falls down, he immediately looks at you to see how you will respond. If you show alarm, he begins to cry. If you smile and coo reassuringly, he will likely get up and go back to playing. When we respond to a young child's gender distress with a lot of energy, we communicate to our child that this new behaviour gives her a lot of power. It's much better not to make a big deal of it one way or the other, while still setting and maintaining appropriate boundaries.

COUPLE DYNAMICS

If you and your spouse are on the same page, consider yourself lucky. Maybe you are even reading this book together: you're a united front. You cooperate and divide up responsibilities by considering your individual strengths and challenges. One of you communicates exceptionally well with your child, and the other bonds and builds memories over shared activities and fun hobbies. When a child knows that both parents have similar rules/boundaries around gender transition, he or she is likely to find greater stability. Sometimes, though, each parent has a different idea about how to make decisions. One parent dives headfirst into researching ROGD, tries to make more strategic decisions and attempts to slow down the social or medical transition. The other parent feels that this is 'overkill' and takes a more lax approach, insisting that the child will figure it out on her own. Sometimes this devolves into an extreme 'good cop, bad cop' dynamic, although it's likely the 'good cop' is actually resigned ('There's nothing we can do anyway'). The more engaged and strategic parent is left feeling angry, abandoned and solely responsible for parenting decisions. Many have reported that their marriages have fallen apart in the wake of a child's gender fixation. Also challenging is the way this may affect your child, who can perceive the 'good cop' as the one who 'knows how to parent', and the other as 'transphobic' and repressive. The 'bad cop' parent is also more likely to be communicating with the school, with potential therapists and health professionals, spending hours researching the latest data and policy, while the 'good cop' parent, largely ignoring the issue, seems to be the main recipient of the child's love and trust.

Whether the marital conflict represents an exacerbation of an existing tension or whether this is the first time a couple has disagreed on a fundamental parenting issue, managing this conflict is crucial. The more you can understand one another's 'whys' and seek to meet in the middle, the better. This advice may be even more important for the resigned parent, though we suspect that he/she isn't reading this book. If you can, explore the following points together with your partner/spouse:

- How were each of you parented (remember the styles in Chapter 4)? What worked or didn't work for you about your parents' style? How does that have an impact on the way you want to behave as a parent?
- Understand where your spouse/partner is coming from. As an experiment, ask yourself, 'What is my spouse's best, most compelling reason for taking that stance?'
- Honour the distress that your partner is feeling. Don't minimise or belittle it.
- Work towards a compromise while honouring your intuition.
- Nurture the relationship. Can you remember what you love about each other? Have a date night and don't talk about parenting, chores or gender.

If it's impossible to work on these things alone, seek out a couples therapist or other means of relationship support.

DIVORCE AND CO-PARENTING

Co-parents who are largely in agreement about how to best support their child can use the principles we've explored thus far. Having continuity in each home will encourage stabilisation in your gender-questioning child. Many of you will be in a different situation: one parent fully supports the social transition and the other doesn't, creating yet another double-life experience for the child travelling from one home to another. The child may hold a great deal of resentment towards the parent who isn't affirming, seeing the apparently lenient parent as the 'cool one'. As explored in Chapter 7, it's important to avoid triangulation where one parent is the saviour, the other the persecutor, and the child is the disempowered victim. In extreme cases this begins to resemble parental alienation syndrome, with the lenient parent turning the child against the other, whether intentionally or otherwise. Sometimes the 'affirmation' is a symptom of negligent parenting rather than a strategic and earnest attempt to do what's best for the child. In other cases, one parent is actively pushing for medical interventions while the other is attempting to slow this down or even fight medical decisions in court. It's not uncommon for the parent who has spent little time researching the psychological and medical implications of transition to advocate for a lenient approach and for giving the child 'time to work it out' over time. 'It's just like being gay, right?' this parent might think. If you're the researching parent in this scenario, it's important to speak privately with the co-parent and explain your concerns. In most cases of disagreement, we recommend attempting to communicate. It may help to enlist a mediator, close friend or relative who is on good terms with both individuals.

SIBLINGS – ON THE FENCE, OR HURT BY THE TRANS ID

Let's return to Laura and her family. When puberty began for her older brother Josh, their relationship started to change. He became less interested in playing with her, and more interested in gaming with his school friends. Laura was struggling to make friends in secondary school and it became painfully obvious that Josh effortlessly possessed social skills that she still found elusive. She would see his friend group sitting together at lunch, a big group of boys, joking loudly and showering Josh with attention for his quick humour and charismatic personality.

Josh was the kind of dynamic, popular kid who lit up the room and easily gained people's attention. This was amplified when he sustained a severe fracture during a soccer game: the family developed a routine revolving around medical appointments, his school schedule and his daily needs. Meanwhile, Laura retreated into the online world, looking for solace and friendship. Subconsciously, she began to associate 'boyhood' with adoration, confidence and social success. Her theory was validated by hours of trans YouTube videos documenting young women's 'transitions', 'gender journeys' and 'transition timelines'. The story was the same: *I was a depressed nobody, and now that I've transitioned to my authentic transboy self, I'm happy.* And thousands of adoring subscribers and fans agreed, co-ruminating on their gender obsession in the comments and on message boards.

Sibling jealousy often lies deep beneath the surface story. Sometimes, the sibling is a high-needs child with neurodevelopmental conditions or chronic health issues. If her brother's explosive tantrums are met with more lenient reactions from parents, a child may come to think life is better as a boy.

As with our discussion of the identified patient (the individual with 'the problem'), speaking directly with your child about her experience of the sibling can help. It's unlikely that she will be intellectually aware of these subtle, subconscious processes, but you can model wisdom and awareness. You can give voice to the real dynamics, even as you recognise that they are not ideal: 'We know that when your brother acts out, we're much more lenient on him than we are with you. We recognise and apologise that this doesn't seem fair. What has that been like for you?' Become mindful of how your energy and time is distributed: it helps for each child to have special ways to connect with his or her parents. Maybe you and your daughter enjoy taking the dog for a walk or going on drives together where you listen to music. Articulate how much you value that special alone time with her.

SIBLING REACTIONS TO THE TRANS IDENTITY

There are a number of ways a trans identity may 'land' with your other children. Whether the siblings are oblivious or indifferent, acting as a passionate 'trans ally' or feeling angry and betrayed, parents may not feel confident when addressing the issue. On one hand, it's wonderful when your kids have each other's backs. On the other, when siblings undermine parenting decisions, it feels impossible to set ground rules.

Younger siblings

Your gender-questioning child might have asked you to tell other siblings about his new identity. Some parents, in the spirit of honesty and transparency, encourage their child to immediately 'come out' to everyone in the family. Children under eight may not understand that sex is constant, and even older children might be confused by the contemporary rhetoric claiming that sex is a spectrum. We feel it's unfair to unnecessarily engage younger siblings, who have emotional and developmental needs of their own. If the younger ones seem oblivious and can be shielded, it's likely best to avoid such a confusing topic for now.

Sometimes this kind of protection is impossible. Your trans-identified child may already be pressuring their younger siblings to use their preferred name and pronouns. Maybe your college-aged child is back home using the new identity, clothing and name. Or maybe, if the impact of medical interventions has become visible, the transition can't be hidden. Your younger children might be asking questions or making remarks. We acknowledge how delicate these situations are. Find some calm moments to speak alone with your other child. Here are some principles you can use in conversation, tailoring the language to suit your personality and context.

Use factual and age-appropriate language. Avoid jargon. Try to contextualise the gender experimentation and help them understand some immutable facts.

1. Sex overrides subjective feelings.

'Your brother can think of himself in a lot of different ways, like playing make-believe or fantasy, but his body is real and it's a male body. The way he thinks about himself doesn't change this fact.'

2. Medically induced changes in appearance are not a sex change. Medicine is not magic.

'We can change our bodies with drugs called "hormones". These can make us more or less hairy, and change the body's shape, but they also have very serious health consequences, like smoking cigarettes, doing drugs or eating too much junk food.'

3. Our values and beliefs are…

'Disliking your body or parts of yourself is normal and can be painful. But we don't believe changing your body is the best way to deal with your difficult feelings. We don't agree with what your brother is doing, but we love him no matter what.'

4. Everyone's feelings matter, including yours.

'It seems you've noticed that your sister is going through something with her clothing/name/body… What do you think is happening for her, and what are your honest thoughts/feelings about it? You're allowed to have ANY kind of opinion or feeling about this, even if you are worried that it would upset others.'

Older siblings

Siblings who feel ambivalent or distressed also need a chance to feel heard. You can build upon the messaging above and ask more open-ended questions. If your child doesn't want to talk, let him know that it's OK but make yourself available should he change his mind. The situation may be complicated to articulate or difficult to process. On the surface, the sibling might seem indifferent, but she may be privately struggling with a great deal of pain. Common feelings include betrayal, confusion, protectiveness, fear or anger. Sometimes parents try to recruit an influential older sibling to join the parental project and redirect the gender-questioning child. While this may be appropriate in certain contexts, it can also place an unfair burden on the recruited sibling.

This young woman talks about her sibling experience:

Having a trans-identified sister with severe mental health problems has been very difficult. We were very close growing up, and it's devastating to see someone who is smart and gifted go down a path that is wrong and irreversible.

I love my mother dearly, but all we did for years was talk about my sister. Seeing my sister's mental and physical state was so painful, I would have nightmares about self-harm and would search my sister's room constantly to find any sharp objects she was using to cut. I would inspect the toilet after she exited as I was so scared that she was following my footsteps to bulimia. During this period, I would have constant panic attacks and chest pains, I found it increasingly difficult to talk to people, and I isolated myself. I found it difficult to study, to be alone with my thoughts. I would constantly watch YouTube as escapism. My grades started to suffer.

Because my sister went to the same school as me, her identity was public and everyone around me suddenly knew. The smug self-satisfaction of teachers approaching me and calling my sister 'your brother' with a knowing look and a smile like they're in the secret club. What do you say? To be seen as progressive and 'on the right side of history', you must perjure yourself: affirm what you know to be untrue, against every experience you've had with this person that you love. To correct would be to admit to being the enemy.

University was a chance to separate myself: no one knew, and so I could say my reality with no pushback; I have a younger sister. But the paranoia is always there, the fear that people will find out and brand me a bigot. One click on my sister's social media page and you will find he/him.

The gender-questioning sibling

You can honour your child's identity exploration while teaching her to respect the needs of others in the family. Point out that it's a violation of others' boundaries when she demands that they use her new boy name/pronouns. This is especially true if her siblings are too young to understand or if they are feeling pressured. Here's an example of how you might communicate this: 'I know you've been experimenting with your identity lately, and that's a healthy, normal thing to do at your age. And being part of a family means that siblings have an impact on each other. Your brother is watching you carefully, and I want to make sure that, just like you, he has a chance to think for himself. When you place demands on your brother, or push your own gender beliefs onto him, I feel concerned about that. Everyone in this family is entitled to his or her own perspective. You can't force us to flip a switch and see each other differently. I know you're trying to work out your own identity, but your brother knows you as his sister, and that's his lived experience.'

Siblings who team up as allies

When a sibling readily adjusts to the new trans identity, it can make your hesitance even more pronounced. You may be harshly questioned by multiple children. The ally-sibling can act as a facilitator, helping to buy clothing, breast binders or make-up behind their parents' backs. The new subversive ideas about gender become a topic of conversation and a way for the kids to bond, pitting themselves against their old, out-of-touch parents. Siblings may shoot parallel death stares about instances of 'misgendering' or may co-lecture Mum about her 'trans-phobia'. Parents may find it especially challenging to erect enforceable boundaries around transition requests. The power dynamic has become skewed, and teens are running the show. It's easy to end all arguments with the phrase 'Anyway, you're just a transphobe.'

Take some time out to reflect on your place of authority in the family. Do you feel you have any? When did you lose it? Is your authority being undermined by your spouse or co-parent? When do you feel most confident as a parent? How can you rebuild your faith in your own authority? Once you've spent some time exploring these ideas, come up with a communication plan. Maintaining a confident, calm, loving tone can help re-establish your role as the authoritative parent. If the kids seem to amplify each other's aggression, maybe an individual discussion with each child is more appropriate.

Social contagion within the family

While parents are focused on how to best support their trans-identified child, a sibling could be watching in the wings, beginning to question his own gender. Unfortunately, this is a common scenario. Having a trans identity becomes a tangible way to call attention to one's distress. A template is created and a domino effect takes place. The multiple trans-identified kids phenomenon may also be the outcome for families who have bought into contemporary gender theories and the idea of actively exploring gender identity.

When you have been trying to slow down the first 'trans kid', a second 'coming out' may feel too much to handle. At this point, you may feel completely exasperated, exhausted and lacking the patience and energy to be strategic. This is a long game and not a short sprint, so we encourage some time to invest in self-care before making any sudden changes. Conversely, you learned a great deal with your first child's exploration of identity, so you may have a clear sense of how to respond with the second child.

EXTENDED FAMILY: SECRECY, BETRAYAL OR COMPETING PERSPECTIVES

Parents are often carrying the psychological burden of their child's mental health distress alone. Fearing the reaction of extended family, parents can become isolated ('There's no way we could explain this to my parents'). Once again, only you know whether talking to your extended family is a good idea. Your gender-questioning child may be private about her struggles and might feel betrayed if you shared her secret, and yet some children beg their parents to tell relatives about their new identity. We don't believe parents should take ownership of the child's coming-out process or help her make announcements. It can be helpful for the young person to take responsibility for the consequences of her actions. When we jump in and ease the coming-out process, we are rescuing our child from the real-world effects of her decisions. In addition, the messaging here should be: 'Exploring your identity is a normal part of growing up, but it's good to take your time and see where things lead, rather than making grand announcements or putting yourself in a position that's hard to walk back from.' And besides, we also need to ask about *your* needs. Do you hate keeping the secret from your family? Do you need their support and understanding for your own sanity and well-being?

If you decide to speak with loved ones, we suggest starting with social contagion instead of gender. Talk about social influence, peer imitation and the various ways teens channel their distress. Eating disorders, cutting, multiple personality disorder and TikTok Tourette's may serve as more familiar examples. You can remind them that the best way to support young people struggling with such issues is to validate their experience, show empathy for their pain and take things slowly to support them through it.

If you can enlist sympathetic relatives who have strong relationships with your children, this could offer a much-needed break from the tension at home. Leaning on loved ones can provide a valuable growth opportunity for your child. It's important for distressed young people to be around those who love and know them best. Could a favourite uncle take your child out for dinner and offer a listening ear? Can your child spend a few weeks with her cousin, aunt and uncle in a different city or country?

One of the most devastating dynamics occurs when well-meaning but misinformed relatives take a highly affirmative stance towards your child's gender questions. They explicitly undermine your parenting decisions and widen the rift between you and your child, making your position even harder to hold. We always encourage maintaining family relationships when possible. Would it help to spend some extended time together, show them literature on ROGD, the risks of medicalisation, detransition, or the caution emerging in certain European countries? Even if they disagree with you on the trans issue, could they support you because they love and care for you and recognise that you are doing what you think is best for your child? If speaking with these relatives gets you nowhere, and they are staunchly pushing for medicalisation, these family members may become an unhelpful influence in your child's life. You may feel deeply betrayed and feel the relationship can never be repaired. There are many parents facing this kind of heartbreak. If this is your situation, it's important to find strength in your parental decisions and find a trusted confidant or support system.

A CHANCE FOR TRANSFORMATION

While we've explored the depths of conflict and devastation that many families experience, we want to highlight a hopeful possibility. Some parents recognise that their child's distress, as well as being an incredible parenting challenge, also offers an opportunity for growth. Parents may say, 'This was the wake-up call our family needed. We leaned in, made some adjustments, and despite the difficulty, we're closer now than ever.' Inspiring and courageous parents have used this experience to honestly take inventory of their family's dynamics, strengths and challenges. We hope the suggestions in this chapter have given you ideas on how to begin the process towards greater strength as a parent.

9

MANAGING CONFLICT
WITH YOUR CHILD

Conflict is an unavoidable aspect of parenting. It famously begins when children are toddlers, abates somewhat when they are primary school age, and often picks up again as they enter adolescence. When gender identity enters the picture, parent–child conflict can become intense. It may be helpful to reflect on how you *feel* about conflict, both in general and with your child. In our experience, many parents of gender-distressed children are loving, attuned – and conflict-averse. They may equate conflict with disconnection and avoid doing anything that will cause discord with their child.

How we feel about conflict will undoubtedly affect how we hold parental authority, in part because society has done much to under-mine parents' position in relation to their children. Therefore, your ability to draw upon your own deep sense of inner authority can make all the difference.

Parental authority comes from within. If you don't feel you're in charge, chances are you're not. A child can sense if a parent has lost his or her way. A parent communicates his or her lack of faith in his or her own authority, in the same way that a teacher who is too tentative signals to students in a classroom that they can discount her. It is an unconscious exchange. To nurture your sense of inner authority, you'll need to find the bedrock where you have faith in your decisions. (We recognise that this can be difficult when you are distressed or pressured.) Take the time you need to care for yourself, so you can make space to connect with your inner knowing. Becoming more familiar with the scientific literature on gender, or talking with others who are knowledgeable on the science, can also help. Try to speak from this place of confidence when interacting with your child. Practise using your strong voice, which is lower in tone, and practise holding your body – shoulders back, strength in the belly, feet planted on the floor – in an unapologetic manner. Also become more aware of your facial expression and learn how to put on your game face when you need it. Your game face is a neutral or serious facial expression that is often displayed by a sports player or gambler, and can be helpful when you need time in a hostile atmosphere to collect your thoughts.

PARENTAL AUTHORITY

As discussed in Chapter 4, Diana Baumrind was a US clinical psychologist who developed an overarching theory about parenting styles and authority, using four main models: authoritative, authoritarian, permissive and uninvolved. We have observed that in the past few decades another style has emerged, which we call 'responsive parenting', and which is characterised by great warmth and attentiveness. Parents invest themselves intensively in their child and in the parenting process. Responsive parents may have significant expectations of their children, and responsive households usually do have rules, but the family tends to be governed by the perceived needs of the child. The underlying assumption is that the child could be psychologically damaged if his needs aren't met.

The culture of 'attachment parenting' and other factors have fostered responsive parenting, encouraging parents to be diligently attuned. Somehow, along the way, parents of this generation absorbed the false belief that discomfort is harmful and that a child's distress is a sign that something is wrong and must be fixed. There can be, as the saying goes, too much of a good thing.

Excessive responsiveness tends to undermine parental authority, because it can be difficult to differentiate between what a child wants and what a child needs. Our parenting becomes overly reactive, gives the child too much power, and risks communicating to kids that they can't tolerate distress.

The assumption underlying responsive parenting – that children will suffer if their needs aren't met and that it is damaging for kids to be unhappy, to suffer or to struggle – has become deeply embedded in our wider culture. Parents are often judged accordingly. We are told that our trans-identifying children need cross-sex hormones, and if we do not assent, our children will be grievously harmed. If we are used to doing everything we can to help our children avoid discomfort, this messaging can shake our confidence in our inner knowing. The child's desire to transition is understood to be a deep-seated need that should be trusted absolutely.

This is one of the ways transgender ideology undermines parental authority. Parents who question a child's desire to medicalise may be made to feel as if they do not know what is best for their child. School administrators and teachers, doctors and therapists may be encouraging parents to prioritise a child's desire to transition, even though the parent has very well-founded concerns.

No matter the age of your child, managing conflict around this issue will require that you get a firm grasp on your parental authority. You are the person who loves your child the most and is the most invested in his well-being. Know also that protecting kids from the worst consequences of their impulses is an important part of parenting. Doing so will not feel good for you and will likely involve making your child angry and upset. This is OK. Gender dysphoric kids can sometimes be suffering greatly, and this is agonising to watch. But sometimes we need to help our children learn that they can tolerate distress. We communicate to them that we know they will be all right. We will provide support, but we trust their resilience.

Parenting through conflict will require that we take an honest inventory of what we can change and what we can't. The Serenity Prayer of Alcoholics Anonymous can help: *Grant me the serenity to accept the things I cannot change, the courage to change the things I can, and the wisdom to know the difference*. Often, there will be more to accept if we have older children. On the other hand, we may have more power and authority than we realised, and we should be unafraid to use it, especially when our children are younger. Often, the final part of the prayer is the hardest.

THE GOAL: AVOID POWER STRUGGLES

Avoiding power struggles is the key to managing conflict effectively. This is not the same as avoiding conflict. In a power struggle, both parent and child are jockeying to achieve dominance over the other, which tends to undermine parental authority and lock parties into rigid positions. Because power struggles set up a situation where there is a winner and a loser, stepping away from them or conceding often involves a loss of face. The way to avoid them is to set clear, enforceable limits, and apply them consistently. The key word is *enforceable*, and this is where the Serenity Prayer is helpful. What kinds of limits can be enforced with children? When our children are young, we can control their access to screens and other media, their sleep environment, how and where they spend their time. If our child is seventeen, there is little we can control. The strategy is the same: identify those things that are in our control and enforce consistent limits. If your child is doing something you don't like but it is beyond your ability to influence, you will have to find acceptance. In general, we have found that when a parent and child get locked into a power struggle around gender, it often makes the child hold on to the trans identification even when it is no longer serving him.

DON'T TALK ABOUT GENDER ALL THE TIME

No matter what the age of your child, avoid making gender the centre of your interactions. Remind her of the big world that exists outside the small, insular world of gender. After all, your child is so much more than her perceived gender! There are many things to share and discover. It is important that we model this for our kids.

You *should* talk about gender sometimes. As stated, it is important that parents register their concerns about gender ideology and medicalisation. Ideally, this should be done matter-of-factly, without heat. The point of such conversations is to plant a seed and invite your child to consider another viewpoint. You'll have to gauge how often to bring up the subject and look for opportunities. The hardest part may be how to take the emotion out of your words when the stakes feel so high. Actively listening – even if you disagree – is likely to build trust and reduce conflict. You can validate your child's feelings without agreeing with her.

AVOID BECOMING AS OBSESSED WITH GENDER AS YOUR CHILD

When our kid becomes trans-identified, many parents begin researching and soon have what we call an 'internet PhD' in the subject. While this is laudable, a parent's preoccupation tends to shift the energy in the relationship, subtly encouraging the kid to dig in her heels even when parents avoid debate. While it's impossible to shut off our concern or *not* notice whether she is wearing the binder today, we need to guard against becoming as preoccupied as she is. As far as our kid goes down the trans rabbit hole, we often go right in after them. This can heighten the sense of underlying tension and may make it more difficult for a child to move through their trans identification and out the other side. The fellowship Al-Anon was founded in recognition that we can become as absorbed by alcoholism as our loved one is absorbed by alcohol. Equally, the Gender Dysphoria Support Network (see Resources) was founded with the same concept in mind – that parents can become as obsessed with the issues related to medical transition as their child is obsessed with transitioning.

LISTENING AND APOLOGISING

No matter the age of your child, listening will be a vital part of de-escalating conflict around gender. Look for opportunities for your child to share his feelings. Teens and young adults may have a lot of anger at their parents. Even if we feel this is unwarranted, it is important to listen and acknowledge how they feel. Offering a sincere apology to our child in response to their perception of having been wounded or failed by us is not the same thing as admitting culpability. The point is to respond to the child's feelings with warmth and empathy, not to litigate who is right or wrong. Apologising even for things you sincerely believe you didn't do signals that you take your child's feelings seriously and that your relationship with him matters more than being right. After all, your child's preoccupation with gender is not really about gender. There is a good chance it is at least in part about his relationship with you, and so you might apologise in a way that feels authentic. Listening, apologising and looking for ways to connect and communicate warmth and love will go a long way to minimising conflict.

DON'T ARGUE

It might be helpful for parents to become familiar with the basic principles of motivational interviewing, a counselling technique aimed at supporting someone in a change process. The listener aims to draw out ideas from the other person in a spirit of collaboration and does not seek to impose an agenda. The listener respects that the other person will have his or her own process and may not have the same goals that the listener does. Through empathy and reflection, the listener helps to bring consciousness to the discrepancy between where the other person is and where he or she would like to be. The listener does not challenge, oppose or criticise, but asks open-ended questions and reflects back the person's strengths. Importantly, counsellors offering motivational interviewing are taught to 'resist the righting reflex' – in other words, to avoid the temptation of correcting someone or telling them what to do. Doing so will probably be ineffective and will likely arouse hostility.

WORK TO MANAGE YOUR OWN FEELINGS

Most of the time, the urge to 'fix' someone by telling them what to do is a response to our anxiety about the person. While it's natural to be anxious when we see our children making poor decisions, our first job is to handle our own anxiety so that we are not making our children responsible for it. This will make it easier for us to stay connected and engaged. You're going to have big feelings about this, but if you can deal with them on your own, it will be easier to approach interactions with your child without these becoming unnecessarily clouded by your emotions.

CONFLICT WITH PREPUBERTAL CHILDREN

If your young child is expressing a desire to dress as the opposite sex or wanting to use a different name or pronouns, you will need to be clear about what you think is best for your child, communicate that compassionately, and hold firm. This may mean ignoring the advice of other parents, even those you have always confided in and trusted. It is important that our decisions are not ruled by fear.

We believe it is best that parents affirm gender-nonconformity while asserting the reality of biology. If at the weekend your son comes out of his bedroom wearing a dress, simply proceed as if nothing is out of the ordinary. If, however, it is his sister's dress, you might react as you would if he had borrowed any other item without permission. Treating gender experimentation in childhood as normal will avoid giving it too much power. On the other hand, it is inappropriate if your son borrows your daughter's underwear and, in this context, you may need to protect your daughter from such behaviour.

While extreme distress might require a change in approach and/or professional input, be careful not to mistake upset for an emergency. This can be difficult, especially when the upset is loudly voiced. It may be challenging to hold your ground in the face of your child's distress or pressure from others such as school employees.

Many behaviours in childhood will self-extinguish if not given oxygen. Think of the little boy with a love of bathroom humour whose mother responds with shocked protestations whenever he makes an inappropriate joke. The child is being reinforced in this behaviour each time his mother reacts. If instead she ignored these jokes, he would likely move through this phase faster. Try to take a low-key approach to your child's gender-nonconformity and avoid making it a contested issue.

CONFLICT WITH TEENS

As children move into the teen years, conflict often increases, and parental influence wanes, though it is still critical. Kids experience the first stirrings of puberty, often accompanied by changes in friends, interests, scholastic expectations and social roles. Children engage more with peers, in real life and online, and peer and social media influence becomes a big factor in how a child understands herself.

You might want to set safety-based limits around tech use, public toilet use and medicalisation. You can refrain from getting your younger child a mobile phone, use parental controls on devices, collect phones at bedtime and turn off the household router. Trying to influence what is out of your control can result in unproductive power struggles. We don't recommend policing clothing or hairstyles, which are difficult to enforce. They also send a message that your child needs to conform to a certain gender presentation, which can work against acceptance of gender-nonconforming behaviour. It is not possible to control what your child's peers call her or what pronouns they use.

While some parents insist that a child uses their birth name at after-school activities, holiday camps or school, this is fertile ground for transgression. It is best to communicate with the adults at the activity or school first.

Even with clear limits and a firm sense of your authority, adolescence can be contentious. Children who were always sweet and loving can shock us with their defiance and nastiness. Even though we had been warned the teen years might be difficult, we honestly never imagined that our pleasant child could turn into this raging monster. If gender troubles coincide with the onset of adolescence, parents may believe the gender issue is the sole cause of the conflict, whereas gender may have been recruited to aid in the developmental task of separation. It may help to keep the rows in context if you remember that conflict and strife with your child are to be expected.

One mum was distraught by the change in her thirteen-year-old, who had begun presenting as a transboy. She and her daughter had always been close and had a sweet ritual of going for afternoon tea after shopping trips. Her daughter now scoffed at the idea. While the loss of connection we feel with our young children as they enter adolescence and the passing of their childhood is heartbreaking for all parents, it is normal. This mum needed to be reminded that her daughter would have probably stopped joining her for tea at thirteen even without the gender issues. Her job was to accept that her daughter was growing and changing, and to provide a safe container for her child's passionate efforts to disentangle herself.

When gender enters the picture, parent–child conflict can become supercharged. Children may be reading online or hearing from peers or teachers that parents are bigots if they don't support their trans identity. We have heard frequent stories about professionals supporting a child in their trans identity against parents' wishes, claiming their child would commit suicide without their support, or chastising parents for being transphobic. Such statements are not backed up by definitive research, completely undermine parental authority and place parents in the role of 'bad guy', adding fuel to otherwise normal teen–parent conflict. These professionals do enormous damage to the child's most important attachment relationship.

CONFLICT WITH ADULT CHILDREN

Having a young adult who is undergoing medical transition can offer a reprieve from conflict, simply because, most of the time, the situation calls for our acceptance. Though it may be gutting to watch our child make decisions that are so clearly harmful, our task is to grieve and move towards acceptance. This can be difficult. And yet, precisely because of our reduced influence in her life, we can gratefully say goodbye to constant conflict.

It is significantly more difficult for parents to influence their adult children's choices – which is the natural order of things. Children are *supposed* to grow up and away from us, not become our clones. But it can be difficult to handle if your adult child appears to reject every single one of your family's values. We have noticed that many children who are enmeshed with one or both parents can find it challenging to individuate, and identifying as trans can be a radical and mentally satisfying way for the adult child to achieve this. It might be helpful to step back, perhaps engage some professional support for yourself, and consider how to provide more positive opportunities for your child to evolve into the independent individual she needs to become.

Holidays and short visits can be fraught for parents of adult children who seem to be lost or unhappy. The parents seek to save the child, who seeks to impress upon them that he can manage fine. Try journalling prior to the visit to articulate the emotions ringing around your head. Ultimately, you might only get the opportunity to land one point. If that's the case, then consider which is the most important, line it up carefully, land it and then leave the conversation. While we often hang around after we have made a key point – usually in the hope that the child will slap her forehead and see the light – it is sometimes best to give her the opportunity to reflect without moving into an argument.

If you are a parent of a vulnerable adult child who has other challenges such as ASD or ADHD, you can find it particularly excruciating to see your child moving towards medical transition, as you know the young adult needs more attention, you know their past cycles of impulsivity and regret, and yet society is telling you to back off. Many young adults attend college or university and become wholly absorbed in identity politics and social justice activism, and all the potential of their brilliant academic experience can go down the drain. At the back of the book we provide a list of many parent groups across the world. Some parents are not natural joiners, and yet it can be profoundly lonely when, for example, your vulnerable adult child is away at college; we recommend you seek support from others.

INDOCTRINATION

Gender-related conflict differs from other parent–child battles in that most trans-identified teens have been subjected to influence from peers, the internet, or both. We have heard several stories of teens and young adults who have formed close connections with older trans adults – online or in person – who encouraged them to transition. Those who have been indoctrinated in gender identity ideology based on the critical social justice model tend to be rigid thinkers who cannot tolerate a challenge to their ideas. The new beliefs replace old world views. Conflict with an indoctrinated person can be intense, and futile.

Many parents are convinced that their bright, perhaps science-oriented child would see the light if presented with the right evidence, but when someone is under the influence of an ideology, any direct challenge to their beliefs may dig that person in further. It is better to give the indoctrinated as little to push against as possible. Connecting with your child, asking sincere questions and listening compassionately to the answers – no matter how odd or exasperating – is a better strategy. Your main challenge will be to self-manage your own emotional responses.

AMBIVALENCE

Ambivalence is normal. We are all ambivalent about almost everything most of the time, and change is a constant in people's lives. Trans-identified kids behave as if this is not the case. They often present with stark certainty – a sign that ambivalent feelings can be difficult to tolerate. It feels good to be sure! So mixed feelings can get split off and given to someone else to hold. In this way, your child can be locked into a position of great certainty, because you are holding their disavowed feelings for them.

When Lisa's youngest child turned one, she started sharing her desire to have another baby with her husband, who wasn't sure. Whenever the topic came up, Lisa would try to persuade him that it was time, and he would give reasons why he didn't feel ready. This went on for several frustrating months until one day, Lisa's husband said he had changed his mind. Maybe it would be nice to have a baby again! At that point, Lisa got in touch with her own hesitation about having a third child. Now it was her husband who was listing all the reasons why they shouldn't delay, and Lisa who was expressing doubt. While Lisa experienced her husband as holding all of the 'no', she could only feel her 'yes'. As soon as her husband softened, she felt the full range of her feelings – including her ambivalence.

If we have a trans-identified child, she doesn't have to feel any doubts, because we are feeling them for her. So sometimes softening our stance can give the child back her ambivalence. That doesn't mean that we need to become a proponent of hormones and surgery. It's a suggestion, rather, that we try containing our opposition so she has some space for her feelings. Refusing to get drawn into playing your child's antagonist is another way to invite an awareness of ambivalence. When we find ourselves playing tug of war, sometimes the most powerful thing we can do is to drop the rope. One mum, life coach and parent educator, 'StoicMom', told one of the authors of this book how she elegantly avoids taking the bait. When her daughter tries to lure her into a combative stance around her intention to medically transition, she invites her daughter to take responsibility for her own decisions. 'It's not what I would do,' she tells her. 'But this is your life. I trust you to make healthy decisions for yourself.'

If our child does speak of her doubts, we will feel tempted to jump on these expressions of ambivalence. This may send her back into her corner of certainty and we may find that she is as closed off as before. It might be better to say something neutral. You could say, 'It seems like a part of you feels really certain that hormones would help you feel better, but another part is scared you might not like all the changes.' This may give her permission to fully consider her feelings.

PROVIDING A SAFE CONTAINER

Being a container for another person's distress means that we give them space to have all kinds of feelings. We put aside our own needs to provide a steady presence and a listening ear. When someone is lashing out at us, being a container can be very difficult. We forget not to take things personally. We lose our cool. This is particularly true if you have many demands on your time – you might have little support from the other parent, and you may also be caring for elderly parents. It can be helpful to remember that your child is struggling, or does not have access to the best parts of herself, or is momentarily impaired in her judgement due to strong emotions. Your gender-questioning teen or young adult is trying to separate from you and prepare himself to face the adult world. He may have been subjected to undue influence, including ideological PSHE lessons at school. Remembering that he may be in the grip of a cult-like belief system can invite compassion and grow our patience.

There is a beautiful image from a Scottish fairy-tale ballad of providing this containing function for someone else. 'Tam Lin' tells the story of the heroine and her betrothed. They are very happy together, until the man is stolen and bewitched by the fairies so that he no longer remembers his beloved. The heroine seeks advice from a wise woman, who tells her that she has only one chance to regain her lover. She must wait until the fairies ride on All Hallows Eve, then she must be quick and pull her lover down from the horse on which he rides, hold him and not let him go. The wise woman warns that he will go through terrible transformations, turning into a lion, a raging fire or a writhing snake. No matter what, she is not to turn him loose. If she can manage to do this for long enough, he will turn back into himself, and they will be reunited. The fairy tale reminds us that when our child is raging and lashing out, we can be a steady, containing presence instead of entering the fray along with him.

CONVERSATIONS

Ideally, the goal is to move away from high emotions and engage in conversations where both people feel that their views are heard and respected, even if the parties disagree. This may seem an impossible goal, but efforts to de-escalate conflict by getting connected, avoiding unnecessary strife and inviting your child to share her thoughts and feelings with you can go a long way. You may have to abandon your memories of the way you were parented – things were done differently in the twentieth century, when children were expected to listen to their parents' superior knowledge – and talk yourself down from a state of high alert.

If your relationship seems strong enough for you to thoughtfully challenge your child's beliefs about gender, pay close attention to what happens *after* such a conversation. If your kid runs out of the room and slams the door to end the discussion but comes downstairs for dinner two hours later and seems genuinely happy to be spending time with you, the relationship can handle a degree of challenge. Possibly some part of your child is even grateful and happy that you are holding the line. If your child sulks for an extended period or you sense heightened tension, perhaps the relationship needs more time to heal before you can have these discussions again. Then it's time to back off and return to the strategy of getting connected and having fun together.

WHAT IF YOUR CHILD DEMANDS AFFIRMATION?

This may even come with the threat of rupture – *you are no longer my parents unless you acknowledge who I really am*. We don't think you should lie about what you think, but we do feel such conflicts are best skirted. We suggest saying something like, 'I'm really trying to get there. I'm asking that you be patient with me. This will take time.' Such a response will avoid the head-on collision your child is trying to provoke.

It might be helpful to point out that no one can force us to change how we think, and none of us has control over how other people see us. You might say, 'You are saying that you want me to respect you, but it sounds as if what you want is for me to agree with you. That's something you can't control.'

THE FEAR OF SUICIDALITY

You might have heard a statistic indicating a 40–41% suicide rate in trans-identified young people. This figure comes from an online survey from 2015 for individuals who identified as transgender. One question asked if they had ever attempted suicide, and 40% of respondents answered that they had.[1] This is an alarmingly high number, but this survey is short on specifics. We don't know whether these individuals were pre- or post- medical transition, if they'd been affirmed in their preferred gender identity, or if other mental health issues were the cause of their reported suicide attempts. We don't know exactly what is meant by a suicide attempt. The only long-term follow-up study of trans individuals post-medical intervention showed considerably higher rates than the general population of suicidal behaviour and psychiatric comorbidity decades after transition.[2] If there's been a suicide in the family or close peer group, the young person may be at greater risk.

Most families are aware of media reports of the risk of suicide among trans-identified youth. Some parents have been told by a doctor or mental health professional that they must support their child's wish to transition if they want to avoid losing their child to suicide: they could either have 'a live son or a dead daughter'. This alarmist message may itself be harmful. Trans-identified young people repeatedly hear that feeling suicidal goes along with being trans. What if telling these kids this is creating a nocebo effect (when a negative outcome occurs because of the belief that a condition will trigger it)? Such reports of high suicide rates among trans-identified youth are also misleading. They are taken from online surveys based on self-report. Better-quality research from the Tavistock Centre showed that suicide among trans-identifying teens was low – 0.03% over a ten-year period.[3] Suicidality among trans-identifying teens is only slightly higher than rates among youths referred to clinics for other mental health difficulties.[4] GIDS at the Tavistock Clinic acknowledge that 'suicide is extremely rare' in relation to trans-identified youth and also that 'the percentages for associated difficulties and self-harm appear to be in line with young people from the LGB population.'[5]

A trans identity often emerges in the context of extremely complex mental health struggles. If your child had previously been self-harming, experiencing a great deal of anxiety or depression or exhibiting disordered eating, you may feel that your child is fragile. A young person might have been recently hospitalised for self-harm, suicidal thoughts or a suicide attempt. Parents are in a difficult position, particularly since the affirmative care model, used in many treatment settings, insists that 'trans kids' are at a greater risk of suicide if the family doesn't affirm the transgender identity.

We completely empathise with parents who do what they can to stabilise their children. We also feel strongly that parents of these unwell teens or young adults should be advised on the most rigorous and effective suicide prevention methods. We consider it highly unethical to confirm and amplify suicidality (a broad term that covers

suicidal thoughts, ideas, ruminations, plans and attempts) in any distressed person. It's wrong to tell a suicidal teen, 'Yes indeed, if you don't
transition you'll be more likely to kill yourself.' Tragically, this has been
relayed to distressed teens (and their parents) hundreds of times under
the affirmative care model.

Any increased risk of suicide is of course alarming to parents and
professionals and must be taken seriously. Trans-identified young
people can be experiencing a great deal of distress. Many may be
burdened with other mental health problems, such as eating disorders
or OCD, which can independently contribute to an increased risk of
suicide, and which ought not to be discounted or minimised. However,
if you have been told by a professional that your child may kill herself if
you do not allow her to access transition interventions, you have been
misinformed and your parental authority has been stripped from you.
Your concerns have been rendered irrelevant, and you may be driven
by fear to get on board with your child's plan. To regain your authority,
you will need to keep a calm head and remember that transition is
statistically not a panacea for suicidal ideation.

There is no robust evidence that transition reduces suicidality in
the long term.[6] A longitudinal study from Sweden found that suicide
was nineteen times higher among those who had transitioned as
compared with age-matched controls (people of the same age who
hadn't transitioned).[7] Another longitudinal study, this time from the
Netherlands, found that suicides were common at all stages of transition, whether people had not yet begun medical intervention or had
been transitioned for some time.[8] The argument that young people
need to be allowed to transition to prevent suicide is not supported by
the evidence.

If you believe your child may be suicidal, attentive professional
care is promptly needed. Warm support and connection from parents
can help a young person remember that he is loved and supported.
Efforts should be made to address existing mental health conditions
and to minimise stressors in the environment. A trained therapist can
assess the situation, plan for safety and provide a stable and consistent
relationship. If you are not happy with the therapist you have engaged,
remember that you are free to find another.

Therapists have been working with depression and suicidality for decades and we know which factors encourage stability, capacity and resilience in the person's life:

- Connectedness with loved ones, extended family and close friends
- Feeling a sense of care and responsibility to oneself and others
- Life skills, coping skills and emotional regulation skills
- Authoritative, confident guidance from a stable family
- Interests, passions and activities the person cares about

Therapists working with suicidal clients find it useful to cultivate:

- A stance of curiosity about the function of the suicidal thoughts
- Space for expression of all feelings
- The ability to tolerate difficult emotions

TRY TO AVOID BEING CONTROLLED BY FEAR

We have spoken to many parents who had threats of potential suicidality used to coerce them to affirm their child's identity. It is healthy for teens to test limits and boundaries. Unfortunately, it is not normal for schools, doctors and therapists to support the adolescent in her challenge to parents.

As already stated, one of the key tasks of growing up is to develop distress tolerance. A big emotion is not an emergency.[9] If we panic every time our child is disturbed, we unwittingly communicate that her big emotion is a bona fide crisis. Often our child's distress triggers our own, and both of us are dysregulated (our emotional response feels out of control) and panicked. If your child tells you he won't be able to feel better unless he goes on hormones right away, you might try reflecting that you trust his capacity to tolerate his painful feelings: 'I know you feel just awful and like you won't be able to stand another minute of feeling this way. I also know that you are resilient. I trust that you will be able to tolerate these feelings. I'm here to help you.' Part of your job as parent is to be the sea wall, able to withstand the high tides of emotion.

What we know about suicide

Professor Michael Biggs, Oxford University

Children who identify as transgender must have their identity affirmed and must be enabled to physically 'transition' – otherwise they will kill themselves. That is one of the most effective arguments used by activists. The most cited statistic is that around half of trans-identified kids have attempted suicide. It is true that children who adopt transgender identities are more likely to contemplate suicide than other children. In one survey conducted in American schools, 41% of trans-identified students reported attempting suicide over their lifetime, compared to 14% of all students.[10] Such statistics, however, are misleading.

Surveys are known to encourage some respondents to exaggerate suicidality.[11] Exaggeration is particularly likely for adolescents who are told that their identity group is prone to suicide.[12] To avoid the biases of self-reported suicidality, we can investigate deaths by suicide. From 2010 to 2020, 15,000 patients were referred to GIDS at the Tavistock Clinic in London, including those on the waiting list. Four of those patients were known or suspected to have died by suicide.[13] Those four deaths were devastating tragedies for the families involved, but it is clear that death by suicide was very rare during this decade.

The annual suicide rate at the London clinic in this period was almost six times higher than the rate for the population of a similar age and sexual composition. That underlines the fact that children who identify as transgender are more likely to be suicidal than their peers. But this vulnerability is not necessarily due to transgender identity or gender dysphoria. Children who identify as transgender are much more likely than their peers to have other psychological challenges, such as eating disorders, depression, anxiety and autism spectrum conditions. All of these are known to increase the risk of suicide.

According to some researchers, transgender adults were less suicidal if they had suppressed puberty with gonadotropin-releasing hormone agonists (puberty blockers) such as Lupron.[14] Using a poor-quality survey, their analysis was marred by methodological errors.[15] Other studies of the effects of cross-sex hormones or surgeries on transgender adults are similarly flawed. According to one study, for example, surgeries reduced the chance of hospitalisation for attempted suicide. The authors subsequently issued a correction, admitting that, when properly analysed, the data revealed no beneficial effect.[16]

In sum, then, people who identify as transgender are at higher risk of suicidal thoughts and acts than the general population. This elevated risk is at least partly due to other challenges associated with transgenderism, such as autism spectrum condition. The absolute risk of death for children is thankfully very low, though suicidal thoughts should not be ignored. There is no robust evidence that medical interventions help to reduce the risk of suicide.

10

SELF-CARE FOR PARENTS

Cheryl had battled with depression for most of her life. With regular therapy and lots of attention to good exercise, diet and sleep habits, she was mostly able to keep the dark days at bay, but then her young adult son announced he was transgender and began to take oestrogen. Cheryl's mental health dropped off a cliff. She was tearful most of the time, and even contemplated suicide.

The plight of parents of trans-identifying young people is uniquely difficult. There are other parenting challenges that are clearly worse, but none are quite like the upside-down experience of seeing your beloved child deny her bodily reality and seek harmful and unnecessary medical procedures – while the world around you cheers her on and condemns you for being a bigot. For many, this harrowing experience can be the most difficult challenge you have ever faced, and yet sympathy from one's family, friends and community may be in short supply.

Difficult experiences bring highly charged emotions. In many of life's most challenging moments, we are aided by containing structures, including ritual, community and religious or spiritual frameworks that help us to make sense of what we are going through and create meaning out of it. When your child rushes headlong towards medical intervention, there are no comforting rituals. No one at church or school will organise meals to be brought round. There are no ancient religious texts that speak to this kind of horrendous loss. Parents are often in the doubly difficult position of facing the worst pain of their lives while having their feelings and experiences invalidated. While we are dealing with devastating loss, we may be told that we should be happy or proud. While going through the agony of grief, others may express their excitement that your child has found his 'authentic self'; we may be told by people who have done no research into the subject that we are wrong to experience entirely normal and understandable emotions. Parents will often have a wide range of feelings, all of which are valid. Below, we explore the most common ones.

DOUBT

Parents receive a lot of conflicting information about trans identification in children. Pressure groups encourage parents to facilitate medical transition, justifying these recommendations with the threat of suicide or poor mental health outcomes. At the time of writing, most major professional organisations in the Western world offer similar advice. Poor-quality research that touts the benefits of medical transition abounds. In recent years, more and more professionals have come forward to express doubts about the affirmative protocol. There are now myriad websites, blogs and organisations supporting parents seeking an alternative to rapid medicalisation. These organisations point to the long-term health effects of transgender medicine and the risk of regret.

Constant self-doubt can be torturous and draining; see-sawing between positions leaves us in a state of perpetual tension and makes it difficult for us to take a firm stance. It can be helpful to remember that *some* doubt is healthy. There is a danger that we as parents will become as dogmatic in our stance as our children are in theirs. Revisiting our decisions, whatever they are, helps us to evaluate whether we need a course correction. It keeps us from being too rigidly committed to a particular path and helps us stay open to new information.

At the same time, standing against the cultural push to medicalise gender-questioning children will require strong conviction. If you are a data- or science-oriented person, try reading the research for yourself. It can help you feel more confident in your decision if you recognise that many of the studies touting the safety and efficacy of these interventions are of low quality.

GUILT

Doubt's close cousin is guilt. You may feel a nagging sense that you did something to 'cause' your child's transgender identification. Parents we have worked with have felt guilty for: having worked while their children were young; having quit their career and stayed home when their children were young; having coddled their child too much; having allowed their child to experience discomfort too much; having pushed them to excel academically; having not pushed them to excel academically; having sought treatment for mental health issues; having not sought treatment for mental health issues. You get the picture. Parents – especially mothers – feel guilty over everything. It is easy to look back at your child's early life and find a reason for her trans identification. In our experience, children adopt a gender identity for any number of reasons and by any number of pathways. The cultural forces affecting this phenomenon are very strong and often out-weigh anything parents do or don't do. It probably isn't possible *not* to wonder whether there is something you could have done (or not done). Developing a practice of self-compassion can help alleviate the obsession and self-blame.

Some parents feel guilt-ridden over not being able to accept their child as trans. Give yourself permission to trust your perspective. You can see that your child is engaged in something self-destructive. If you have an older child and need to accept her transition, it does not mean that you must agree with it or celebrate it.

FEAR

If our young child is struggling with gender, we may be fearful of the world he will have to navigate. Will the other children tease him because of his gender-nonconformity? Will teachers or other adults encourage him to think of himself as female? It can heighten our terror when we hear messaging from pressure groups or the media that tell us he may become suicidal.

If your child has socially transitioned, you may dread hormones. If your child begins hormones, the fear of surgery is never far away.

Parents often live in a constant state of vigilance, monitoring every small aspect of their child's presentation, hoping for signs of desistance. They live in dread that the news will come that the surgery has been scheduled. Such a state of constant hyperarousal can go on for years, and can take a toll on our mental and physical health. When your head is seething with anxiety, it's challenging to maintain a relaxed and calm tone with your child.

GRIEF

If you have a young gender-questioning child, you may feel grief over the loss of simplicity and the hoped-for fantasy of a happy, carefree childhood.

When a young teen announces a trans identity, you may feel grief over the end of childhood innocence and the loss of a conflict-free relationship. Mourning the end of this stage is entirely appropriate. Your child has chosen gender to separate from you, although you may wish he had picked some other way. Because of the threat of medicalisation, professing a trans identity is unlikely to be a beneficial way to individuate, but the impulse behind the act is healthy.

Psychologist Carl Pickhardt has written that the purpose of adolescence is to break the spell of childhood.[1] The dawning of the teen years can be a time to mourn the rewarding stage of early parenthood. Give yourself permission to grieve in whatever way feels right to you. Take an afternoon off to write in your journal, take a walk alone in nature or spend time with a close friend. Your child has his own work to do to grow towards independence, but your experience and feelings matter.

If you have an older child, you may be mourning the future you had imagined – the academic achievement, the career, the wedding, the children, future decades of closeness. One mum had a daughter who had always dreamed of going to a top university. The whole family was elated when she was admitted. Shortly afterwards, she declared a trans identity and began taking testosterone, dropped out of school and began working a series of low-wage jobs. This mum found she had many things to mourn, including her daughter's health after several serious medical issues, and her daughter's beauty and innocence. And she had to mourn the bright future she had imagined. These are real losses, and it is OK to grieve them, even if your child seems to be thriving in her new identity.

If you have a young adult who has medicalised, you may feel you have lost your child even though she lives with you still. You may not be allowed to refer to the daughter you once knew. Some parents are asked to remove old family photos. Many estrange themselves from their families, replacing them with a trans-identified peer group. In this case, the loss may feel even more acute. You may wonder if you will ever be reconciled.

If you were to lose a child to addiction, disease or even a cult, you would be likely to find support among other communities, whereas many parents find themselves alone in their anguish when they lose a child to a trans identification. Rituals can help us make meaning of pain. Taking a walk in the wilderness, burning a candle or planting a tree are possible ways to create a ritual of mourning and honour your complex feelings.

In 1969, Elisabeth Kübler-Ross's *On Death and Dying* identified five stages of grief – denial, anger, bargaining, depression and acceptance.[2] Anger and acceptance are so important that we've given them their own sections below. Bargaining may have special relevance: you may feel that if you do or say exactly the right thing at the right time, you will persuade your child to reconcile with her biological sex. Parents agonise over the search for the exact combination of words that will properly communicate their concerns, as if there is a magic formula that will break the spell. But parents are unlikely to be the ones to penetrate a child's defences; and parents often have little sway if their child is a young adult. Staying stuck too long in the bargaining phase is exhausting, and may lead us to try things that could push the young adult away.

Losing a child is a universal experience. Even when nothing goes awry, our children still grow up and leave us. The ancient story of Demeter and Persephone speaks to the universal quality of this experience. Persephone is gathering flowers not far from her mother when Hades carries her off to the underworld. Like many mothers of young girls who announce a sudden trans identification, Demeter is frightened and enraged. She goes looking everywhere for help. Who has seen her daughter and might know where she is? Only the goddess Hecate can provide some information, for she heard the young woman's cries. Demeter wanders for days, searching. At last, she sinks into grief. The crops cease to grow, and famine ravages the land. Eventually Persephone is returned to her mother, but only in spring and summer. She has become a great goddess in her own right, and now rules in the underworld.

There are many ways to interpret this, but it's important to note that Persephone cannot stay with her mother forever. Demeter passes through many stages – bargaining, anger, depression and denial – before she accepts the new status of herself and her beloved daughter.

AMBIGUOUS LOSS

The term describes a situation in which a loved one is no longer present in the way she once was but is not clearly gone either. Losing someone to dementia is an example: the person's character is changing, but they continue to be present physically. When a loss is ambiguous, it is more difficult to mourn, because we don't have closure. This can keep us in emotional limbo. Likewise, if you have a young teen, you may be mourning the easy relationship you once had and trying to steer your child away from medicalisation. If you have a young adult child, you may be coming to terms with her fate while still hoping she will detransition. If your child has estranged himself, you have to live with his absence and the hope that he will one day reconcile.

If your adult child has been medically transitioned for several years and their mental health is good – perhaps their career and relationships are going well – then your challenge is to graciously accept something you might have long campaigned against. This could be the long-term outcome, and waiting for detransition can become inappropriate. Equally, if you have an adult child who is living a life that seems miserable, but they remain fully absorbed in their trans identity, it can be debilitating to focus on their decision to medically transition. Sometimes we just have to accept the good in a relationship and let go of the rest.

HOPE

You may find yourself caught in an endless loop of hope and crushing disappointment. If your child is older, try to cultivate a healthy, loving detachment. We will never stop caring about what happens to our children. We will never stop worrying about them. But at some point we need to recognise that they are their own person, with their own destiny.

DISAPPOINTMENT

Most of us had children to experience the pleasure of loving and raising a child. As they grow, we have hopes and dreams for their future. If our bright, talented child forsakes his interests and pours all his energy into transition, we may rightfully feel disappointed. Plenty of people will tell parents that their hopes and dreams for their children shouldn't matter, but we have our feelings and shouldn't be made to feel guilty for them. Feelings just *are* – there are no right or wrong ones. Parents often feel ashamed for admitting that they are disappointed in their children's choices. While it is unlikely to be helpful to share these feelings with your child, it is nevertheless important that you give yourself permission to have the full range of reactions.

SHAME, EMBARRASSMENT AND DISGUST

Many parents have confided that they feel ashamed of their trans-identified child. Their children are often struggling with mental health issues or have dropped out of college. When you run into another mum from your child's old playgroup, it can sting to admit that your son is pursuing a path you know is self-destructive. As a result, some parents avoid places where they may meet old friends and acquaintances.

Disgust is a visceral core emotion. It can't be rationalised away. When we see our daughter who used to look happy and well groomed but is now covered in hair and acne and walks around in a cloud of gloom, we can feel disgust. It is almost as if these young women are trying to make themselves look as unattractive as possible.

Parents of young men report that it is excruciating to see their son affect a woman's voice or walk with a swish in his hips. Seeing their lanky, broad-shouldered 6'2" son dressed in women's clothing and wearing make-up can elicit revulsion. Some of these young men will become very interested in porn. They may dress up in sexy women's outfits or leave sex toys lying around their bedroom. It can be challenging for any parent to be confronted with their child's sexuality, especially when their interests have usurped others and are maladaptive.

It is painful to realise that we feel ashamed of or disgusted by our child. However, feelings that can't be expressed have a way of festering and making us feel worse in the long run. Journalling can be a safe way to give voice to unsayable feelings, help us gain perspective, reduce anxiety and decrease unhelpful rumination. Journalling on a computer or on a digital app may offer greater security and privacy. Speaking to a trusted therapist or at a parent support group can be another way to give voice to your distress.

ANGER

We have yet to meet a parent of a trans-identifying child who doesn't feel a tremendous amount of rage. Many parents have had direct encounters with therapists and other professionals who encouraged their children to believe they were trans. Worse than that, these therapists often chastised the parents for having doubts or questions. The degree of betrayal families and children have suffered at the hands of some professionals is difficult to fathom. The rage that mothers and fathers feel towards those responsible knows no bounds. Some parents have friends or family members who encouraged a child's trans identity against parental wishes. Usually, such relationships do not recover.

There is great energy in anger, and it can motivate us to take steps to protect our child. It can spur us on to activism that helps alert others about the dangers of rapid medicalisation. One mum learned that her child's therapist was encouraging her daughter to start testosterone as quickly as possible. The therapist was trans herself and had not explored any of the other complex factors at work in this young person's life. The enraged mother set up a meeting and had a direct confrontation with the therapist. Her anger helped her to feel clear about what was right for her daughter and to take a strong stand to protect her interests. This mum was subsequently able to take other strong steps to help her daughter come through her gender confusion without resorting to medicalisation.

When anger loops in repetitive arcs and goes nowhere, it breeds bitterness and resentment. Such anger can be corrosive. If you find yourself spending a lot of time in dark ruminations, you may have crossed the line. If you have lost your sense of humour, that is another sure sign that things are out of balance. Even gallows humour can help us weather a difficult experience.

If you find that you are in a negative, angry cycle, take a break from reading about trans issues. Try to remember that life is full of many things besides gender. Reconnect with something you love. Take a break from thinking about your kid. You had a life before her – you did things you loved. It may be difficult to imagine feeling that way again. For example, one mum made a point of noticing something positive every morning. Some days it was just her morning cup of coffee.

It's easy to focus on what's wrong in our life. The human brain is wired to give more attention to what's not going right than what is. Focusing on the positive takes conscious effort. Maybe your window box or garden is particularly glorious. Maybe work is a welcome respite. Some parents feel very grateful for the new friends they meet as they seek support from other parents of trans-identified children.

Many parents feel an extraordinary amount of anger at their child. It is important that you don't judge yourself for having this perfectly normal reaction. You have spent her whole life nurturing and protecting her, and now she is engaged in behaviours that are likely to cause real harm. Also, some trans-identifying kids can be highly provocative. They may say truly awful things to us. Even parents with the patience of a saint can feel riled when tested in this way.

These feelings are normal and healthy, and we should give ourselves permission to have them without justifying or minimising them. At the same time, we must be judicious about what we do with our emotions. Obviously we want to avoid angry outbursts at our children. We don't want to berate, reject or harangue them.

There is a simple technique that may be helpful. The goal is to let yourself give full expression to your feelings in whatever way you like – in your imagination. Allowing yourself to experience your feelings safely can bring relief and clarity. Close the door, turn off your phone and give yourself thirty minutes to imagine doing or saying whatever your anger wishes you could. Maybe you'd like to lock her in her room or scream at her. Maybe you would like to confront the doctors or therapists who enabled his transition and let your rage pour forth. The point is not to ruminate on dark fantasies of revenge but to imagine expressing your anger fully.

Though we always advise parents *not* to vent their anger at their child, just about every parent we know has lost their cool at least once with her trans-identified kid. If this happens, don't be too hard on yourself. It's OK not to be perfect. Moreover, authenticity can bring about healthy outcomes, and such incidents can clear the air. They often take our kids by surprise and let them know that we care – and know – a good deal more than they thought we did. We have rarely seen a case when a parental outburst did any significant damage, even though parents often worry that they have blown it. The power of these incidents is usually that they *weren't* planned or scripted.

To summarise, allow yourself to have your feelings; avoid expressing your angry or heated feelings to your child; however, if you become angry, don't beat yourself up about it.

SUICIDALITY IN PARENTS

The parents we have worked with are often extremely distressed, and it is not uncommon for parents to contemplate suicide. It can make us feel as though life is no longer worth living if we think that our much-loved children are destroying their health, especially in service to a new ideology that favours abstract ideas above biological reality. If you have any vulnerability to depression or other mental health issues, these problems can be exacerbated by your child pursuing medicalisation. If you find yourself considering suicide, get professional support. Many parents fear they will be chastised for being unsupportive of their children. This is a legitimate concern. The Global Exploratory Therapy Association has a directory of therapists familiar with gender issues from an exploratory perspective. Try to find an experienced, seasoned therapist. Someone with a psycho-dynamic orientation may be more open to a range of experiences without expressing judgement.

DIFFERENT APPROACHES TO COPING

There are no simple solutions here, but we do have some suggestions.

Seek support

Choose a therapist carefully. The directory at the Global Exploratory Therapy Association is a good place to start. Sympathetic family members and friends can be sanity-saving, and there are growing numbers of support groups for parents, both online and in person.

This is a marathon, not a sprint, and parents are at considerable risk of burnout. You might need to take regular breaks away from it all to ensure you retain a sense of self- and other-compassion, including therapeutic support for yourself.

We have noticed that it can sometimes be more effective for a parent to undergo counselling rather than the child. Often the parent is in deeper distress, as they are confronting reality in a way that their children are not yet able to, and so the child is shielded from the harsh-ness of the life before him. Also, the therapist can act as a springboard for parents to help them evaluate how best to reconnect with their teen – how to figure out what works, what doesn't work, and how each challenge should be handled.

Activism

Some parents find that activism transforms their suffering and makes it meaningful. It can give us a sense of purpose. Perhaps best of all, it can connect us with others. There have been many wonderful friendships that have been sparked by those working to shed light on this medical scandal – not the least of which is ours!

Becoming an activist has downsides as well. First, our child may become aware of our efforts. This could be damaging, and in our opinion, your relationship with your child ought to come first. Even if they don't find out about your activity, you may find yourself sneaking around, posting clandestinely under pseudonyms. You might convince yourself you're doing something positive when in fact it's a displacement activity. Activism can create tension in the family that can exacerbate conflict, and we risk getting as obsessed with gender as our child, who can unconsciously sense what is happening. Just as we want to promote flexibility in our children, we should try to model it as well. Life is about more than gender!

One mum had an active, anonymous Twitter account where she posted frequently. She decided to step away. It was during her four-month Twitter break that her son began to desist. This may have been a coincidence, but it's worth taking note.

Acceptance

When we have kids, we expect that they will grow up to be adults whom we like and respect and who in turn will want to spend time with us. As therapists, we know that this is not everyone's fate. It isn't unusual to have an adult child who you feel is making terrible decisions, whom you don't like, or with whom you don't share common values. Some parents must face a painful rupture when their child marries someone objectionable. Maybe the spouse has very different politics, is impossible to talk to or has a serious mental health or substance abuse issue. You may feel anger and disdain for her poor choices. You will likely find the birth of grandchildren and other milestones to be ambivalent. You may secretly wish for the day when your child will come to her senses, leave her husband and come back to the fold. And sometimes this *does* happen. As in the case of a medical transition, if we try to influence our child to leave this inappropriate partner, we will likely push her further away. We have no choice other than to release our child to her fate.

You can only control your own actions. No matter what the reason, it's genuinely tragic when our expectations go so badly awry. In our anguish, we may want to exert our influence, lash out, or even withdraw from the relationship. These impulses are unlikely to change the situation.

As stated, if you have an adult child, working towards acceptance can bring a modicum of peace and allows us to move forward; we did the best we could, but things have not worked out as we hoped. For most of us, raising our children will be the most important thing we ever do. It can be devastating to see such a distressing turn in the life of our child. Yet nothing can take away our memories of enjoying life with our child. No matter what he does, we can give ourselves permission to feel proud of how we parented.

Some trans-identified young people do well in their new life. If our young adult child is happy and thriving in her trans identification, we can try to feel proud of her accomplishments even while we have concerns.

Reinvest in your own life

Whether you can exert influence or not, you can control how you conduct your own life. Have you always wanted to take piano lessons? Now might be the time. Have you let dear friendships lapse? Maybe you need to schedule a weekend away together. Many parents report that their renewed interest in Russian literature or yoga has allowed them a few hours each week of respite from rumination. Your dreams for her may have been dashed, but what about your dreams for yourself? Investing in ourselves will allow us to disengage from the exhausting hypervigilance and will also send a healthy message to our children: *I love you, but I also have my own life.*

Self-compassion

Self-compassion is the gentle practice of turning towards ourselves with empathy and tenderness. The psychologist Kristin Neff has researched and written about self-compassion.[3] There are many free resources on her website (see Resources for her book). When we are distressed, we can acknowledge that we are suffering and even provide a comforting physical gesture such as placing our hand on our heart. Though simple, the practice of self-compassion is powerful. It takes time to cultivate, but it can be a real help in our darkest hours.

A spiritual perspective

If you have a faith tradition, you will likely find it reassuring to engage in prayer or worship. If you do not have such a belief, you can still find comfort by getting in touch with your spirituality. Carl Jung observed that we all have a need to relate to something larger than ourselves, and doing so can bring a sense of meaning to our lives. You may find comfort by being in natural settings that inspire awe, or volunteering to help others. Poetry, music, literature or art can be touchstones that connect us with our most ennobling impulses.

The universality of suffering

The heartache of seeing a child lose his way is nothing new. Young adult children may go astray for any number of reasons, including mental illness, addiction or a bad relationship.

There is a Buddhist parable to help remind us that we are not alone in our suffering. A woman's young child had died. She sought out the Buddha and demanded he bring her boy back to life. The Buddha replied that he could do so if she could bring him a mustard seed from a home that had not been touched by loss. The mother searched far and wide, but she was unable to find such a home. It can be very healing to recognise that we are having a universal experience, and it connects us with humanity.

Making meaning

In his memoir about surviving the Holocaust, Viktor Frankl wrote about the relationship between suffering and meaning: 'If there is meaning in life at all, then there must be a meaning in suffering.

Suffering is an ineradicable part of life, even as fate and death. The way in which a man accepts his fate and all the suffering it entails, the way in which he takes up his cross, gives him ample opportunity – even in the most difficult circumstances – to add a deeper meaning to his life. It may remain brave, dignified, and unselfish.'[4]

Finding meaning in our suffering may look like finding a deep compassion for ourselves and our child. It may mean that we become more alive to the beauty around us, that we cultivate an intention to enjoy our connections with friends and family, and are awake to our own human vulnerability.

Showing up as the parent you want to be

Lisa Salamone, certified life coach for mums of ROGD teens/ young adults and host of The Gender Wise Mama *podcast*

When envisioning showing up as the parent you want to be for your gender-questioning teen, it's important to first have awareness around how you're currently feeling.

Why does this matter? Emotions are the fuel for our behaviour. Every single thing we do in our lives is because of how we feel or how we think we will feel. Every decision we make, every dream we fulfil and every relationship we create is based on how we want to feel.

Humans don't like how negative emotions feel and naturally want to resist, react or avoid them. But by doing this, we and our relationships suffer. By allowing negative emotions with curiosity, non-judgement and self-compassion, we begin to gain leverage over them and model the same for our struggling teen.

Think about what you want. Likely, it's to have your teen change her behaviour by desisting or detransitioning. If you go a layer deeper, asking yourself why you want this, often it's because you will feel a better emotion than what you are currently feeling. Maybe you're feeling fear, worry, panic, anger – negative emotions that feel internally threatening and overwhelming.

External focus on your teen can lead to 'control mode' parenting of debating, yelling, pleading, all in an attempt to fix him. You're stuck trying to change something outside yourself (your teen), hoping it will change something within you (your emotions). You attach your emotional well-being to your teen's actions. If he just did things the way you want him to, he would be safe and OK – and by him being safe and OK, you would feel OK.

Instead, allow your negative emotions. Welcoming them as you would a guest into your home will lessen their intensity and duration. This skill of emotional self-regulation allows you to also gain insight into your teen's emotions, creating connection on a deeper level. When your teen knows you're there for her, she can enjoy a sense of safety and trust that lessens her own defence.

Showing up means being mentally and emotionally present for your teen and first requires being mentally and emotionally present with yourself. Focusing less on him and more on the things within your control – how YOU think, feel and behave – you will start to see the ripple effect of your internal change and show up as the parent you want to be.

11

ALIENATION AND ESTRANGEMENT

Parental alienation has been on the rise in recent years, and most of the time it is the adult child who initiates the separation. Some researchers believe that estrangement may affect more than one in five UK families.[1] Psychologist Joshua Coleman is a specialist in family estrangement and the author of *Rules of Estrangement: Why Adult Children Cut Ties and How to Heal the Conflict*. He notes that, in former times, relationships between children and their parents were governed by the demands of duty and obligation. Now, adult children judge their relationship with their parents according to whether it sustains their personal growth and fulfilment.[2] This change in how the family is viewed is happening as many parents are investing more intensively in their children. We have seen parents who have lovingly and selflessly provided for their child in every way possible, only to have that young adult estrange himself upon reaching adulthood. This is devastating.

In our experience, estrangement is a real concern among families that have a trans-identified young adult. Some parents may choose to decrease or cut off contact with a young adult who has been abusive, threatening, violent, disruptive or repeatedly provocative. This is a painful but understandable choice. While we support parents to protect their families, we generally advise against choosing estrangement. It is better to be in touch, even if doing so brings pain, although establishing good boundaries in your dealings with any adult child is important. Life is long, and there can be many twists and turns in our relationships that we can't foresee. Many trans-identified young people struggle with medical problems, mental health problems or vocational difficulties, and may one day need their parents' support.

ALIENATION

Alienation is often an unfortunate sequela (the consequence of a previous traumatic issue) of a child's trans identification. By alienation, we mean a tendency for the child to withdraw from his or her parents, resent their influence and view them as the enemy. Aspects of transgender ideology as promulgated online can promote parental alienation, as children are taught to believe that their parents hate them or wish them ill if full-throated acclamation is not immediately forthcoming. Accusations of transphobia are easily lodged against any parent who hesitates or questions transition. Because of this, a child's announcement often brings an almost immediate sense of separation.

Cassandra's daughter Becca had just completed her first year of secondary school. She had become isolated from her former friend group, who turned against her because of something Becca had said. Cassandra and Becca had always been close, and Cassandra was an attentive and attuned mother. It pained her to see Becca become sad that year, but it bothered her even more that Becca became withdrawn. As a child, Becca would always seek out her mother for comfort when she had had a hard day at school, or someone had hurt her feelings. Now, at thirteen, she didn't want to talk about what was clearly bothering her. Whereas Becca's goals for herself had previously been roughly aligned with her parents' hopes, these agendas now sharply diverged – something Cassandra found even more troubling. Becca was no longer interested in doing well in school or participating in the activities that had always meant so much to her. Conflict ensued. Whereas Becca and her parents had seemed to be on the same team, now they were more like enemy combatants. Becca began to treat her mother with disdain and hostility. The trust between them was gone.

Although it's standard for children to turn away from parents and towards peers at the beginning of adolescence, this healthy developmental impulse can become supercharged by the dynamics around a child's trans identification. Under normal circumstances, the distance between a parent and child during adolescence is a precursor to a new relationship as a young adult enters her twenties, but ongoing conflict over a transgender identity can lead to estrangement once the child becomes independent.

Although indoctrination is a strong word, we believe that it describes what happens when a young person spends hours each day consuming media about a belief system. One detransitioner pointed out that, when you join a cult, you are often asked to listen to lectures or watch movies for several hours a day. She spent much more time than that every day watching transition timeline videos or engaging with other trans-identified young people on social media platforms. A child may hole himself up in the fortress of the bedroom and escape into the endless online world.

Recent research about online radicalisation is relevant.[3] While on these platforms, a child is likely to learn the whole range of transgender talking points. These can include beliefs such as: if you are wondering if you are trans, then you probably are; you need to stop puberty as quickly as possible and begin transition; and if your parents don't support you, then they are toxic and you should cut them off.

For younger teens, we encourage parents to research parental controls via software options or your internet service provider. Be aware that kids are often able to subvert controls, though. With younger children, you may make access to a smartphone conditional on their giving you their PIN code. It's good to establish a habit that phones stay out of bedrooms overnight. This can be a commitment the whole family makes. Yes, it may mean buying an alarm clock! Apple phones have the Downtime option (go to Settings, then Screen Time), and routers can be turned off. If it's difficult to get your child off his phone, get him a mountain bike, suggest camping, picnicking, bouldering, kayaking, safe sea swimming – whatever it takes to ignite his imagination.

ADDRESSING ALIENATION

There is a relatively simple formula for addressing alienation: reduce unnecessary conflict and increase fun, warmth and connectedness.

Look at the areas in which you and your child frequently have conflicts, and reassess. It's important to have expectations and to set consistent boundaries, but are there areas where you can let things go? Maybe it's OK if he quits the swim team, or hardly ever tidies his room.

Make sure to create space to have fun. Fun and play are ways of connecting. In mammals, play is an attachment behaviour that helps individuals feel closer to one another. Play might look like going for a fun vacation or breaking out the board games, but humour is another form of play. If you can find it in you to be light-hearted, silly or even self-deprecating and make your child laugh, you have found a wonderful way to connect.

Reducing your child's dependence on peers can be accomplished by centring family life in your daily activities. The book *Hold On to Your Kids* by Gordon Neufeld and Gabor Maté provides powerful advice about how to reduce peer influence. Establish or reassert family rituals such as walking the dog or regular family trips to the movies. If you've stopped eating dinner together, reintroduce this at the weekend, and build on it. During school breaks or long weekends, suggest two or three outing options for them to choose from. Go camping or visit beloved cousins. Family activities and travel will naturally limit time online. For single parents, it may be harder without another adult to back you up. Small wins are a great start.

ESTRANGEMENT

We define estrangement as a total or near-total lack of contact between two family members, and have mostly seen this happen where there is significant conflict between parents and their adult child. They have disagreed over some aspect of the child's transition, and communication has broken down. The child may be suffering from significant mental health issues. Usually, we see her announcing her intention to cease contact. This may be accompanied by strident statements or ultimatums that her parents acknowledge her identity as a male, use male pronouns, or similar demands. The estrangement may be supported by other adults, including family members, step-parents, friends and even school staff. Occasionally, estrangement happens in a less dramatic way. The young person simply stops responding to texts or phone calls. He may resist visits from parents and avoid family events and holidays.

It is difficult not to wonder what you did wrong. As other parents celebrate their child's launch into adulthood, you may find yourself mired in grief and shame, unable to share in the communal Facebook posting about graduations, first apartments and first jobs. You may fear that others will assume you are the terrible, abusive parent that your child accuses you of being. Most of all, you may feel heartbroken that you have apparently lost your child whom you have loved and cherished.

We have worked with parents who were convinced that their child would never estrange themselves and were shocked when it happened. Asserting parental authority and setting boundaries is often successful with younger teens, but as our children approach eighteen, by repeatedly sending them articles or talking to them about our concerns, this is something to push against – and at this age they tend to push away. Accepting your children's decision makes it less likely that they will cut you off.

Many parents are dismayed to hear this. But acceptance doesn't mean you agree that your child was born in the wrong body and needs to take hormones and have surgery. It doesn't mean you're not allowed to be heartsick or feel broken and angry. Acceptance and loving detachment mean you acknowledge that you have diminishing influence. Doing so may help prevent your child estranging himself from you and allow you to move on in a healthier manner. None of us can live our children's lives for them. Even though we may feel sure they are making a mistake, we must release them to their fate when they are adults.

As your child moves forward with medical transition, perhaps making plans for surgeries, you may feel an urgent need to do everything possible to forestall these developments. Parents may consider using all means necessary to stop the ticking clock – perhaps withdrawing finances or staging a family intervention. We understand parents' desires to know they did everything they could. We have even known some unusual situations in which these steps made a difference, although there were often special circumstances in each case that made them unique. For example, one mum made financial support for university dependent on her daughter refraining from medical transition, and the daughter desisted. In the same time frame, the young woman had become close friends with another desister. It is likely that the new friendship had a significant influence on the outcome. There is no perfect answer here.

FACTORS AT PLAY IN CASES OF ESTRANGEMENT

Estrangement also happens when parents have done everything to support their child's transition. Affirming our child is not a guarantee that our relationship will be harmonious. There is anecdotal evidence that significant conflict exists among families who have supported a child's transition. Estrangement is a complex phenomenon, and there are always multiple factors. Below, we consider some of the major contributors.

Need for separation and individuation

Adult children often initiate a degree of separation in young adulthood. This might take the form of less frequent phone calls and visits, or young people might let their parents know they are intentionally 'taking a break'. Though such separations can be painful, they may also be a healthy part of a young person establishing her independence. Such separations can resolve within a few months and be the precursor to a warm, connected relationship with an adult child. When such separations are initiated with rancour and/or with the intent to be permanent, they can be devastating.

Most parents who come to us have been devoted to their children. It seems especially cruel and unfair when these children, who have been so carefully nurtured, turn upon their parents. It may be that such kids have an especially intense need to separate precisely *because* they have been so attached to you, suggesting that parents should encourage independence as a task of adolescence. As discussed, a transgender identification can be used by teens to address a wide variety of developmental needs. For an adolescent natal female, announcing a trans identity serves to meet the need to distance herself from her mother ('I'm so much not like you that I'm not even a woman!') while it communicates her need for increased care and attention.

Supporting a teen in finding a job, getting a driving licence, travelling without parents or applying to college are all ways that we can provide gentle nudges towards separation.

Changes in cultural expectations

As Joshua Coleman has pointed out, we used to believe that honouring our parents was critically important. Now we are more likely to evaluate whether we perceive them to be supportive of our happiness. A culture of grievance has taken hold, and young people have been encouraged to be vigilant for perceived persecution. Parents are often the first to be suspected. One popular meme shows an illustration of a small child with large pink and blue wings that resemble the transgender flag. The parents wield an outsized pair of scissors, ready to snip off these wings. The caption reads: 'Refuse to be your child's first bully!' Such emotive messaging prepares young people to view their parents as the enemy, and can colour a child's view of childhood. For example, it is easy to find online quizzes that determine whether your parents are abusive or toxic with subjective questions such as 'When you make a mistake, do your parents make you feel bad?' These poorly constructed quizzes can easily lead one to the conclusion that, indeed, your parents are emotionally abusive.

Undue influence

Undue influence occurs when someone's free will and judgement are impaired by manipulation, deception, appeals to authority, or other pressures. When Julie's sixteen-year-old daughter announced a trans identification, Julie took her to an LGBT-friendly counsellor to help her daughter explore the issues she was facing. Instead, Julie was called into the room with the therapist and told – in front of her daughter – that she must accept her 'son' right away. The therapist also suggested that Julie seek treatment to deal with her 'transphobia'.

Professionals who offer teens and young adults such a polarised, binary way of understanding their parents' reactions are ignoring any existing comorbidities, promoting their own ideological world view and exerting undue influence that can promote alienation and estrangement. Cultural scripts that encourage children to see their parents as oppressive, rejecting or the adversary can help to destroy the attachment relationship.

Divorce or separation

Divorce is a strong predictor of later estrangement between parent and child.[4] Divorce may place loyalty binds upon a child, who may feel she must pick a side even when parents do their best not to impose such an expectation. Unfortunately, it isn't uncommon for a child's transgender identity to become a significant fault line. Strong disagreement can lead to marital breakdown. This can lead to the child estranging herself from the 'unsupportive' parent, sometimes with involvement from social services. If this is your experience, you will need to dig deep to find patience, tolerance and understanding towards the other parent, who likely believes they are acting in the child's best interests.

Unrealistic expectations

We may not realise that the enormous significance we attach to parenting can be experienced as a burden by our children. Have we become overly reliant on them to give our lives a sense of purpose? Does seeing them take a path different from the one we hoped for make us feel as though our life is over? Do we have trouble imagining a future without them?

Expecting our children to provide our life with meaning can be stifling, even when this expectation is unconscious. This may encourage them to pull away from us.

If your child estranges himself, this may prompt you to reflect on your values, beliefs and hopes. Self-examination may remind us to find meaning and purpose within ourselves and not look to our children for it.

ADDRESSING ESTRANGEMENT

The good news is that there are steps you can take to improve the situation. In our experience, some cases of estrangement partially resolve within a year or two. Deciding the best path forward will depend on the nature of the estrangement, your child's mental health status, and the quality of your previous relationship.

In cases of formal estrangement, where your child has made an explicit announcement stating that he does not wish to be in contact with you, proceed with caution – any attempt to connect may be taken as a violation of his wishes. We recommend giving your young adult child plenty of space. A single text to affirm your love and a reminder that you will always be there for him may be all the contact one ought to attempt at first. If there is no negative reaction, you might send another brief, reassuring text or email some time later. If your child responds with anger and demands that you stop contacting him, you may have no choice but to back off for a while. You may want to send one final communication such as: 'We want you to know that we received your message and will respect your wishes. We won't try to contact you again, but please know that we love you unconditionally and will always be here for you.'

Joshua Coleman recommends writing an amends letter to a child who has become estranged.[5] This can be appropriate for the formally or informally estranged child. According to Coleman, the letter should be unreservedly conciliatory. Parents should apologise for whatever wrongs their child has accused them of and agree to the child's requests without defensiveness. This doesn't mean you should provide financial support for medical procedures, but it might mean agreeing to use a new name or pronoun. There ought to be no hedging. Do not say, 'We need to agree to disagree' or 'I'm sorry that you feel I haven't been supportive in the ways you would have liked.' While you ought to avoid fawning, being directly dishonest or self-blaming, you should be clear, direct and to the point – and concede the argument completely. Many parents may find writing such a letter difficult. The point is to recognise that the conflict is not about who is right or wrong, and it is not about gender. It is about your child's feelings of hurt and anger and the quality of the relationship between you. We have seen these letters make a big difference. On the other hand, the amends letter is not for everyone. Sometimes parents need to set boundaries; some have experienced emotional and/or physical abuse, theft, violence, inappropriate sexual acting out or endangerment of siblings. Parents will need to make the choice that feels most right for them.

If your child has informally estranged herself – there has been no declaration, but she avoids interacting with you – we recommend brief, occasional texts or emails that are warm but not overly emotional. Many parents find it easiest to communicate about a beloved family pet. Sending a picture of the cat along with a friendly but neutral note every so often can be a way of staying in touch. As always, it is important to monitor effect. If your child responds to these communications with anger, it is probably best to reduce the frequency of communication. If she doesn't answer but you know the messages are being read, you may choose to continue in this vein.

We know one mum who set up an email account for her daughter's favourite childhood toy, which she had continued to sleep with up until she left home. This mum wrote charming short emails from the toy to her daughter, sometimes including funny, self-deprecating stories about 'Mum'. Though this strategy didn't bring about an immediate shift, it gave the mum a non-threatening way to stay in touch with her daughter and paved the way to an eventual rapprochement.

Any time a child is estranged, the goal is to make it as easy as possible for the child to come back. This will require removing all possible obstacles so contact can be painless. We sometimes talk to parents about easing the way home by metaphorically keeping the path mown and the porch light on. Small reminders that you continue to care for your child remind her that you are there for her. A time will come when our kids need help – financially, emotionally, or both. You want them to know they can come to you for that help easily and without shame.

There are some basic dos and don'ts when dealing with estranged adult children:

- **Don't** look for reassurance from your child about your parenting, her decisions or her feelings about you.
- **Don't** make tacit demands on your child with professions of love that are overly emotional. Remember, most of us experience hearing 'I love you' as a demand for a reciprocated confession. This doesn't mean you should never say it, but we would recommend doing so matter-of-factly and only occasionally.
- **Don't** justify or explain yourself. It signals that you are looking for something from your kid, such as forgiveness or understanding. This is likely to drive him further away, and doing so will give him an inappropriate amount of power.
- **Don't** be intrusive. It can be difficult to gauge the right amount of contact. When in doubt, less is probably better.
- **Do** be warm and reassuring.
- **Do** keep communication brief and light-hearted.
- **Do** keep your child up to date on family happenings. You want to let her know she is still part of the family.
- **Do** offer help as appropriate. If your child is moving or gets ill, offer to help her.
- **Do** occasionally send gifts or money. The best gifts are practical. For example, one mum sent her daughter gift certificates to her favourite takeaway restaurants and food shops. Make sure not to give a gift with a pointed agenda. Sending pretty underwear or pyjamas to your trans-identified daughter is not a good idea.
- **Do** consider delegating communication to one parent. It may be easier for a rapprochement to happen with one parent initially. Sometimes it's the relationship with Mum that has been the most fraught and emotional. It might be that Dad can strike a more detached, less demanding tone. Or it might be that Mum is the one with the best communication skills. Whichever parent takes the lead, it's important to communicate that *both* parents are wanting to connect with the estranged child. If your child is only in touch with your affirming ex-partner, do what you can to de-escalate conflict and stay in touch in whatever small ways you can. This is a long game.

If your child does start to communicate with you again, you might find yourself wanting to make a full repair quickly. Resist the urge to rush. Tune into your child's reactions and allow that to guide you. There will likely be starts and stops. Reconnecting can be a long road.

Child and parental estrangement

Joshua Coleman, PhD

Many of the parents in my practice whose children have transitioned or expressed a desire to transition became estranged as a result. This is typically because they didn't immediately embrace the decision to transition; questioned the need to transition or the rush to surgery; challenged the safety and advisability of hormones; or they refused to adopt the new name and gender. As a result, the parent became cast as unsupportive, unloving, and worse, transphobic.

Let me start by saying that having worries, concerns or doubts about your child's expressed desire to transition does not make you a bad person or an unloving parent. In many ways, it is predicated on the opposite: a desire to be thoughtful, careful and considered in a decision that has lifelong implications for your child.

In addition, it is unfair and wrong of society to shame anxious or reticent parents as being prejudiced for a decision so monumental to their children's well-being. It is no small task to accept that the child you thought of as a girl is a boy – or that they should now be considered as one. It is unrealistic to assume that parents should almost overnight be able to change pronouns from *he* to *she* or *they*. To have your child's physical appearance changed before your eyes. Worse, for those who have children with mental illness, to worry that the transition will either worsen their unhappiness or fail to address the underlying causes.

But, once your child is grown, they get to decide who to keep in or kick out of their lives. From that perspective, you don't have the kind of power to influence them in the ways that you might have done when they were younger. Your desire to influence them by refusing to support their decision or adopt their preferred use of names and pronouns will only further alienate them from you and weaken whatever potential influence you might wish to have in their lives. In other words, your reasonable doubts and concerns will quickly be proof of your transphobia and your lack of love and support.

I recommend that you defer to your adult child's preferences, for the following reasons:

1. Your child will experience you as more respectful of his or her wishes, and that willingness improves your chances of reconciliation and lessens your chances of estrangement.
2. Your child may feel more hurt or rejected by your reticence or resistance than you realise. If you're willing to be more flexible, they will feel more cared about by you and less inclined to distance themselves.
3. Accepting the adult child's viewpoint encourages them to reduce their feelings of opposition or defensiveness. This creates a better opportunity for a more collaborative or nuanced version of you or the past to occur.

You can continue to assert that your child is wrong, that you refuse to accept their terms if you want to. But you can either be right or you can have your child in your life. You may not be able to have both.

We're aware that some parents might not subscribe to Coleman's viewpoint. Parents have told us that they prefer to keep their integrity and don't feel able or inclined to follow his advice. As with all suggestions in this book, we recommend that you take what you need and leave the rest. You are the world authority on what has happened, and you undoubtedly have a good deal more insight into the relationship dynamics at play than anyone else.

12

DESISTANCE

Desistance is the process of reversing a transition that was only social (e.g. by reverting to a birth name and no longer seeking medical transition). It is often, but not always, associated with the individual becoming more comfortable in his own skin. Nobody can be sure why some people move beyond their distressing feelings and others don't. Although there is no magic formula, we have noticed how several small insights can work better than one large insight – and these small insights are more effective when building self-awareness and expanding the young person's world view than when relating specifically to gender.

Desistance often involves a reckoning, a coming to terms with who you are, the limitations you face and the consequences of your choices. This solitary process can lead an individual to connect more deeply with themselves, so they can better understand their own thoughts and feelings. This can happen even when the person is very young.

From our work in clinical practice, desistance seems to require a lot of sensitivity, care and consideration. Often the child will have fully immersed themselves in their identity and so they might feel embarrassed about admitting that what they spoke about so trenchantly for so long is now being discarded. It makes them feel fake or even silly. The phrase 'it's only a phase' has become a derogatory way for society to describe the intense experiences young people have while they are in the midst of forming their identities. Many people are unaware of the psychosocial stages of the young person and don't realise that these so-called 'phases' are exactly how the process of identity exploration works.

IS IT DESISTANCE?

Parents often ask if their teen is showing signs of desistance because their child has started wearing a dress or is no longer using her trans name. There does not seem to be a hard and fast rule. Often initial desistance happens at home, and there can be a baffling time as the young person may continue to present as a girl at home and a boy in school for some years. This is excruciating for many parents, who feel an intense need for reassurance from their child that she is desisting. It feels too cruel to dare to hope and then watch the child relapse back into an identity that is neither comfortable nor satisfying, but sadly this often happens. Recovery is seldom a linear process, and often it is a drawn-out scenario of one step forward, two steps back, two steps forward and one step back, then a step forward, then a step sideways. It can be incredibly difficult to track and not helpful to try.

Often, any sign of movement is preferable to the stagnant paralysis that hits so many gender dysphoric youth – although some young people cycle through different gender identities at a fast pace, with no intention of desisting. Natal girls can speak happily about breaking the barriers of gender by being a femme boy and wearing a dress. We have also heard reports about natal girls 'going stealth' and dressing as a girl even though they consider themselves to be (according to queer theory and gender identity theory) a boy. Nonetheless, the process of desistance typically begins with some signs of change, such as a new name or a different style. Many desist by moving from trans to non-binary and then deciding they no longer require medical intervention. This means they remain under the trans umbrella, retain their new name and pronouns and don't lose their friendships or community. It is a way to retreat from the trans identity with dignity and zero fuss. Parents might have questions, but this is seldom beneficial for the child. They may have rejected the theory driving the trans identification and feel embarrassed and even belligerent about everything that happened.

They may never want to speak about it, especially if they have lost or are in danger of losing their friend group, thereby losing both their faith and their community.

Some people can feel deeply disoriented by their move towards desistance. They might have been embedded within the LGBTQ+ community and felt horrified when they began to think heretical thoughts about their gender identity. If this is your child, watch out for signs of sadness and even depression. They might have believed that all their problems were going to be solved and now be experiencing the cold, sharp shock of reality, stuck being themselves with no road to follow to guaranteed happiness. The feeling that their friends are involved in a belief system that seems to be harmful may trigger loneliness and alienation. A cynical outlook towards institutions, education and political systems is a common response.

Stella's story of desistance

When I think back to the few years I spent desisting as a child, I remember feeling excruciating shame, a pathological sense of secrecy and a determination, above all else, to save face. Although everyone else in my life didn't take me madly seriously – I was only a kid – it was incredibly important to me. I felt utterly mortified by the whole thing.

I had painted myself into a corner and I couldn't find a way out without being laughed at. This meant – to my intense way of thinking – that I had no choice but to remain in the same position forever. I simply could not face the idea of people patronisingly smiling at me. Had I been asked, 'Which is more important, that nobody finds out or that you remain stuck like this forever?' I wouldn't have hesitated to answer, 'That nobody finds out.' I'm still quite baffled at my intense sense of shame about it all, and yet I have come to believe that my desistance was a natural result of my burgeoning sexual development and this was why it felt so private.

Because of my own personal experiences, I know that if I was living with a child who was desisting I would try hard not to notice any changes that suggested desistance – indeed I would not even raise an eyelash let alone an eyebrow at a change of style. I would instead focus my efforts on trying to have mind-expanding and engaging conversations with my child and helping them develop a sense of gentleness and self-compassion towards themselves.

THE RATE OF DESISTANCE

Across all the long-term studies carried out on gender dysphoria in early childhood, the vast majority of gender dysphoric children desist by early adulthood.[1] Although we know that desistance is the most likely outcome for gender dysphoric young children when they are allowed to go through their puberty naturally, we have very little research about the current cohort who have presented with adolescent-onset gender dysphoria over the last decade or so. Nor do we know if desistance among the new phenomenon of ROGD youth will be different to other cohorts. We also don't know how the current focus on gender identity and the availability of puberty blockers and social transition will affect the long-term outcomes for childhood-onset gender dysphoria. Everyone is operating in a vacuum of information.

One thing we do know is that historically the most likely psycho-sexual outcome for gender dysphoric children is a homosexual sexual orientation without gender dysphoria in adulthood, and so parents might need to keep in mind that same-sex attraction is more likely if their young child is gender-nonconforming.[2] As suggested in Stella's story above, it is arguable that the beginning of sexual attraction is the process that could lead many minors to desist. One of the pernicious aspects of puberty blockers is that with the blocking of sexual development, the likelihood of the child coming to terms with his sexual orientation is almost zero – how can an individual know he is gay if his sexual development is blocked?

Another worrying issue related to puberty blockers is that, without sexual attraction, the child is in danger of remaining wholly focused on themselves. As children we are asexual and self-focused. Then, as adolescence begins, we become more interested in other people. There are certain developmental milestones that adolescents need to over-come in order to become functioning adults, including the ability to form lasting relationships. The loneliness that many teenagers feel is often the beginning of the existential ache and the sexual awakening that ultimately drives so many to seek a mate for life – if we didn't feel that, then perhaps few of us would seek a partner, settle down and start a family. Nor perhaps would we become so focused on developing our ability to maintain a long-lasting relationship. And so the loneliness of adolescence may serve a purpose; it may cultivate a desire to learn how to bond deeply with other people.

CHILD-ONSET AND ADOLESCENT-ONSET DESISTANCE

Young children who desist generally do so as part of their evolution as an individual. Somewhere around puberty – before, during or after – children can come to realise there are limits to their magical thinking. It doesn't matter how much force of will they bring to the situation, how much they can convince the world they are a girl rather than a boy, or vice versa: in the end, nature is far bigger than they are. They become more conscious of their relationships with other people.

The process of puberty can be incredibly difficult for the gender-distressed child. They already have a dislike of their own biological sex, and they often experience intense misogyny or misandry. They don't want to grow up to become a man or a woman – the thought horrifies them, and their bodies can feel out of control. But it is often this very process that leads them to begin the long road towards self-acceptance, and so it can be difficult but worthwhile at the same time.

However, puberty does not always lead to desistance – it might lead some further into a trans identity, and can lead to maladaptive coping mechanisms, such as eating disorders or body dysmorphia. A child who is desisting is going through a serious challenge to their sense of self and might need some extra love and attention. The desister might need to be around people who can handle their emotions and questions. They might become questioning of society, or of the family's values. As puberty and developing sexual awareness are typically involved in childhood desistance, this can feel embarrassing and very private. It might not be appropriate for parents to intrude or speak about it. It depends on the individual child.

Adolescent-onset desistance has a very different quality, and this process often involves leaving a community where a young person once felt an important sense of belonging. Desisting adolescents might have developed their critical thinking skills and consequently find it difficult to be around people who are mindlessly accepting of theories that don't make sense any more. This can lead to a loss of friendship, loss of community and a loss of faith in a certain belief system. It can feel devastating for the young person.

WHAT IS THE PARENT'S ROLE?

Stress levels for parents can hit the roof during desistance. Most desisting children seem to want to quietly try out the new desisted identity and see if it's for them, and we encourage parents to allow their children this freedom without becoming over-involved. Young children who previously proclaimed from the rooftops that they were a boy or a girl often become more private as they are quietly coming to terms with themselves.

Action might be more helpful than conversation in the initial stages. Perhaps the child might go on a holiday somewhere completely different or join a new club where nobody knows them. Finding new places with new people can help the child to continue their exploration of identity where there are no preconceived notions about them. Desistance is typically another stage in the process of exploring identity for young people, and it will be easier if they meet new people to try out this new identity.

Most parents seek desistance for their child; however, most children fear desistance – perhaps because they believe it somehow demeans their dignity. This process has all the ingredients for a long-drawn-out power struggle, and we recommend you try your best to avoid this.

Parents seek desistance typically because they have read about the heavy burden on the body that comes with medical transition. The stakes seem very high: potential infertility, impaired sexual functioning and many health complications can arise from medical transition. Parents look to the long-term future of their children, and many come to the conclusion that the medicalised life is a difficult one. Parents have life experiences that a young person may not be able to imagine. For example, you can be hit hard in your thirties by the need to have a baby, but very few young people can truly imagine this sense of urgency. Although some might seek their child's desistance because of what is called 'transphobia', the vast majority of parents we have worked with have nothing against trans people and are simply fearful of medical complications and the psychological distress they believe will unfold when the promised new life doesn't deliver.

It may not be helpful for children or young people to analyse their gender identity while they are in the middle of desisting. It might be more appropriate for these kids to engage in pursuits that encourage them to work with their bodies – this might be rowing, horse riding, yoga, climbing or any other activity that challenges them physically and is not focused upon sex or gender. Opportunities to connect with nature can also help and come in many guises – caring for a new pet, gardening, hiking, freshwater swimming.

Desistance is often an intensely private experience and, as far as possible, we recommend that you don't comment on your child's apparent desistance – keep speaking about interesting subjects, and wait for them to come to you.

A parent's story

I am writing this on my daughter's twenty-third birthday, six years after she told me she was trans. As I type, the spellcheck version I have on my computer still marks the word desister as an error, yet I know that desisters like my daughter exist. Despite the fact that she gradually desisted from her trans identity and did not incur any physical changes to her body, I have had difficulty recovering from those years when she was identifying as trans and seeking medical interventions. Possibly because I was forced to gamble with my child's well-being and the gaslighting I experienced from the healthcare system and the mainstream media whenever I raised my concerns.

The affirmation model only allows parental input if the parent agrees with whatever medical course of action or narrative the child has decided for themselves. I sensed early on that if I voiced my concerns about irreversible medical interventions too strongly there would be the risk of social services or a 'well-meaning' adult getting involved. That would possibly result in my child accessing those interventions without being challenged and therefore without fully understanding the risks and limitations of those procedures. As a defensive move, to try and keep my child from seeking the help of another adult who would not be as concerned with the long-term outcome, I decided to play a subversive game. I pretended to facilitate her desire to transition while at the same time delaying and spreading out her appointments with the clinicians who were willing to mindlessly follow her lead. By doing that it bought me time to gather information and gave my child a chance to explore her identity without any physical or legal changes. It also meant I was playing with fire.

Today, I struggle with that decision. On the one hand, given the political and legal climate where I live, it may very well have kept my daughter from medicalising, given she did not require at seventeen my consent to do so. On the other hand, it may have prolonged the pain my daughter and our family experienced unnecessarily and possibly intensified her gender dysphoria and trans identity. Due to diagnostic overshadowing [ignoring existing comorbidities], the medical system did not allow me to be a partner in care. Our preference for exploratory therapy and differential diagnoses as a first step and medical interventions only as a last resort was not an option my husband and I were given. Even though my daughter escaped physically unscathed, it came at a cost, as her depressive symptoms worsened during that time. I was also forced to neglect my younger child and ageing parents as I recognised the medical system was not going to properly evaluate my child before medicalising, and I had to find my own resources during a time when clinicians and the community at large were telling me I should be doing everything I could to facilitate and quicken the medical transition.

How did my daughter avoid receiving unnecessary medical interventions? I believe there are many variables involved. Parents who put in just as much effort and time as my husband and I did, trying to avoid medicalisation, have had children medicalise and/or are estranged from them. I feel for those parents and recognise that I could just as easily be experiencing their pain. My heart also breaks for those parents who, in the absence of information on desistance, felt they had no option but to support the medicalisation of their children and now find themselves trying to find support services for detransitioners. Another word that my computer's spellcheck refuses to acknowledge.

The same parent sent us this account of how she fielded her child's desistance:

1   I stayed calm when she told me she had plans to medicalise. I affirmed her distress but emphasised that the risks of medicalisation needed to be examined thoroughly.

2   I never purchased a binder for her, and to my knowledge she never had access to one. She did dress and cut her hair to look like a boy.

3   Due to delayed organisational skills, possibly caused by her autism, she did not take the initiative on her own to seek adult services even though she qualified for them, and therefore I was able to delay her access to interventions while distracting her with non-pharmacological ones that related to her special interests. I recognise that her ASD made her socially vulnerable and most likely was one of the biggest contributors to her trans identity in the first place.

4   Her non-confrontational and introverted personality seemed to keep her from making public statements about her pronouns, etc. and she did not force the issue at school, so there were no formal changes to her name on school documents or legal ones. Again, those personality traits also probably made her socially vulnerable and a target for gender ideology.

5   By fluke, I came across a radio programme about the different presentation of females and ASD, which my daughter fitted. Over time she became open to exploring ASD and was willing to undergo an assessment. The sensory and social challenges that she had experienced since childhood began to make more sense to her and perhaps provided her with a more realistic reason why she had certain struggles.

6   My husband and I were on the same page of accepting a transition as a last resort after everything else was exhausted but were making every effort to try all other options first.

7   We focused on diverting her attention and tailoring her extra-curricular activities to her strengths and found ways to budget and the time to do so.

8   I told my daughter the truth. That medical interventions were only cosmetic and could not change one's sex, so she would ultimately be living in an in-between space.

9   While she stayed in the same high school till she graduated, I found a six-week intensive summer school programme in another district and an evening volunteer position, both in her areas of interest, that kept her busy and exhausted. As I noticed a change in her and she

talked less about transitioning during that break from her regular school, it gave me hope that medicalisation could be avoided.

10 At the time my daughter declared her desire to transition she only had a basic phone. I discovered she was periodically on Tumblr while she was using the family computer in the kitchen, although at that time I thought it was a fan art site and did not recognise the dangers. So, while she did not have a private space or unlimited time to view things, I mistakenly thought that as the computer was in a common area it was 'safe'.

11 I was able to speak with older LGBTQ individuals who supported my concerns about medicalisation and were shocked at the lack of safeguards, which also helped me resist my daughter's insistence at the time that she thought she needed testosterone.

12 Fortunately, we did not experience interference from social services, the school or a 'glitter' parent, so no other adults that I know of were trying to access gender-affirming services for her. Although I did have a former friend with a 'saviour complex' tell me she would be happy to have my daughter live with her while she transitioned if I could not cope with it. This is where it gets weird. I don't know if in some ways by 'playing along' with my daughter's request to use her preferred name and pronouns in the home and 'pretend-ing' to be on board with transition in front of the clinicians, while asking them non-confrontationally about the medical risks and co-occurring conditions, if that helped prevent interference from social services and 'well-meaning adults'. Or did 'playing along' result in my daughter identifying longer than she would have if I had taken a harder line, given that she was sixteen when she first told me? I instinctively felt the need to be subversive as a means to hold on to my daughter and avoid her seeking help from other adults or teens that were not as concerned about her future as I was.

13 Luckily, my daughter had developed a technical skill and talent early that was not only recognised by her biased parents but also by her high school teachers. Fortunately, this skill has practical job applications, and it was in this area that my husband and I added additional resources as a means of distraction during the time she was identifying. Again, there was luck involved, as the city where

we live happens to be a hub for this type of work. I was able to find a two-year post-high school programme in this field that naturally accommodated her ASD (she did not have a formal diagnosis at the time so would not have been eligible for any services). It was a structured programme of only forty students separated into two cohorts. In a regular university first-year programme she would have been completely lost. I think the change to a structured programme where all the courses, except for first-year English, were related to her special interest that had nothing to do with gender, aided her desistance.

THE COMPLEXITY OF DESISTANCE

We have worked with many desisters who have evocatively described their intense feelings of self-loathing: this needs to be addressed, as the desire to medically transition can often be rooted in an urge to flee from yourself. Your child might have been unaware of their unconscious feelings, and sometimes – but not always – the process of desistance can involve the first green shoots of self-acceptance. It can be useful to seek out films, art, literature or music that appeal to your child: the focus should be on coming-of-age scenarios where the individual deepens their self-knowledge through self-reflection and contemplation about the nature of life.

You have a lot of opportunities to explain well-thought-out points when your children are prepubescent, but role-modelling is generally more effective once young people move into adolescence. A positive impact of desistance is that a certain level of softness and flexibility might arrive, as, perhaps for the first time, your child comes to terms with their fallible self. You can also be changed by this experience, and you might find yourself living in a manner that suits you better. Practising self-compassion and other-compassion, combined with self-acceptance and other-acceptance, might feel irrelevant to you; however, once your child has moved into adolescence, the most influential way you can address any given problem is by becoming an effective role model for a healthy way of being. If your teen has learned to be self-critical through role-modelling negative parental behaviour, this might be a good time to attend to a dysfunctional bad habit. The inner critic can be a ruling force, and your child – and you – might need to learn how to talk back. Some people find that repeating mantras (also known as affirmations) can be valuable, such as 'I'm good enough' or 'Good enough is good enough' or 'The perfect is the enemy of the good.' It doesn't matter what the mantra is, so long as it speaks to the person repeating it. Although some people don't like mantras, others can feel comforted by repeating short, reassuring phrases.

Although desistance usually begins tentatively, handling it can also be challenging for the young person. This is a difficult process that requires vast levels of flexibility, forgiveness, gentleness and compassion. After years of blow-ups from their kid when they got the slightest thing wrong, parents are often afraid to hope their child might be coming around to a place of self-acceptance, and terrified their behaviour might somehow inadvertently stop the desistance. We don't know how many potential desisters reverted to a trans identity at a crucial point in a potential desistance. Nor do we know if there are common triggers among detransitioners, or similarities among desisters, that could offer important information about how to prevent an inappropriate medical transition. As ever, all parents can do is try their best to manage any given situation and hope that their love sees them through.

PARENTAL RESPONSES

Parents at this stage are often burned out, sick of walking the emotional tightrope, and can lose their tempers easily. Yet, as mentioned before, sometimes an authentic blowout can have an unexpectedly positive impact: parents are not therapists, and the genuine love sometimes evident in raw emotion can move a young person from feeling disaffected towards a more empathic position. Nonetheless, we have noticed that a similar response to the initial 'coming out' is often the most beneficial, meaning that you do and say little and instead focus on role-modelling a healthy, functioning life while helping the child to expand their options. Parents should strive to be sensitive, authentic and compassionate, neither over- nor under-reacting but supportively neutral.

Some children are happy for their parents to help them prepare the narrative. For example, eight-year-old Joey was returning to school as a boy after the holidays, having identified as a girl for three years. He was anxious about fielding questions regarding his new identity. His parents helped him by engaging in some role plays:

CHILD NO.1 [PLAYED BY DAD]: Hey, Joella, why are you looking like a boy now?

JOEY: I was experimenting with my identity, but I know I was born a boy and I'm cool with that now.

CHILD NO.2 [PLAYED BY MUM]: Which bathrooms are you going to use? My mum says it's not right.

JOEY: I'm going to use the boys' bathroom.

CHILD NO.1 [PLAYED BY DAD]: Hey, Joella, are you a boy or a girl?

JOEY: I'm a boy. I lived like a girl for a few years, but that's over now.

As you can see, there is nothing particularly complicated to say – it is the courage and the steadfastness that is challenging to maintain. Parents might ease the tension by telling the child that it will take a while, and that you'll one day have a celebration when a certain annoying kid at school gets over it. In the meantime, it can be helpful if parents seek out a peer group who have never known Joey as a girl, as he would then see that resistance is mainly based upon habit. He might need a lot of support in the form of softness, tenderness, treats and authentic acknowledgement that this is difficult and that you're very proud of him for the way he's handling it.

In another scenario, a teen who is desisting may need to learn to stay away from triggering friendships or risky scenarios such as the disappointed trans group. Our peers can have a significant impact on our mental well-being and parents can help the adolescent to ascertain which peers are supportive. Perhaps your teen becomes upset when she goes to a particular event but is otherwise OK. The more they can anticipate patterns of behaviour, the easier they may find it to develop the ability to cope. Maybe spending an hour in their friends' company is pleasant but they tend to become hostile when it is longer. It is often productive if the teen can learn to think analytically about upcoming situations, foresee any issues and think or chat about them beforehand so they aren't caught off guard.

RELAPSE

Although it is a normal part of any recovery process, relapse can be devastating for loved ones to behold and can lead to deep feelings of despair. Mental health conditions can be cunning, baffling and cruel. If your child is in deep distress and then moves out of it to become happier but then, often with little warning or apparent reason, relapses back into an emotionally painful place, you might feel overwhelmed and inclined to give up. Relapse is a well-known phenomenon – many of us need to go one more time, or ten more times, around the circuit before we fully come to a place of self-acceptance and mental peace.

Emotional relapse is when the person's thoughts are placing them at higher risk of relapsing. She might be revisiting old sites online, experiencing isolation or anxiety or engaging in poor self-care. Physical relapse can involve a physical demonstration of the old identity including style, mannerisms and/or voice. Mental relapse can involve 'euphoric recall' when individuals look at their experiences through rose-tinted glasses. They might miss their old friends, their old sense of belonging and having a purpose. They could benefit from seeking out new communities and other ways to live purposefully.

Flexibility and boundaries are as important as ever, but none of us is perfect and you'll wear yourself out if you try to be. If your child is relapsing, you might need to expand your personal strategies for your own well-being. Yoga works for some, conversations with friends for others. You might seek out parent groups, or find some one-to-one counselling.

THE FALLOUT ON PARENTS

The impact on the family of gender-related distress and subsequent desistance can be devastating. You might feel a compelling need to speak the truth about what happened. You might feel traumatised, or you might have lost your faith in institutions, in doctors and in the fabric of society as in horror you watched other adults' attempts to lead your precious child down an inappropriate path, alienate you and dismiss your genuine concerns as 'transphobic'. If you feel undone by what happened we urge you to seek further emotional support; this can be a ruinous event in a person's life, and some extra support can help carry the load.

13

DETRANSITION

After years of walking the gender tightrope throughout secondary school, Heather's son David medicalised once he was at university. Heather worked hard to find a new equilibrium for herself and accept the changes happening in her family, but she also found hope following detransitioners on Twitter. 'If they can come out of this, I know David can too,' she told herself.

RATES OF DETRANSITION

Before the era of ROGD and gender-affirming care, it was widely understood that rates of detransition and regret were exceedingly low. One systematic review reported regret rates under 1%.[1] However, this study had significant weaknesses: inadequate methodologies, short follow-up periods (not allowing enough time for potential regret to develop), and very high – as much as 36% – lost-to-follow-up rates (many respondents became uncontactable) call into question the reliability of the analysis.[2] It is possible that regret and/or detransition has been higher in the past, but there are not enough robust, high-quality studies that can offer meaningful data on this subject.

Previous research on regret and detransition was conducted before the phenomenon of ROGD became widespread, around 2014 to 2015, and before the clinical approach towards gender dysphoria switched from watchful waiting to the gender-affirmative approach. An autogynephilic natal male who transitioned in his forties after a lengthy process of assessment and therapy is a very different situation to an eighteen-year-old lesbian who decides she is transgender after consuming a lot of social media content, and who begins taking testosterone after a single visit to a US clinic. Rates of regret and detransition might therefore be significantly different between these two groups. Since we suspect that ROGD is in part due to the misattribution of psychological and social difficulties to being innately (or 'truly') trans, we would expect to see higher rates of regret in the ROGD group. Some of the little research we have notes that only about a quarter of those who detransition let their doctors know.[3] A recent study found that only 70% of the trans-identified participants (average age nineteen) were still taking cross-sex hormones after four years.[4] Detransitioners are growing more visible and, at the time of writing, a community for detransitioners on Reddit (www.reddit.com/r/detrans/) has more than 47,000 members.

Recent research indicates that rates of detransition are higher in those who fitted the ROGD profile when they were trans-identified. UK studies conducted in 2022 and 2021 found rates of detransition of 9.8% and 6.9% respectively.[5] Those who study high-control groups such as cults note that roughly 90% of members eventually leave.[6] We believe that detransition rates in the ROGD cohort may become widespread, especially as awareness of detransition increases.

WHAT CAN PARENTS DO?

Detransitioners tell us that this is one of parents' most common questions. Frustratingly, the answer is usually 'nothing'. Detransitioners report that they gradually came to understand that transition wasn't helping them, or that their understanding of sex and gender evolved.

One young woman recalls trans-identified friends giving her a lot of online affirmation that she was really a guy. When the validating voices were no longer available and she was alone in her room, the knowledge that she was a woman who had had her breasts and uterus removed landed with a heavy thud. This was the beginning of her detransition process. Another detransitioner recounts the sudden epiphany that transition had not made her life better, and that she had been unhappier since she transitioned. This revelation began a process where she came to understand herself again as female. Many detransitioners report that medical complications first led them to stop taking hormones, and then from this a process of moving away from trans identification first began.

These stories underscore the very personal nature of the decision to detransition. Whereas the decision to transition is often taken after considerable encouragement from peers, detransition is often a very solitary experience, at least initially. It is unlikely that you will spark the sought-after realisation. While you may not be able to find a magic formula to encourage detransition in your daughter, you can help her stay in touch with her previous incarnation by engaging in familiar rituals, including her in family events and finding ways to enjoy each other's company.

Assuming a trans identification is often an unconscious effort to address complex needs. Many young women have a difficult relation-ship with their anger and aggression. Coming out as trans may be the first way they've been able to express the anger that is often a necessary part of establishing an independent sense of self. Therefore, whatever needs the child was trying to meet with the trans identification have likely not gone away. As painful as it is for us to watch, young adults need space to make their own decisions and mistakes away from our prying eyes.

Throughout our years of working with gender dysphoric young people, we have not yet heard of a parent's intervention solely leading to a decision to detransition. In most cases the decision was taken once the young person had established herself away from home. We think it's best for you to focus on reinvesting in yourself while showing up in your child's life as the parent you would most like to be. However, interventions have been used to great effect for people with addiction, and this could be helpful if the timing is right.

THE EXCEPTION – WHEN AN INTERVENTION MIGHT BE APPROPRIATE

Directly confronting your child and asking them to consider detransition is always going to be risky. And yet sometimes circumstances line up and give an opportunity to provide forthright feedback. If delivered at the right time, in the right way and for the right reason, such a reaction may be clarifying for the trans-identified young adult. In general, we would recommend a gentle, loving confrontation only when all the following criteria are met:

- You have found a place of acceptance and detachment towards your child and are not offering feedback in a grasping or controlling fashion. You can honestly say that you recognise your child's decisions are beyond your control.
- You and your child have a stable, connected, warm relationship. She trusts you, and you are a safe place for her.
- Your child appears to have doubts of her own or feels confused or ambivalent.
- You can offer the feedback about a specific issue that is tied to visible consequences. For example, if your daughter is facing significant health concerns following hormone treatment, you might be able to speak honestly at a crisis point, such as during another trip to the hospital.

If all these criteria are met, deliver straightforward feedback in a brief, dispassionate style. Report the facts and avoid offering your opinion. Avoid the temptation to lecture or harangue. Less is more. Framing it as a question allows her to be in charge: 'This is the third time you've had to go to hospital in the past two months, and it seems like these symptoms are directly connected to the testosterone. Do you see this as a potential problem?' Once you've offered this, don't keep going. Let her make the connections.

Offering such an intervention is unlikely to result in a sudden decision to detransition, but it may help a young adult to re-evaluate the path she has chosen.

WHAT IF MY CHILD DETRANSITIONS?

It is likely that you will be the last to know, particularly if you have been vocal in the past about your concerns. We all need to be taken seriously, especially when we are young. Deciding to detransition means a potential loss of face. If your child gets off a medical pathway, you might be overcome with relief and joy to know she is no longer harming her body. You don't have to say 'I told you so!' for your child to confront the humiliating reality that your concerns were right all along.

If your child detransitions, expect little fanfare. He may even hide it from you. There may never be a formal announcement. You may notice a change in presentation and eventually a request to go back to the old name and pronouns. It's best to meet these changes with complete nonchalance. Try to avoid gleefulness. This is a sensitive and vulnerable time for your child, and he needs space.

WHAT TO EXPECT FOR YOUR RELATIONSHIP

We have known of cases where the parent–child bond is renewed and the relationship feels closer than ever, but in general this is not the case. If you enthusiastically supported your child's access to medical interventions and she later detransitions, she may feel angry and betrayed. She may secretly be grateful that you tried to put the brakes on but feel too embarrassed and ashamed to admit this. There may well be residual anger about what she likely experienced as your efforts to control her.

There is likely to be lingering resentment on both sides. Don't be disappointed if your child's detransition doesn't look like the return of the prodigal son. Be gentle with yourself – and with your child. Allow time and space for both of you to have a range of feelings.

It is likely that things will never go back to 'normal', and that is how it should be. Remember that a child's trans identification is often a misplaced but healthy impulse to separate and become her own person. When our children are young adults, all parents must come to terms with ruptures that may have occurred during adolescence. We must accept that our child is her own person who may not be what we hoped for or expected. Our job is to celebrate the child we have.

OUR CHILD'S NEEDS

Some detransitioners we know made the decision because of spiralling mental or physical health issues. And this often sparks other crises. Detransitioners report losing their social circles. Isolation and fear of being ostracised can result. They may feel a profound sense of disorientation as the framework that guided their decisions for years is swept away, often rapidly. Your child may be happy to receive help from you, but he's more likely to look elsewhere. Some detransitioners feel guilt for what they put their parents through and are reluctant to ask for anything. They may feel ashamed of what they have done. Leaning on parents can feel too much like a regression, and it is healthier for the young person to solve his own problems. Communicating love, acceptance and a willingness to help gives the detransitioner a sense of security at an unstable time.

Medical

Detransitioners may need medical guidance to go off hormones or, in cases where gonads were removed, get on the appropriate dose of replacement hormones. Health consequences can range from the distressing but cosmetic (such as hair loss) to the severe and life-altering (such as bone density issues or bladder problems). Finding medical professionals versed in the needs of this population is difficult at this time. The Society for Evidence-Based Gender Medicine (SEGM) is one place to start when looking for medical help. Genspect's Beyond Trans programme offers a range of support, and funds therapy for anyone who has been hurt by medical transition.

Educational and vocational

It isn't uncommon for trans-identified young adults to decide against college, drop out of university or take time off work due to mental health issues. Therefore, at the time they detransition, many young people find they are lagging behind their peers and consequently the prospect of higher education may be daunting – especially because the current culture at most Western universities is likely to be hostile to detransitioners – and they may need support in finding creative ways to finish a degree. Since trans-identifying young people tend to be bright, it can often be very disappointing for parents to see a traditional educational route abandoned, but our kids will need us to accept wherever they are. As heartbroken as we may feel, we must try to keep our feelings to ourselves and be there for our child.

Offering support for a young adult to continue studies or establish themselves professionally might involve paying for tuition, allowing the young person to move back home, assisting them to get a car or helping them generate ideas about the best way forward. Your child may be reluctant to take much from you, and financial assistance is often the easiest to accept. It may be difficult for parents if your young adult seems happy to take your money but won't share their plans or their struggles. This is uncomfortable territory, and excessive generosity can engender unhealthy dependence. The goal is to provide some scaffolding to allow the young person to become independent. It's best to communicate clearly how much you can provide and at what intervals, but be wary of having any strings attached as this may compromise a young person's autonomy.

Mental health

Many detransitioners had complex mental health needs before they decided to transition, including eating disorders, OCD, ADHD, autism, depression, anxiety or experience of trauma. These issues are likely still present and, in some cases, may be exacerbated. In addition, there may be new emotions: regret, despair, self-blame, a feeling of isolation. Your loving, supportive, non-judgemental presence may be more important than ever.

In our experience, suicidal ideation appears to be high during the first year or two after detransition, although there is little data on this.

Many detransitioners feel self-conscious about their altered appearance or voice. You may even be the person your young adult is most comfortable socialising with. Make sure she knows she can come home whenever she likes. Offer to include her in family trips and vacations and contrive to be in her town occasionally to take her out to lunch or dinner.

Young adults are not necessarily good at asking for our help or showing us gratitude. If you have lived through a decade with them as an angry, sullen teenager who wanted nothing to do with you, it can come as a surprise that they might need your companionship now. It can be hard to know what they need, as they likely don't even know themselves. It might be helpful to think of the relationship in terms of an experiment. If you call or text more frequently, how does he respond? If he seems reluctantly grateful to hear from you, keep doing it. If he spends his week off on holiday with you, did he enjoy it? If so, maybe suggest another trip.

If your detransitioned child is under eighteen, you might offer to help her find resources. Genspect's Beyond Trans programme offers support for detransitioners. Many therapists at the Global Exploratory Therapy Association are familiar with working with these issues. Older detransitioned children will likely prefer to find their own way and it will probably be important for you to let them. Offer resources only if they ask.

YOUR NEEDS

Young adult detransitioners frequently have plenty of needs, but parents also have needs. It is always important not to neglect your own needs.

As your child comes to terms with what she has lost, you will have your own grieving to do. If you supported your child's transition, you may feel tremendous guilt and sadness. Coming to terms with your role in your child's transition will require you to have your own process. Though it might be appropriate to share certain thoughts with your child, you cannot look to them to provide reassurance.

If you opposed your child's transition, there may be long-term damage to your connection. Intense conflict in adolescence often has its own half-life even after the child grows up and the issues are seemingly resolved. Resentment may be exacerbated by your adult child's shame and embarrassment that you were, in the end, right. You may need to work towards mourning and acceptance of the lost years.

If your detransitioned child has lasting health consequences, you will have to mourn her loss of optimal health. You may have to mourn the loss of fertility or ability to breastfeed. If you have lost the prospect of biologically related grandchildren, you may experience this as a heavy blow. All these are compounded if your child is struggling with the same grief.

Joe and Christine had tried to be attentive and concerned parents to Kayla, who had struggled through one mental health crisis after another since she was thirteen. First there had been a severe eating disorder. Kayla's mother quit her job because Kayla's care was so demanding. The expensive inpatient treatment ate through much of the family's savings. A few years later, Kayla announced that she was trans. She was insistent and demanded immediate access to hormones and surgeries. Her parents were quickly supportive, as they had been told by the therapist that Kayla's being trans had been the root cause of the other issues all along, and that transition would cure her. They helped pay for Kayla's therapy, and later hormones and expensive surgeries. When Kayla detransitioned three years later, she became depressed and suicidal. Her parents were sympathetic, but they were also understandably weary of having Kayla's mental health issues dictating their family's lives. Although it can be difficult to admit, you may be angry at your child for taking the family on this wild and difficult ride.

You may need to make meaning of what has happened to yourself and your children. Activism can be a way to perhaps prevent future tragedies. If parents and child are on the same page, parents may be able to speak publicly about their experiences. These efforts allow some to turn their suffering into soul-making.

You are more than your gender

April Lidinsky and Ken Smith

In our experience, a young person and their parents may share many emotional challenges during detransition.

Our daughter, who transitioned to live as male for a brief time as a young adult, with testosterone and a double mastectomy, decided to detransition a few difficult months after the surgery. While it was hard for her to tell us she had changed her mind about the medical interventions, her bravery paved a path forward for all of us.

It is understandable that people who detransition might be embarrassed or ashamed to admit they have made a mistake, particularly to family and friends who supported their transition. Similarly, parents may feel they have emotionally or financially helped their child participate in a poor medical decision. Parents may face challenges in explaining to others their child's decision to detransition.

Our detransitioning daughter threw us all this life preserver, a piece of wisdom adapted from a Maya Angelou quotation: *We all did the best we could with the information we had at the time*. That reminder helped release all of us from feelings of shame and anguish about what in retrospect was a harmful decision for our child. It took effort not to dwell on what felt like a series of mistakes and instead to consider our past selves with compassion and to focus on supporting our child's journey forward.

As she began creating a post-detransition life, our child shared with us the simple advice she'd wished a therapist had said to her when she was in the depths of a depression that led to her desire to transition: *Try getting off the internet, getting enough sleep, drinking enough water and eating healthy food, getting a job that gives you dignity, and remembering that you are more than your gender*. That advice was helpful for us too, as we supported her evolution as an increasingly forward-looking person with hobbies and new interests (including more time outdoors), and a wider range of friends. That advice, it turns out, is healthy for all of us.

Our young adult child and our family went through those times well aware of many loud voices in our society speaking with great confidence about what they felt was surely best, not just for themselves, but also for others they had never met. In time, there was enough space, enough peace and support, enough courage, for her to take her own bearings for her life. We hope everyone struggling with the complexities of gender can find enough quiet, enough support, enough time, to discover and choose what is healthy for them.

14

HOW TO ROW BACK AFTER AFFIRMATION

Claire looked at the smiling faces in the support group for parents of trans teens and wondered why she couldn't conjure up the appropriate level of enthusiasm. Claire, her husband Justin and their daughter Beth had been through an incredibly turbulent year, beginning with Beth's mental health crisis at fourteen. Unbeknownst to them, she had been struggling with self-harm and depressive thoughts. Almost a year before, Janice, the mother of Beth's best friend, had called Claire to alert her to cryptic and disturbing posts on Beth's Instagram. She had posted a 'goodbye' message, implying that she was going to kill herself. Claire and Justin went into crisis mode. There was a series of hospitalisations. Rather than stabilise Beth's mood, the week-long visits to the mental health clinics only ramped up her teenage angst. They found more social media posts about her 'mental illness' where Beth seemed to glorify forced hospitalisation. Their happy and loving daughter had become dark and mysterious.

When the hospital psychiatrist referred to Beth as 'Benjamin', Justin suggested they were looking at the wrong file. The doctor corrected Justin and informed the couple that Beth had been 'identifying' as a boy for eight months and had requested they use 'he/him pronouns' at home. Her previously non-existent 'gender dysphoria' was scribbled unceremoniously in her hospital records as one of many diagnoses and the 'discharge plan' included a referral for 'Benjamin' to a local trans health clinic. Justin and Claire didn't understand how their daughter could possibly be a boy and suspected that some of the trans-related content on her phone had something to do with this. Surely the staff at the clinic would come to the same conclusion. Justin assured Claire that careful assessments would easily reveal to the mental health professionals that Beth was not really trans. In the first meeting at the clinic, however, Beth's parents were told to 'meet the child wherever he is'. While Beth was having an individual evaluation with a gender specialist, Justin and Claire were ushered into the support group. In each meeting, they were 'educated' about the importance of following their child on 'his gender journey'.

The clinic followed a gender-affirmative protocol, offering an array of possible social and medical interventions. Puberty-blocking drugs could be used to 'pause' development and give 'Benjamin' time to think. Therapists at the clinic frequently reminded Justin and Claire about 'Benjamin's' recent suicidal ideations. Claire and Justin were in a constant fog of terror and confusion: 'What kind of parent would rather have a dead daughter than a live son? Maybe we just need to love, accept and support our trans child. We didn't even know our kid was suicidal, maybe there are other big things we didn't know!' These thoughts kept the couple up at night. They vacillated between trying incredibly hard to be the kind of parents idealised at the clinic and alternatively feeling that something was terribly wrong. But this was also punctuated by moments of hopefulness with each confident and urgent prescription from the clinic's doctors. After all, these were psy-chiatrists with prestigious degrees and a seemingly functional medical system backing their recommendations.

So the couple advocated for their daughter to be called Benjamin at school. They got her name legally changed. Despite the outward 'support', they were feeling worn down by the pressure. They had an unshakable sense that something was 'off'. On 'Benjamin's bad mental health days' (as the clinic called them), Claire and Justin were encour-aged to try harder with the pronouns and avoid 'misgendering'. If they could make themselves believe their daughter was really a boy, 'he' would feel validated and 'his' mental health would improve. This prom-ise was hardly being fulfilled: 'Benjamin's' relief was short-lived with each transition step. Only pacified by the new name and pronouns for a short while, 'Benjamin' soon proceeded to the next demand: puberty blockers. Justin and Claire reluctantly agreed to the 'pause button', which metaphorically sounded like a much-needed break for everyone. They hoped that, finally, Benjamin would stabilise after a difficult and chaotic year, but after ten months, and approaching sixteen, 'Benjamin' asked about 'starting T'. It struck Claire like a lightning bolt: her child was on a medical conveyor belt with no end in sight. That night, Claire began googling 'my child says she's trans'. Claire was frantically typing, reading and sending Justin everything she could find. She allowed herself to consider all the questions she'd been encouraged to repress at the clinic. The ferocious internet searches lasted every night for weeks, and all the pieces began to fall into place: the ROGD cohort, the pressure to affirm at the clinic, the detransition stories. And there were thousands of other parents like Claire, who loved their children, who were open-minded about LGBT issues, and yet still felt deeply hesitant about socially and medically transitioning their kid.

When the couple learned that puberty blockers and cross-sex hormones for children are completely experimental, being used off-label, and guarantee future sterilisation and a litany of medical complications, they found themselves once again in panic mode. A horrible, gut-wrenching dread set in: 'What have we done? How could we have been led into this? Why didn't we trust our instincts?'

Coming into awareness can be an excruciating process, especially if you suspect you might have made a mistake regarding your child. This is a parent's worst nightmare. And we want to express how brave you are to begin facing this head-on. You may be one of thousands who were emphatically instructed to believe that 'support' means helping your child transition. Some surgeons are even promoting their gender-affirming surgeries on social media platforms popular with young adolescents.[1] We view the gender-affirmation enterprise as a grave failure of medical institutions, and not parents' fault.

Offering support to your child when she is most vulnerable is an attachment behaviour that pays long-term dividends in your relationship. In other words, when you consistently and lovingly accommodate your child, you strengthen your relationship and connection, and this bond will help your family correct its course and move forward. We understand that many parents found it counter-intuitive *not to* affirm their child at first. But another important aspect of attachment is providing your child with the information she needs to orient towards reality and truth. When you know more, you can make better parenting decisions. We commend you for taking courageous steps to reconfigure your instincts and shift your strategy in a different direction. We'll offer some big-picture ideas and specific strategies to help you course-correct. Our big hope is that when it comes to parenting your child, you learn to trust yourself again, or maybe trust yourself for the first time.

GENERAL PRINCIPLES

1. Self-awareness and self-trust

There have been so many voices telling you how to parent. You may feel that you've been written out of your child's life, but we believe that your parental instincts and wisdom are the crucial foundation to your child's well-being. Consider taking a break from social media, web articles or parenting resources. Go for walks in nature and spend time reflecting alone. Journal, reflect, meditate, observe your emotions and thoughts. What arises when you clear away the distracting advice from everyone else? Reflect on your strengths and challenges: when you're compromised due to work stress, marital issues, poor sleeping habits or neglecting your self-care, how does that impact on you? What can you do to avoid these pitfalls?

2. Build a plan and focus on the process

Now is the time to slow down, think beyond the 'crisis'. Cultivate awareness of your family's strengths and vulnerabilities. What can you do to improve relationships and support your child's well-being? Think of yourself: who is on *your* team? How will you handle the announcement to your child; to the school; to family and friends? This chapter will help you build and begin implementing this plan, one step at a time.

3. Be truthful

Telling the truth can be very empowering. Can you begin telling the truth in both small and large ways? It is valuable to begin to align your behaviour and words more closely with how you truly think and feel. This is a special opportunity to model changing your mind because you've learned something new. Perhaps your child will do the same too.

4. Step confidently into your role as a parent

Your child is doing what he is supposed to: experimenting, taking risks, trying to figure out how to live in his body. Children look for the edges of their parents' authority. And parents do what they are supposed to: keep them safe, say no when necessary and erect flexible guard rails to guide them on their path. Avoid enabling your child's self-destructive behaviour. When there's a big argument, can you reconnect and repair without self-deprecation? Visualise yourself communicating in ways that are heartfelt and confident.

5. Have some faith in your child

Show faith in your child's ability to grow. Moods, tension, even puberty will pass. Usually, the only way out is through. Our greatest difficulties offer the most potent opportunities for transformation. Can you believe in your daughter's resilience? Can you believe the bond with your son, the one you've been nurturing for years, is strong enough to withstand heated arguments and disappointments? What good is a bond if it is never tested?

6. Prioritise expansive experiences

Affirmation directs much of a family's energy towards the child's gender identity. This narrows the focus and gives young people more power than they can reasonably manage. Instead, broaden your child's perspective and help her to build a more robust repertoire of activities. Take cross-country road trips or plan vacations with your teen that include his favourite gaming conventions or landmarks. If your family has ancestral origins from another country, help your child reconnect with this part of his or her identity. Visiting the homeland of past generations can build new memories and restore old linkages with the past. Families reported that such adventures have helped them repair relationships and support more flexible thinking in their children. Thinking *beyond gender* is a crucial element in many stories of desistance.

TAKE ACTION

Service providers

It's crucial that you are not working at cross purposes with other important adult figures in your child's life. Unfortunately, you may need to seek out new doctors, paediatricians or therapists who will support and cooperate with you as you row back. If you've been attending a gender clinic regularly, you may recognise that the clinic is not operating with your child's long-term best interests in mind. Even if you've decided you want to switch providers, it can be difficult to identify physicians who don't advocate for the affirmative model of care. Here is where some creativity can be helpful. Rather than thinking about 'gender experts', consider practitioners from other areas of medicine who may be proficient in the use of the interventions or hormones themselves. For example, if your child has already begun puberty blockers, you can contact endocrinologists who have experience with precocious puberty, since puberty-blocking drugs are often used to treat this condition in very young children. For older teens who have already begun cross-sex hormones, consider endocrinologists who specialise in anabolic recovery or anabolic steroid withdrawal. These physicians help athletes restore their hormonal health after having used illegal anabolic steroids. Experts in precocious puberty and anabolic recovery will be highly knowledgeable about the impact of these drugs (respectively) and might be able to offer helpful guidance without the ideological bent of many 'gender doctors'.

For a list of therapists and mental health professionals who use an exploratory approach to gender issues, please refer to the resource list at the back of this book.

Schools

Parents might ask themselves: 'Is my child's school environment conducive to desistance?' A social transition at school can exacerbate a teen's distress and may engrain the identity exploration into a more fixed state. 'Coming out' creates a pressure to live up to the new role of 'trans kid', which includes 'passing' and taking various steps, such as altering one's appearance and name and requesting new pronouns. Furthermore, the child's body and appearance, which had always signalled their birth sex, have become a betrayal of the 'true self' and must be treated as the enemy. Schools often fail to recognise the impact social affirmation can have on future decisions to medicalise the identity. We recommend that you directly engage the administrators or leaders within the school to discuss your family's new requests. We find it's helpful to adopt a collaborative and confident tone when advocating for your child and requesting new accommodations or rowing back old ones. You can reference Chapter 8 and the school-related resources at the end of the book for more specific ideas on how to discuss such issues. If the school won't support your decisions, or if they prove to be combative or condescending, this may not be a workable relationship. Many families have decided to change schools, begin homeschooling or look for alternative solutions for education. Some families have even moved to a new town, state, county or country in order to find an educational setting aligned with their values.

Family and friends

As you learn more about the shaky foundations of gender-affirming medicine, we hope you have strong relationships with loved ones where you can share your discoveries. Those who are earnestly doing what they think is best are likely an important part of your child's life and should be included. Help them understand why you're seeing things differently now. Share your plan and ask them to be a part of it. Explain the context: let them know that there's a raging controversy in medicine about the best way to support gender-questioning kids. Point out what convinced you to change your approach. With young siblings, you can be more authoritative and directive. Older siblings may need to understand your position or may not agree. We hope that loved ones in your child's life will be grateful to know about the risks involved in social and medical affirmation. They may, however, maintain their position about affirmation being the best way to support your child. If loved ones insist on undermining your position, you might have to make very painful decisions about how to navigate this complicated dynamic, trusting yourself to do what's best for your child and your relationship.

SOCIAL TRANSITION WITHOUT MEDICALISATION

If you are rethinking your child's social transition, it's important to be direct about your change in strategy. You will need to talk to your child. Social transition puts too heavy a burden on the young person, so you can help ease that burden by stepping into a clear, warm, but authoritative stance. With a prepubertal daughter you might make the announcement by saying: 'When we changed your name and started saying you're a boy, we did that because we thought it was the best idea at the time. We have been doing a lot of thinking, reading and reflecting, and we don't think that was the right decision. We ARE our bodies, and you will always be a girl. We need to tell you the truth about that. We are going to make some changes to help you deal with your gender issues in a better way.' With young teens, you might share more details about your decision to change course. You'll be modelling a spirit of flexible problem-solving: 'We've tried this strategy, it seems to be creating even more distress, so we need to go back to the drawing board. We've decided to put gender aside for now and work on other ways to help you feel better. We want to help you improve the overall quality of your life, work on our rela-tionships, build enriching activities and hobbies and think about your long-term well-being.'

Over the course of a few weeks, you can then clarify what changes you will be making with the school, doctors or therapists, any legal name changes, and other important aspects of your child's life. When age-appropriate, offer your child options: 'Would you like us to talk to your teachers about this at your current school, or would you prefer to change schools and have a fresh start?' Your family may consider experimenting with different ways to present your child's gender. For example, your child could introduce himself as a boy or go into the men's toilets with Dad at the shopping centre. Use age-appropriate play, sketches or toys to visualise, role-play and practise. Find out what scares or excites your child about these steps and validate his feelings. Continue to show confidence that he can make adjustments, even if it's a bit scary.

Once you've clarified the logistical aspects of your plan and you've begun to implement those, you will have to continue helping your child come to terms with reality. This process will likely elicit a variety of different emotions from your child, such as anger and sadness. Ultimately, we hope your child or teen comes to a place of peace which brings relief.

To aid in the process of affirming reality for your child, you might read books together about gender-nonconforming children who identify with their natal sex. Ask open-ended questions and have discussions, but use clear statements to reiterate facts about what's true. You're introducing the idea that self-expression isn't dependent on one's biological sex.

If your prepubertal child has a fear of puberty or growing into a woman or man, remember that social transition likely amplified that fear, or, worse yet, might have created that fear in the first place. Now you can introduce a more hopeful way to think about growing up and accepting the body. Puberty is normal, healthy, and necessary for us to grow into ourselves.

You might also discuss the burden of keeping secrets. Ask what your child's experience is like when strangers or other children are unaware of their birth sex. In age-appropriate ways, talk about the issues that arise when we erect a dramatic false self and hide our true self (ironic, we know). Explain that we are all made up of different parts: strong, soft, feminine, masculine. And that we can embody all of this without hiding our biological sex or pretending to be someone else.

ACKNOWLEDGE THE UTILITY OF A TRANS IDENTITY

If affirmation has led to some improvements in mental health and stability, the identity has served an important need. We can imagine a life raft, helping someone cross a river to arrive safely on the opposite shore. But it's not useful to drag the heavy life raft around on dry land. There comes a time when putting down the identity is the best way to move on. When discussing these concepts, it's helpful to use the third person, keeping the identity separate. For example, in the case of a son, Caleb, who identifies as 'Crystal', consider saying, 'I can see that for the last six months, being Crystal has really helped you in some ways. What do you think being Crystal has helped you to do differently?' Listen for ways that the child has taken helpful actions that have improved his life. Remember that he, as a person, is doing hard work. 'I see! So as Crystal you've taken more risks socially and connected with new friends! I'm so proud of you for doing that! Now seems like a good time to show that same bravery and strength as yourself; as Caleb.'

Similarly, in the case of a girl who adopted a trans identity after a traumatic situation, you can honour the protection and strength April may derive from being 'Max': 'I can see that becoming Max has helped you to feel safer and more protected in your body. Feeling safe is so important, especially after everything you've been through. I wonder if you can find different ways of feeling strong and protected, regardless of your gender identity. After all, wouldn't any girl who's been through that kind of trauma *also* deserve to feel safe in her body?' or 'We would hate for you to give up on April or, worse, take your anger out on her. You deserve compassion and time to heal as April, but it seems you've tried to throw her away and replace her with Max.' It might be helpful to point out to your child that the traits of the opposite-sex person they cultivated are really a part of them. We are all immensely complex. As Walt Whitman wrote, 'I contain multitudes.' You might frame for your child that desisting from a trans identity will allow them to develop all of their multitudes as they no longer need to be confined by the need to enact the stereotypes of the opposite sex but can continue to have a relationship with those aspects of themselves that the trans identity highlighted. You might offer something like the following: 'Crystal will always be a part of you! Those parts of yourself aren't going away.'

SOCIAL TRANSITION WITH MEDICALISATION

If your child's well-being has deteriorated with medical transition, you can refer to the dialogue examples above emphasising the need for a new strategy and a focus outside of gender. However, if your child is doing well, is emotionally stabilised and you have a strong relationship, we recommend beginning your announcement strategy with some education about the value of puberty. Going through it helps a young person clarify her identity and sexuality. Muscles and bones are strengthened, cognition further develops, and social experiences change dramatically. You might discuss how puberty blockers are a medical avoidance strategy and that relying on them implies that your child lacks strength and resilience. Your child might interpret the puberty blockers as a 'pause button', but this euphemism is far from the truth, with 96–98% of children on blockers progressing to cross-sex hormones.[2] Discuss the health risks you've learned about.

When your child has been on puberty blockers and is now pushing for the next step, whether that be surgery or cross-sex hormones, point out the pattern you're observing – that each step seems to increase the need for the next. Here is where parental authority and structure become exceptionally important. If your child is in distress, then by definition she is not best placed to think through long-term consequences. Explain the medical and psychological risks of staying on this hamster wheel and model the ability to take a different action with the new information you have. The ability to change course once you're better educated is precisely the kind of flexibility you want to demonstrate for your child.

It's certainly more challenging to come back from medicalisation with an older teen, but only you can gauge the best course of action here. If your teen is a minor and you signed off on their medical treatments, or even facilitated their medical transition, you'll need to explain exactly why you want to now walk things back. It might help to describe why you agreed to medical interventions in the first place. Were you in crisis mode? Were you misled by medical professionals? Explain to your child why you've had a change of perspective, and spend some time exploring alternatives. Even if your child doesn't come to see herself as a detransitioner, you should explore safe, healthy ways for her to manage gender dysphoria. Alternatively, you can discuss trans-identified people who no longer choose to medicalise because of the health concerns. Miles McKenna, for example, is a well-known FTM YouTuber who decided to stop testosterone for health reasons, but still identifies as a transman. There are many ways to express yourself and deal with your distress without being dependent on drugs.

ADULT CHILDREN

Children who no longer live at home will ultimately be responsible for figuring out how to deal with this situation. This is precisely what can make parenting adults so difficult. You will have to make decisions about how to engage your child in these discussions. What do you need to say to pacify your conscience? Many parents want to know they did all they could to communicate honestly with their child. Especially as you come to learn new and important information that has incredible implications for your child's health, you should share what you feel compelled to. After that, you will need to trust your child to figure out what is best for herself. You should of course remain available as a sounding board. If you've remained close, your child might continue to seek your input. If this is your relationship, it's truly a gift! But many young adult children will make it clear that they need to make autonomous decisions about their identity, health and body.

It is not too late

Rose Marie Patrick

I socially transitioned my son at age four, and before his eighth birthday, my spouse and I made the decision to go back to his birth name and pronouns, and firmly and lovingly hold him in the reality that he was born a boy, and therefore could not be female.

I had forced myself to believe my son could be transgender and 'know' at a very young age. I made myself believe this despite all of my own instincts screaming against it.

Once I allowed myself to listen to my doubts, the anguish came in like a tidal wave – we had 'led' him into this cross-sex identity by telling him that he could be born male but feel like a girl inside. Was it too late to lead him out?

It took us almost two years to painstakingly come to the decision: it was not too late. We had led our son into this, and therefore we were responsible for leading him out.

And so I sat my son under a large maple tree in our backyard and told him that males cannot be female, and we would be going back to his birth name and pronouns. I said, 'Honey, I know that this is something you feel you cannot live without. But you *will* be able to live without it. And you will actually be happier.'

I expected my son to be angry, and he was. What I did not expect was that, the very next day, he would feel incredible relief. I could tangibly feel that he had laid this adult burden down.

The early days were hard. My son does not like change. We had to trust that time would heal. Two years later, he is happy, blossoming and growing, and has found peace in being a boy.

It is not too late. The path may be hard, and it will take great courage and resolve. Trust your instincts and your love for your child. You – not the experts – are your child's best bet.

15

IT'S NOT *REALLY* ABOUT GENDER

The fact that you're reading this means you're now well versed in the issues around parenting a gender-questioning child. We hope it has been clarifying and validating to have your suspicions confirmed: your child has been influenced, the identity doesn't seem authentic, and there are thousands of other families going through this same experience! While we advocate for parents to research and reach their own conclusions, we want to caution you against developing a parallel obsession: while your child has become obsessed with gender identity, you have become obsessed with gender as well. Now is a good time to remember that it's not just about gender.

Have you ever asked your child why she thinks she's a boy? Have you ever highlighted the regressive reliance on stereotypes necessary for a child to identify as trans? Most parents with a gender-questioning child have gone through a litany of questions, hoping to understand their child's baffling decision that they are transgender. The answers usually involve some iteration of 'I don't know, I can't explain it. How do you know you're a woman, Mum? You just know!' What young person can tolerate being interrogated on a deeply held personal belief about his identity? We might think of these conversations as being 'lost in the detail'. When parents analyse the mannerisms, clothing, play preferences and appearance of their child, looking to confirm or disconfirm the 'transness', they are lost in the detail. Ironically, the same process of combing over one's life history looking for 'trans clues' is encouraged by trans influencers online and LGBT school clubs, and might have led your child to the trans conclusion in the first place.

A few years into a child's experimentation with gender identity, many parents come to observe a kind of arc. Initially, there were huge demands, a lot of heated emotions and a great deal of chaos and conflict in the family. Then things settled. The raging demands lessened, the child continued doing normal teen stuff, and the family found a liveable rhythm while the trans identity loomed beneath the surface. But nonetheless life moved forward. Parents notice that investing energy into areas of life that have *nothing* to do with gender seems to be helpful to their teen: staying busy, getting a part-time job, finding good friends, getting outdoors, having fun. And parents also need to work on areas of life outside the gender conflict: improving the family dynamic, minding their own mental health, enjoying low-pressure moments with their kid, working on their relationships, etc. Borrowing from the stories we've heard from hundreds of families, we'll summarise what this whole trans identity *could* be about for your child. Then we'll look at the opportunities (yes, opportunities) that you are presented with as you lean into one of the most bewildering and challenging parenting experiences of them all.

So, if this is not about 'gender', what *is* it about?

We imagine you could easily answer this question for yourself. You've likely spent countless hours mulling over your child's underlying struggles, social circumstances, her gifts and her challenges, hypothesising about what's *really* going on. We'll outline a few possibilities that also serve as a summary of what we've discussed.

THE SEDUCTION OF TRANSFORMING ONE'S LIFE

We are all vulnerable to the seductive idea that a single solution will resolve our painful and difficult problems. After struggling for years with seemingly complex and intractable difficulties, maybe your child is betting it all on 'trans'. The willingness to sacrifice for the chance of transformation may feel powerful and all-consuming. She may be stuck, thinking this is the only way out of her dark slump. Usually, however, time and circumstance necessitate a change of course, a new mindset, and growth will happen, even after long periods of intractable fixation. When living inauthentically, eventually, something's got to give.

FINDING ONE'S PLACE IN THE WORLD

We all want to belong, especially during adolescence and young adulthood. Feeling like part of a tribe is a crucial developmental task that often leads us into experimenting with identity and evolving. In today's climate, trying to fulfil the desire to be part of a 'community' can become both compulsive and perpetually unsatisfying. The unconditional and mutual care that young people are seeking is difficult to come by, despite the declarations of belonging that immediately follow a 'coming out'. If your child has managed to develop meaningful and caring relationships irrespective of his new gender identity, more power to him! Many young people will discover that their search for connection is not over and continue seeking out these important relationships within and outside the LGBT community.

SEPARATING FROM ONE'S PARENTS

Finding ways to differentiate oneself from Mum and Dad is as old as time. Since our culture retains few symbolic ways to usher children into adolescence and adulthood, young people have been carving out their own path for decades. The adoption of a transgender identity, and social and medical transition, offer adolescents a prefabricated, easily accessible and culturally salient way to individuate. We believe this is a maladaptive process for ROGD kids, with potentially long-term consequences. But even when young people are not struggling with gender issues, they also run this risk. Addiction issues and self-sabotage are not uncommon aspects of adolescence. Once a young person feels sufficiently autonomous, they usually experience another identity shift, and may set aside the experiments and personas that helped them move into adulthood.

LEARNING ABOUT ONE'S VULNERABILITY

Desisters and detransitioners have learned a harsh lesson about their vulnerability. To have been so certain about a life-changing decision, only to have that become a source of regret, is a painful initiation into the world of adult consequences. They have also learned a lesson about trust, as they placed their faith in doctors and therapists who had themselves been swept up in a social contagion and medical scandal. Sensing one's own vulnerability can lead to an incredible strength, as individuals harmed by transition tap into their new-found wisdom.

For so many of you, the fear and anxiety about your child's safety have ploughed into your life and disrupted everything. Yet we have worked with many parents who find growth and healing through this surreal experience. Some even report gratitude that their child's gender-questioning has made them aware of what wasn't working and has given them ways to improve their relationships and their lives. Sometimes a parent will tell us, 'My child and I are closer than we've ever been.' Yet for others with estranged children, this seems like an impossible dream. We think you can find growth and healing through this experience *regardless* of how things are going with your child. Here are some ideas for you.

Parents, you are not a failure

As a parent with a gender-questioning child, you may hold your child's desistance or detransition as the measure of your worth. We've met hundreds of families with vastly different parenting styles, financial circumstances, beliefs and lifestyles, and all of them have a distressed gender-questioning child. Now is not the time to beat yourself up. Now is not the time to blame yourself for not having the predictive power to know this would happen. Now is the time to accept the current situation and do your best to embody the person you want to be.

Radical acceptance and holding the tension

Accepting the current situation means that you hold complicated feelings simultaneously. We call this 'holding the tension of the opposites'. You are terrified about your child's well-being while also striving to trust her own growth process. It means you can unconditionally love your child even while being angry with him. You can feel rage at the medical scandal taking place while also committing to stay present with your child in the middle of this crisis.

You may need to find other ways to participate. We do not recommend endlessly debating with your child or trying to 'make them' desist. Instead, you may channel your energy towards rebuilding your own life, becoming involved in advocacy work in this area, or by putting the gender wars aside. One mother describes taking back her life:

> When I discovered my daughter was deeply entrenched in gender ideology, it shattered my ego and threw me into a dark state of desperation and impotence. I tried 'all the things' to get her to desist, yet she dug in deeper. Knowing I couldn't control her experience, I decided to take charge of my own.
>
> My daughter was trying to opt out of womanhood, so I decided to model a womanhood I thought she might find attractive. I reframed this experience and accepted what I came to see as my daughter's invitation for me to heal myself. I sought out ancient wisdom to remind me that humans have great capacity to overcome suffering, and that deep pain is what forges us into our strongest selves. I embraced the idea that the thing we focus on tends to expand. I turned my attention to those positive aspects of myself, of her, and of my family that would see us through this excruciating circumstance – and every time we all laughed together, I allowed it to comfort me and to communicate, 'We'll be OK, we've got this.'
>
> I also tuned into myself and nurtured a relationship that I had ached for in the past – a trusting relationship with my intuition. I pursued awe and wonder to remind me that I am both insignificant and part of the gorgeous fabric of the universe. Instead of

letting this break my spirit, I allowed it to break my heart open, and I ended up falling in love with the richness of life. I let go of my stranglehold on my daughter's future, because I recognise that's her work now. I try to be a mother who models how to move through the hardest of things and come out the other side stronger, wiser and more compassionate. As I write this, my adult daughter still identifies as transgender, but I'm not afraid any more.

Trust the process

We recognise that many young people caught up in gender identity exploration will move through this unscathed. They may experience some profound social and psychological confusion, but ultimately, if they don't medicalise, they will one day put this behind them. For others, medicalising their identity will leave marks on their body, even if they eventually detransition. As therapists, we believe that living inauthentically is unsustainable for our mental well-being. At some point, something will shift. We can't predict when or how or what that shift will entail. Nonetheless, we invite you to trust the process of your child's development and your own parenting. If you have a younger child, you know the importance of holding your authority. When you lean in with love and structure, sometimes it will be impossible to know if you are having an impact: trust the process. If you have an older child who is taking risks with his body, and you feel uncertain about his ability to care for himself: trust the process. If you are developing habits that are nurturing to your body, mind and spirit, this too is a slow churn: trust the process.

Rediscover yourself

You've probably sacrificed many aspects of your life for your child. This began long before the gender struggle. From the minute he was born, you meticulously curated a life where he could thrive. It didn't always work out as you expected, but you continued to reanalyse, make changes, find support and provide as much as you could to parent him well. You might have put aside your own passions in service of this parenting project. You might have lost your own identity. Ironically, the more focused you became on him, the harder he wrestled himself out of your gaze. We encourage you not to lose yourself in this process. Can you find the gifts hidden within this struggle? Can you hear the calling to reconnect with your own intuition, with your own sense of self, with who you are becoming as a person? As you work through the ideas and offerings in this book, we encourage you to think of this not as a mission to save your child but as a project to discover your own strength. There is much wisdom and vitality to be cultivated here – not despite this crisis, but because the crisis itself may awaken undiscovered parts of your soul.

Be good to yourself. This is an unfolding medical scandal. You, your child and society are in the middle of a process. Few of us understand what's going on, and none of us know where this is going. You and your family have been caught up in something larger, an enormous cultural maelstrom from which it is difficult to emerge with your sanity intact. For many parents, this will be the hardest experience you've ever faced. This journey may alter the way you understand the world. It may test your strength and courage. Facing this test will require an act of heroism. A hundred years ago, the American poet Max Ehrmann penned 'Desiderata', which has offered solace to many undergoing such a trial. We will leave you with his words of fortitude and comfort:

Nurture strength of spirit to shield you in sudden misfortune. But do not distress yourself with dark imaginings. Many fears are born of fatigue and loneliness.

Beyond a wholesome discipline, be gentle with yourself. You are a child of the universe no less than the trees and the stars; you have a right to be here.

And whether or not it is clear to you, no doubt the universe is unfolding as it should. Therefore be at peace with God, whatever you conceive Him to be. And whatever your labors and aspirations, in the noisy confusion of life, keep peace in your soul. With all its sham, drudgery and broken dreams, it is still a beautiful world.

Appendix 1

WHAT IS GENDER?

The word *gender* has been the subject of much debate in recent years. Some people think gender is more important than our biological sex, while others say it doesn't exist. Up until relatively recently, the word *gender* was used interchangeably with the word *sex* and intended to mean male or female. Now *gender* denotes a person's social or cultural status as masculine, feminine or something else. The following sections provides some context to the controversies around this word.

QUEER THEORY

A good deal of the current thinking associated with trans identification is connected to queer theory. With roots in sociology and literary criticism, what queer theory asserts is explicitly postmodern: objective reality is rejected and fluidity and incoherence are celebrated. Indeed, queer theory is one reason why many parents feel baffled when they ask their child why they want to transition – the young person's answers are often obtuse and highly theoretical. This theory views society as a system of power and privilege, and promotes the subversion of norms as a liberating and politically necessary act, including commonly held notions of what it is to be a boy or a girl. Parents are not so influenced by the cultural zeitgeist and can find it difficult to understand why their daughter, who has always been conventionally feminine, suddenly decides she is a 'femme boy'.

Queer theory emerged mostly from gay and lesbian studies, women's studies and writers such as Judith Butler, Gayle Rubin, Sandy Stone and Susan Stryker in the late 1980s and early 1990s. Butler's theories on gender in childhood were underpinned by the work of Michel Foucault and her aim was to liberate any links between sex and gender as she believed that gender could be a flexible state; free-floating and not influenced by other factors. A free and flexible identity alongside an understanding of gender as a performance is now considered a core concept in queer theory.

Initially, queer theory was mostly discussed in academia. It wasn't until the rise of social justice activism, critical theory and identity politics that it arrived on the internet and seeped into young people's perceptions of life. Many young people who are turning towards gender identity are often quirky, intelligent and socially awkward. Their brains enjoy the mental gymnastics involved in a world where everything is questionable and nothing is fixed. There is no universally accepted scientific or historical truth. There is no linear experience of adult life. The boundaries need to be blurred so that the oppressive systems of power and privilege are subverted.

Historically, the word *queer* was understood to mean odd or outside social norms; now, according to queer theory, everything can be 'queered', e.g. with concepts such as queer history, queer time, queer death. For example, the concept of *queer time* offers an alternative to the notion of age and stage development and suggests that there is no need to discontinue a particular practice or behaviour because you are 'too old' for it.[1] This also takes the pressure off a young person to treat their achievements as if they are to be ticked off a list, where they can tell themselves and other people, 'We might reach significant life events later or never at all, we might be considered inexperienced for our age, but that doesn't mean there is anything wrong with us.'

Parents tend to take the whole issue deadly seriously – and their kids sometimes do as well – but at the same time young people often enjoy engaging in a playful fluidity that is intellectual and invites transgression. Cerebral young minds tend to find queer theory compelling. Yet this theory can also be destabilising. Just as children enjoy it when their parents offer no boundaries but also feel unsettled and insecure because they experience the burden of responsibility on their shoulders, young people can feel disconcerted and adrift if they are too immersed in a world view that undermines all fixed categories.

It is valuable for you to learn how to speak about these theories without projecting an air of clueless exasperation. If you can understand the basics and speak knowledgeably about these ideas, you will better understand why your child enjoys playing with language-based identities. This will also reduce the glamorous secrecy surrounding the trans identity – which often bewitches young people into thinking they are operating within an edgy, subversive world.

GENDER IDENTITY THEORY

While queer theory is a language-based, cerebral concept that tells us anybody can identify in any way they wish, gender identity theory holds a very different standpoint. Nonetheless, the general conclusion reached by both theories is similar: everybody who seeks medical transition should receive it, no matter what their age.[2]

Gender identity theory is based upon a belief that we all have a gender identity. Similar to the concept of the Catholic soul, it is personally subjective, unidentifiable, invisible, untestable and therefore unfalsifiable, but it can also change over time – indeed, anyone can change their gender identity any number of times. This concept was initially developed by two clinicians in the 1950s and 1960s, John Money and Robert Stoller. The work of John Money has been harshly criticised as unethical, and you might want to read up about Money's work so you can speak about the origin of gender identity theory. Essentially, Money was convinced that an infant could be socialised to be raised either male or female. He used this theory on an infant male, Bruce/David Reimer, whose penis was damaged during a botched circumcision. Money recommended that Bruce should be operated on and raised as a girl. Bruce's parents reluctantly followed the doctor's advice. For the first few years Money presented Reimer as evidence that his theories on gender identity were proven, but in the long term this experiment did not work out. Reimer experienced distress growing up, and when he learned the truth about being born male, he changed his name to

David and began to live socially as a boy. As an adult he underwent operations to construct a neopenis, married and tried to settle down. Tragically, Reimer died by suicide when he was thirty-eight.

Some people believe there is a biological reason for gender-related distress and that gender dysphoria is caused, for example, by a female foetus being exposed to too much testosterone, but to date there is no robust evidence to support this. Nor is there any scientific data to support the theory of an innate gender identity. People who subscribe to the biological model often mention differences of sexual development (DSDs, also known as intersex conditions) as proof that there is somehow a biological component to our identity. There are more than forty different conditions where sexual development does not rigidly adhere to the typical male or female pathway, but this does not mean sex isn't binary.

If your child has a DSD, we recommend you do not confuse the issue further with gender identity theory and instead swot up on the biological basis of being male or female. It's important to note that the concept of 'intersex' is widening considerably and that some people inaccurately describe anyone who does not follow rigid rules pertaining to male or female biology as 'intersex'. The philosopher Kathleen Stock points out that, according to some people, she could be considered as 'intersex' by some as she lost an ovary in early adulthood.[3]

A DEVELOPMENTAL MODEL OF UNDERSTANDING GENDER DYSPHORIA

As clinicians working in the field of gender, we hold a developmental model of understanding gender dysphoria. This means that we perceive gender as a concept related to the social norms associated with being male or female. These norms often rely upon regressive stereotyping, but sometimes they can be helpful to categorise group behaviour. Within our framework, gender dysphoria is a symptom of distress for a variety of reasons that could be biological, psychological and/or social. The biopsychosocial factors that underlie a person's distress can be important to explore, as they can bring about a deeper understanding of gender. This theory suggests that our bodies, our hormones, our experiences and many other influencing factors shape our minds and our behaviour. Holding a holistic view of the individual, the developmental model takes the whole person into account and suggests that it is worthwhile to explore all the facets of a person's identity.

Today, most teenagers who seek medical transition are swayed by a combination of queer theory and gender identity theory, though some of these teens don't know much about these belief systems – and nor do they realise these academic ideas have influenced their thinking. Parents, on the other hand, are less likely to have assimilated the zeitgeist and can feel uneasy about these theories. Initially, medical transition was focused solely on genital surgeries until the 1990s, when testosterone and oestrogen began to be marketed as representative of the essence of manhood and womanhood and there was a move towards hormonal treatment. Gender identity theory tends to suggest that certain people need to take testosterone or oestrogen to help their external appearance match their inner identity. Meanwhile, queer theory suggests that people can dabble in hormones to create their individual identity. A developmental approach to gender-related distress typically involves learning about how the imposition of gender roles might affect an individual, while building self-awareness, self-acceptance and, perhaps, tolerance of distress.

Appendix 2

SOCIAL AND CULTURAL MOVEMENTS THAT CAN SHAPE GENDER-RELATED DISTRESS

As you look at your politically engaged child who uses so much jargon that they almost speak a different language, you may be left scratching your head, wondering what has happened. In our examination of this subject, we have come to realise that many factors have contributed to the sudden and unexpected focus on gender identity in the twenty-first century. The following is not an exhaustive list but instead a snapshot of the various movements affecting young people's thinking today.

IDENTITY POLITICS

The concept of identity politics gained traction in the late twentieth century arguably because of the rise in popularity of what is called 'intersectionality', which considers the range of different ways an individual can be oppressed. This is embedded within critical theory, which seeks to critique and challenge power structures. While this is a potentially valuable political perspective, a consequence of identity politics is that certain groups, including heterosexuals, are viewed as part of the oppressor class. Many young people reject the heteronormative mindset (the belief that heterosexuality is the normal sexual orientation) because they don't want to be perceived as an oppressor.

Young people aren't always aware that their thinking is influenced by critical theory and identity politics, but they do know from their day-to-day lives that being a white, middle-class 'cis-het' teen is a heavy burden to shoulder. It's hard to be told you're privileged when you feel desperately unhappy, ill at ease and socially excluded. When they look online, distressed young people may feel relieved when they begin to believe their 'true' tribe is among the oppressed.

These days, technology, social justice activism and trans activism offer youths the opportunity to be part of the solution. Those of us who know our history understand that there have been many cultural revolutions through the ages with young people coming together to strive for a better world. It's heady and exciting and easy to create a feeling of 'us and them', and beguiling to hear that the world's problems will be solved by subverting the power and privilege of the oppressor class. Conversations about the Bolshevik Revolution, the civil rights movements across the world, the Cultural Revolution in China and the peace and love movement in the 1960s can be enlightening: the young person may come to realise that although there are multiple ways to improve the world, many before them also thought they had the answers, only to find that life was a good deal more complicated.

With the advent of the internet and social media, there has been a massive increase in humankind's ability to exchange information. Previously, if a teenager wanted to understand identity politics, they would have had to read a dense book – nowadays they can watch a YouTube video and feel educated. If your child has lost their way, it might be helpful for them to fully understand this complex subject. As the seventeenth-century poet Alexander Pope warns us, 'A little learning is a dangerous thing.'

SOCIAL JUSTICE ACTIVISM

The social justice framework seeks 'equity' in terms of the distribution of wealth, opportunities and privileges within a society. A concept that can be traced back to the work of Plato and Aristotle, the term 'social justice' originates from the eighteenth century.[1] There are some common elements: the duty of the state to distribute resources fairly, the protection of human dignity, and the importance of affirmative action to seek equal opportunities for everybody.[2] These concepts are noble and aspirational, but many parents who consult with us become antagonistic towards the concept of social justice, identity politics, queer theory and other conceptual frameworks linked to their child's LGBTQ+ identity. Parents often feel that these ideas are at the root of the desire to transition – though they should instead be an opportunity to engage in thought-provoking conversations.

DIAGNOSIS CREEP

An added challenge today is the phenomenon of 'diagnosis creep'. Diagnosis creep refers to the tendency for disease categories to evolve to include many more people. In the case of mental health issues, diagnosis creep tends to happen organically as people identify with certain disorders as a way of understanding themselves or gaining access to care or resources. The clinical definition in the *DSM-5* (see Appendix 3) is a reaction to a life-threatening event, but in popular usage, the word 'trauma' is often invoked to refer to any event that resulted in emotional upset. This issue seems to have arisen due to consumer-driven healthcare, where expanding medical definitions increase the numbers suffering from, for example, ASD, ADHD and gender dysphoria. In mental health, diagnosis creep is associated with the phenomenon of diagnosis-seeking. Young people may find that having a mental health diagnosis confers a sense of specialness and belonging. For example, young people on the social media platform Tumblr frequently include a list of mental health issues in their bios, including depression, anxiety or ADHD. The focus on intersectionality and identity politics (especially at college or university) has led many young people to brandish their diagnoses as a form of valorising oppression.

A core developmental task of adolescence is to come to terms with who we are and where we come from. You can help with this by exploring different aspects of your own personal history, so children might learn to acknowledge their entire selves, not one specific aspect that seems so central to their identity. The more you can expand the narrative, the more your children will begin to respect their own complexity.

A GENDERED WORLD

There have been major improvements in the 'battle of the sexes' with regards to issues such as equal pay; however, there has been a very specific regression in relation to children. Defining children according to their sex has been gaining pace since the 1990s, a trend primarily driven by business interests – there is more profit to be gained from having a blue aisle and a pink aisle in the toy shops and the baby clothing stores. Most kids don't particularly mind being pushed towards one or the other, but a minority of children dislike it, and gender-diverse kids absolutely loathe it.

Many young girls we work with don't feel 'pretty' enough to be a girl, and many young boys don't feel 'masculine' enough to be a boy. Whereas in the 1970s and 1980s female teenagers often had short hair and wore what could be described as 'boyish' clothes, these days teenage girls with short hair are often perceived to be communicating a political statement, and boys are expected to conform to rigid gendered expectations – playing contact sports, supporting a football team, engaging in weight training. Young people have always been conscious of how they look; however, these days the intensity around appearance is reaching worrying levels.

Appendix 3

GENDER DYSPHORIA: DIAGNOSIS AND DEFINITIONS

Historically, gender-related distress has been given a range of different labels and definitions. Renaming and redefinition is not uncommon in the medical world, and many other conditions have cycled through different names and descriptions.

Gender dysphoria was previously known as gender identity disorder and was diagnosed among two main cohorts – middle-aged males and young, mostly male children. The current extraordinary rise in the number of adolescents seeking medical treatment has come out of the blue in less than a decade and so the medical profession, the research and our understanding of this phenomenon are all lagging behind the culture.

In 1931 Dora Richter is said to be the first person to have transsexual surgery. The focus then was mostly on surgical operations rather than hormone treatment to signify a change of sex, and in 1952 Christine Jorgensen was the first American to publicly acknowledge that she was a 'transsexual', the term used at the time. There was a growth in the number of gender identity clinics in the US in the 1960s and 1970s. In 1979, the first standards of care for transsexuals were published by the Harry Benjamin International Gender Dysphoria Association, which later came to be known as the World Professional Association of Transgender Health (WPATH). Until relatively recently, this was a fringe subject that few were interested in and so WPATH's position as the world authority on transgender health was unchallenged. In recent years, however, there has been a proliferation of organisations that have been established to challenge their position, and there is a significant rising tide of criticism about their standards of care.

THE WORLD HEALTH ORGANIZATION (WHO) AND THE *INTERNATIONAL CLASSIFICATION OF DISEASES* (*ICD*)

The WHO publishes the *ICD*. In 1990, the WHO included the diagnosis of 'transsexualism' in the *ICD-10*, then in 1994 this was replaced with 'gender identity disorder'. In 2018, the diagnostic category was again changed, this time redefining 'gender identity-related health' as 'gender incongruence of adolescence and adult-hood' and 'gender incongruence of childhood', respectively.[1] This moved gender issues out of the chapter relating to 'Mental and behavioural disorders' and into 'Conditions related to sexual health'. However, this move also attracted criticism for implicitly suggesting that children as young as three diagnosed with gender dysphoria can now be described as having a 'sexual health problem'. Among the critics were Dr Lucy Griffin and Dr Katie Clyde, in *World Psychiatry*: 'We note that *ICD-11* has dropped gender dysphoria from its chapter on mental and behavioural disorders and moved it to the chapter on sexual health. What then, is the exact nature of this sexual health disorder? Are children necessarily prescribed puberty blockers and cross-sex hormones because they suffer from a sexual health issue?'[2]

This move discounts the impact of socialisation and raises questions about the nature of sexual health and mental health. The decision reflects current thinking that 'trans-related and gender-diverse identities are not conditions of mental ill-health, and that classifying them as such can cause enormous stigma.'[3] Many have objected to this statement, which in itself stigmatises mental health.

THE AMERICAN PSYCHIATRIC ASSOCIATION (APA) AND THE *DIAGNOSTIC AND STATISTICAL MANUAL OF MENTAL DISORDERS* (DSM)

The APA publishes the *DSM*, and the latest edition, the *DSM-5-TR*, classifies gender-related distress differently to the WHO and the *ICD*. The *DSM-5-TR* views gender dysphoria as a diagnosable mental health condition that refers to the 'distress that accompanies the incongruence between one's experienced and expressed gender and one's assigned or natal gender'.[4] The *DSM-5* provides one overarching diagnosis of gender dysphoria, with separate specific criteria for adolescents and adults and another for children.

Clinical diagnosis of childhood-onset gender dysphoria

According to the *DSM-5-TR*, the following criteria are necessary for a diagnosis of gender dysphoria in childhood. When we examine these, it becomes clear that they rely heavily on sexual stereotypes. If you wish to parent your child free from stereotypes, you may not agree with these criteria. No matter what your position, if your child is suffering from gender-related distress, they will benefit from you knowing the details of what is required for a diagnosis of gender dysphoria, and so it is worth acquainting yourself with this information.

The *DSM-5-TR* defines gender dysphoria in children as a marked incongruence between one's experienced/expressed gender and assigned gender, lasting at least six months, as manifested by at least six of the following (one of which must be the first criterion):

- A strong desire to be of the other gender or an insistence that one is the other gender (or some alternative gender different from one's assigned gender)
- In boys (assigned gender), a strong preference for cross-dressing or simulating female attire; or in girls (assigned gender), a strong preference for wearing only typical masculine clothing and a strong resistance to the wearing of typical feminine clothing
- A strong preference for cross-gender roles in make-believe play or fantasy play

- A strong preference for the toys, games or activities stereotypically used or engaged in by the other gender
- A strong preference for playmates of the other gender
- In boys (assigned gender), a strong rejection of typically masculine toys, games, and activities and a strong avoidance of rough-and-tumble play; or in girls (assigned gender), a strong rejection of typically feminine toys, games, and activities
- A strong dislike of one's sexual anatomy
- A strong desire for the physical sex characteristics that match one's experienced gender.[5]

As with the diagnostic criteria for adolescents and adults, the condition must also be associated with clinically significant distress or impairment in social, occupational, or other important areas of functioning.[6]

Adolescent- and adult-onset gender dysphoria

The *DSM-5-TR* chose to position the adolescents within the same framework as the adults, perhaps because prior to the last ten years there was little information available about this cohort. We believe that the recent focus on adolescent-onset gender dysphoria may one day lead to more specific criteria for adolescents.

The *DSM-5-TR* defines gender dysphoria in adolescents and adults as a marked incongruence between one's experienced/expressed gender and their assigned gender, lasting at least six months, as manifested by at least two of the following:

- A marked incongruence between one's experienced/expressed gender and primary and/or secondary sex characteristics (or in young adolescents, the anticipated secondary sex characteristics)
- A strong desire to be rid of one's primary and/or secondary sex characteristics because of a marked incongruence with one's experienced/expressed gender (or in young adolescents, a desire to prevent the development of the anticipated secondary sex characteristics)
- A strong desire for the primary and/or secondary sex characteristics of the other gender

- A strong desire to be of the other gender (or some alternative gender different from one's assigned gender)
- A strong desire to be treated as the other gender (or some alternative gender different from one's assigned gender)
- A strong conviction that one has the typical feelings and reactions of the other gender (or some alternative gender different from one's assigned gender).[7]

In order to meet criteria for the diagnosis, the condition must also be associated with clinically significant distress or impairment in social, occupational, or other important areas of functioning.[8]

Appendix 4

APPROACHES TO TREATMENT

As there is little consensus about what is gender, gender identity and gender dysphoria, it is no surprise that there are many different approaches offered to help alleviate the mental distress experienced by those with gender dysphoria. In this section we outline some common approaches, so you can feel equipped to speak with any mental health professional about your child's distress.

THE GENDER-AFFIRMATIVE APPROACH

In the world of therapy, the gender-affirmative approach is the new kid in town. Never before in the history of psychotherapy has it been suggested that therapists do little more than nod along affirmatively to whatever the client might say. While this might make the client feel good in the short term, it can lead to some hasty decisions that cause distress in the long term, and can lead to the individual being convinced that an external solution will resolve an internal problem. Although the gender-affirmative approach might offer therapeutic *support*, it doesn't offer a more valuable therapeutic *process*, which ideally brings about greater self-awareness and the ability to self-reflect. For example, the Samaritans is a great organisation that offers listening help to whoever calls their phone line, but the support callers receive is nothing like attending therapy sessions, which require a good deal more interactive commitment and effort.

Although we believe it is important to be sensitive to the fact that a child coming out as trans is very different to a child coming out as gay, gender-affirmative therapists conflate these two experiences and respond in a similar way to either presentation. Some therapists may follow the gender-affirmative approach because they believe gender is innate. Other therapists have been schooled in queer theory, a key aspect of which is the idea that everyone is free to identify as they wish. Queer theory is all about playing with language and subverting everything we 'know' to be true, so there are no valid challenges to an individual's self-declared identity, no matter what age or circumstance.[1] Body modification procedures are a choice, and any attempt to question this can be construed as a form of oppression.

The gender-affirmative approach positions therapists (and parents) as facilitators who need to help every child, no matter what age, to transition. When discussing the gender-affirmative approach with your child, it can be helpful to explore the uneasy feelings that can arise when you seek help and the person just nods along to everything you say, without fully engaging with you.

We have come to believe that the gender-affirmative approach is an inadequate model that fails to consider the complexity of the individual and the biopsychosocial factors that can have a significant influence on the person's development. Many gender-affirming therapists also do not explore the significant medical, psychological and social risks and unknown outcomes associated with transition. This can allow the young person to engage in magical thinking when honest examination and compassionate critical thinking would be far more helpful. From our clinical practice we favour a more depth-oriented approach, underpinned by conventional exploratory psychotherapy, and if your child is attending a gender-affirmative clinician, we urge you to consider other options.

PSYCHOTHERAPY

Conventional psychotherapy has been with us for many years. This type of therapeutic treatment uses 'talk therapy' to help people who are experiencing mental illness and/or emotional distress. Psychotherapy can help eliminate or reduce troubling symptoms so the individual might function better. Effective psychotherapy often brings about increased self-awareness and insight, which can lead to an increase in well-being and resilience. There are many different types of psychotherapy, for example psychoanalysis, cognitive behavioural therapy (CBT) and person-centred counselling. Research suggests that it is often the relationship between the therapist and the individual that matters most.

There is no 'one-size-fits-all' approach. Therapists may seek a deeper understanding of why a teenager feels constricted by the narrow-minded gendered expectations that are integral to being a teenager today. This therapy can be very beneficial for gay, lesbian and bisexual youth, as they are often gender-nonconforming and may experience distress when they reach puberty and begin to come to terms with their sexual orientation. Many young people come out as gay and later come out as trans. The psychotherapeutic process allows the space for any issue to be freely explored in a neutrally supportive fashion, with attention given to the differing nature of each experience, so the young person feels able to explore their psyche without toxic shame or pressurising speed.

EXPLORATORY THERAPY

The exploratory approach has evolved in recent years by therapists who wish to provide a thoughtful and careful therapeutic process with no ideological agenda. It's for anybody who wishes to explore their gender identity or who might be struggling with body acceptance, self-acceptance, internalised homophobia and other related issues. Exploratory therapy treats identity development as a complex, gradual process that can have several influencing factors and be affected by other mental health issues. Exploratory therapy is also body affirming, as it helps individuals to accept themselves as they are, while recognising that our identities are not static but continuously evolve during our lifetimes.

THE WATCHFUL WAITING APPROACH

Prior to the recent explosion of young people seeking treatment for gender issues, psychologists and parents tended to utilise the 'watchful waiting' approach. This is used in the treatment of other issues – for example, when a clinician closely watches a patient who presents with a severe headache but does not automatically recommend brain surgery or other interventions unless further symptoms appear. This approach is often employed when the risks of treatment are greater than the possible benefits. For example, prescribing puberty blockers to a thirteen-year-old can create more problems than it solves.

Many believe the watchful waiting approach is not sufficient these days, as the cultural context today is very different to how it was previously. Some teens are spending vast amounts of time online, nurturing their trans identity as if it were a bonsai tree. They attach all their hopes and dreams to their new identity, entrenching the view that medical transition is the only possible route out of their distress. 'Watchful waiting' entails loosely monitoring the situation and not doing anything to further exacerbate the issue – but when a young person is spending extended periods of time online, this may not be the best course of action.

THE TRAUMA-INFORMED MODEL

This model of care assumes that an individual is likely to have a history of trauma. For example, a disproportionate number of looked-after or foster children identify as trans, and many of these children have a history of trauma that can be overshadowed by a diagnosis of gender dysphoria. It is important that carers and guardians ensure they obtain the right support by being fully informed about the child's challenges. In this model, all the difficult experiences the person has had to contend with are explored, and attempts are made to come to terms with the underlying trauma and how this is affecting their gender dysphoria.

CONVERSION 'THERAPY'

Conversion 'therapy' – trying, for instance, to force gay patients to become straight – is an outdated pseudoscientific approach that has been fully discredited. We place the phrase 'therapy' in inverted commas as a way of highlighting the fact that we do not believe that this is therapy. Instead, this is a cruel and authoritarian practice no longer credibly associated with any form of psychotherapy. This brutal treatment imposed the therapist's beliefs, values, opinions and even goals upon the client. This 'treatment' is now, thankfully, seldom offered and found instead mostly among religious zealots. We do not believe it is helpful for parents of gender-questioning young people to engage a so-called 'conversion therapist' who promises to 'convert' your child – this is very likely to cause a good deal more harm than good.

Psychotherapy has a long history of helping clients explore their issues in an open-ended fashion without imposing an agenda. Therapists help trans-identified young people develop better self-awareness by providing a neutral space for exploration, and one result of this may be that they no longer identify as trans. This is in no way the same thing as conversion therapy.

Appendix 5

CHILD AND ADOLESCENT DEVELOPMENT

In the first years of a child's life, observing the rapid pace of acquiring new skills and abilities is a source of wonder and excitement for parents. It's remarkable to witness: a child derives a pure thrill in a peek-a-boo game or stumbles as she learns to walk with more stability.

Developmental psychologist Dr Erik Erikson theorises that each stage of life poses a fundamental question. During early childhood, between the ages of three and five, children ask, 'Am I good or bad?'[1] During these years, there is a focus on play, exploration and initiative. Make-believe and fantasy play an important role in the lives of young children. They may not be able to distinguish easily between fantasy and reality. For example, a popular chant from childhood, 'Step on a crack and break your mother's back' conjured horrifying imagery, so we deliberately hopped between paving slabs. Magical thinking is also expressed in childhood before the development of 'sex constancy'. This cognitive ability, which develops between the ages of approximately five and eight, allows children to understand that sex cannot be changed with clothing or hairstyles. For example, a four-year-old may believe that a male classmate 'becomes a girl' if he puts on a dress and wig. By age eight, the child would know her classmate is just a 'boy wearing a dress'.

Adolescence is a time of turbulent change, thrilling possibilities and existential dilemmas. According to Erikson's stages of development, the main question during adolescence is 'Who am I'? We reinvent ourselves, moving from childhood to adulthood. Developmental psychologists, building upon Erikson's theories, have identified other important areas of change during adolescence, including cognition and judgement, body and sexuality, relationship to authority, ethics and morality, and sociability. During the teenage years, considerations and conflicts may arise.

COGNITION AND JUDGEMENT

While the cognition and judgement of the child are more basic, the development of nuanced cognitive skills in adolescence is dramatic and has profound effects on how teens think and understand the world around them. Adolescents begin to move away from magical thinking, in which two unrelated events are thought to be causally linked. Their capacity for abstract thinking strengthens, and teens begin to contemplate consequences in a more logical manner. Teens are still subject to degrees of magical thinking, however, as they continue to develop their understanding of cause and effect. Furthermore, teenagers are notoriously more impulsive than adults, and an adolescent can make decisions based on emotional reactivity, not careful deliberation. Depending on their personalities, some teens will act out by taking risks while others may anxiously withdraw, refusing to engage with social life altogether. Under the duress of adolescence, with their cognitive development in this state of flux, and with the adoption of new ideas about gender, transition and identity, it's easy to see how teens buy into the transition fantasy. They come to believe they can change sex, that medical interventions will make everything better, and that a new life of happiness awaits them on the other side of social or medical transition.

RELATIONSHIP TO AUTHORITY, SEEKING AUTONOMY

Parents are often the stars of the show for children up until puberty. You can blithely inform the child of the family's judgement and values on any given subject and most children absorb this like a sponge. Then, during adolescence, the nature of parent–child relationships changes dramatically. The eagerness to please their parents fades, and your son or daughter becomes more oriented towards peers (whether in-person or virtual). Teens begin to question the values of the family and may become combative, challenging your authority or keeping secrets. Society and its authoritative hierarchies arouse suspicion as the adolescent attempts to develop autonomy and become an authority in their own life. Social difficulties like bullying at school and psychological vulnerabilities like autistic traits can impede this process. The familiar role of the obedient child is shed and an existential loneliness may set in: with greater independence comes a degree of isolation. A teen may seek out alternative and maladaptive means of individuation and rebellion, such as self-harm or drug use. They may be susceptible to extremism and radicalisation. It's also common for teens to indulge in persecution fantasies about their parents: Mum and Dad don't understand me; if it weren't for their stupid rules and restrictions, I could be truly happy.

Gender-questioning young people make bold and mature-sounding proclamations about identity, surgeries and hormone treatments. Still, many of them are behind the curve in acquiring the life skills that facilitate true independence: an eighteen-year-old refuses to drive, a fifteen-year-old is too timid to order her own food at restaurants, a young man relies heavily on his parents to manage meal preparation, medical appointments, laundry and basic hygiene. Yet the innate drive to be independent powers on and finds other ways to express itself through labels, assertive declarations and demands for 'pronouns'. We might consider this as a misplaced attempt to become an authority figure in one's own life.

ETHICS AND MORALITY

What is the point of life? Why is society structured this way? How can things be so unfair? Although some children give consideration to these questions, most don't, and it is typically in adolescence that bright, sensitive teens begin to ask themselves deeper questions about the nature of life. They seek answers by interrogating traditions and mores that were taken at face value in childhood, or experiment with new belief systems and moral frameworks. Because they are intellectually open and malleable, this is a time characterised by rejecting the old and experimenting with the new. Veganism, atheism, new political ideas or religious exploration can dominate the intellectual life of a passionate teen. This intellectual flexibility can spark meaningful drives towards positive behaviours, like volunteering, or campaigning for philanthropic ideals. Yet it also makes teens particularly vulnerable to adopting radical and dangerous belief systems, which often include the attempt to fulfil utopian fantasies by any means necessary. Signs of radicalisation may include a sudden change in behaviour, alterations in friend groups, isolation from family and friends, adoption of scripted or unfamiliar speech, an unwillingness or inability to discuss her views, a newly disrespectful attitude towards others, and increased levels of anger and secretiveness, especially around internet use.[2]

A new, subversive framework for understanding sex, gender and sexuality has great appeal to the open-minded and analytical teenager. It's powerful to think that your parents' values, the assumption that you're 'cis' and the subtle and overt gender norms you've embodied over the years can now be questioned and rejected outright. So a historically gender-conforming girl may come to believe she's trans if she thinks her female gender identity has been imposed on her. Or perhaps your son, if he hadn't been 'suppressing' his transness, would never have been so heteronormative. These gender identity beliefs prompt young people to rake over their life histories, searching for proof that they were always transgender.

SOCIABILITY

Attachment relationships change dramatically during the teenage years. Peers begin to hold an outsized influence over adolescents as kids move away from parents towards their friends. Some parents can feel displaced or rejected in favour of a new best friend or friend group. And sadly, a lack of friendships in adolescence increases the chance of mental health issues. Being friendless in middle school (age

11–14) is associated with greater vulnerability to the negative impacts of bullying.[3] So developing strong and influential peer relationships is important and can be a healthy part of separating and individuating (becoming one's own person) from parents. But there are also dangers involved. Research demonstrates that teens take greater risks and behave more impulsively when in the presence of peers.[4] A cautious and deliberate child may suddenly claim to want 'top surgery' or cross-sex hormone injections, with little apparent concern about the ramifications. More than a few parents have said, 'This kid doesn't even like to take aspirin! I don't understand how she wants to inject testosterone into her body!' When a peer group, not to mention the culture more broadly, has normalised and even glorified a medically hazardous intervention, it's no surprise our teen feels so drawn to have it.

Taking gender out of the equation can help us contextualise this copycat behaviour from a developmental perspective. We can all remember 'phases' that were peer-induced in our own adolescent years. We listened to the same music as our friends, dressed like them, watched the same TV shows and adopted similar mannerisms and hobbies. For some of us, being a social outcast is what bonded us with our peers, and that outsider persona became an integral part of our identity. For others, it was an athletic hobby, artistic endeavour or a focus on academic achievement. Gender-questioning teens can find acceptance and community through a school LGBT club, when a close friend 'comes out', or in the realm of virtual relationships. For those teenagers who don't have friends in real life, hour upon hour can be spent developing celebratory, intense and powerful new relationships on social media platforms. In online chat forums, young people who begin questioning their identity find a flood of validation, encouragement and complimentary support which further pushes them to adopt a transgender identity. Should there be any scepticism from parents or friends, young people are told that this resistance is 'transphobia' and an indicator that they are being misunderstood and marginalised. They are encouraged to keep going with the trans identity and thus become their 'authentic self' (a term used often in such online groups). Being 'trans' plays double duty: it allows a young person to have instant connections, and as a glorified misfit they can suffer beautifully with other 'oppressed' groups on the fringes of society. Young people who come to feel guilty about their 'privilege' or status as an 'oppressor' can shed those punitive labels as they move into a coveted marginalised category by changing pronouns and coming out as trans. The 'heteronormative cis' kid becomes an insider in a group of closely bonded outsiders.

Appendix 6

COMMON COEXISTING CONDITIONS

Many parents of gender-distressed kids report considerable additional challenges as their children are dealing with other issues. In this section we note common coexisting conditions that are often experienced by young people with gender dysphoria.

AUTISM SPECTRUM DISORDER (ASD)

ASD is a developmental condition. People with ASD often have a number of traits that may influence how they experience gender-related distress. In Chapter 2, we discuss the impact of this condition in relation to ROGD kids.

Many individuals with ASD have difficulties with social communication and interaction. They can find it hard to make friends, and although they sometimes prefer to be alone, their solitary life may lead to a profound sense of loneliness. Autistic people might find it difficult to understand what others are thinking or feeling and find it exhausting to figure out the social context. Consequently, they can become very anxious about social situations. We have noticed in our work that isolation can be alleviated by the sense of belonging that an online community can offer. The well-known difficulties with making eye contact are not an issue online and the screen can offer a welcome protective distance in social interactions, so the young person can begin to prefer this as a way to socialise with other people. This can lead to intense friendships forming with people online and a corresponding lack of interest in real-life interactions.

Autistic people may understand language in a very literal manner, for example they may not grasp sarcasm or metaphorical language. For this reason parents need to be extremely careful if they, for example, choose to use a different pronoun or agree that their daughter is no longer a girl but instead a transboy. To a neurotypical brain it might seem obvious that there is a certain play with language being carried out, but this may not be the case for the more neurodiverse.

Restricted or repetitive behaviours or interests are often evident in people with ASD, and they might also be inclined towards hyperfixation. If the autistic person becomes hyperfixated upon a trans identity it can be difficult to figure out the difference between a hyperfixation and an intense desire to be perceived as another gender.

Autistic people are often non-conforming in a variety of ways. Their brains are often logic-oriented, and so they do not see any need to follow the silly rules society chooses to impose upon us. For this reason many autistic people can be gender-nonconforming. They often have sensory issues, and so when they find clothes they are comfortable wearing, they can be extremely reluctant to wear anything else. They also tend to become anxious about change and prefer to keep the same routines in place. This combination of traits might mean your young son insists on wearing a certain dress and will refuse all entreaties to wear anything else. They may also find the changes that happen during puberty extremely difficult to tolerate.

It is notable that autism in females is often overlooked, and so if you have a gender dysphoric girl who shows many of these traits it could be helpful to seek a diagnosis. Autistic girls may have hidden signs of autism and instead have learned to 'fit in' by copying others. They seem to be more likely to hide their feelings, and so their parents can often be surprised at the diagnosis of ASD when it finally arrives.

Some parents have reported that the diagnosis of ASD provided the young person with much-needed insight into their challenges, while others have recounted how their child believed their diagnosis of ASD was significant proof that they were in fact 'truly trans', as it is well known that autism is disproportionately high among members of the trans community.

People with autism tend to feel comfortable with rules that are explicit and rigid, and the many rules involved in being part of the trans community can be very appealing. There are codes stipulating which pronouns can be used, and what language is and is not OK. In addition, the transition pathway offers a clear road forward which can feel comforting for an autistic person, who may feel pretty disembodied and alienated from their physicality.

Parents can help their autistic child by building their self-awareness about their autistic traits and how medical transition might seem to be attractive but will not necessarily bring about the best long-term outcomes. Extreme caution around any changes in language is recommended, as it will be difficult to reverse course. Instead, a clear and detailed framework of how the parents view their trans identification – and also how it should be managed – can be the most helpful way to approach gender-related distress in a person with ASD.

ATTENTION DEFICIT HYPERACTIVITY DISORDER (ADHD)

ADHD is a common neurodevelopmental disorder that affects a young person's executive functioning. People with ADHD have difficulty with impulse control, and so if they have a desire to transition, they can become utterly consumed by this and begin a campaign of attrition that will be familiar to their parents. ADHD can bring about an overwhelming need for instant gratification, and so young people with ADHD will want to begin the transition process immediately. Parents of children with ADHD can often feel worn down and unable to cope with their child's intensity. Their children's executive functioning might lead them to have difficulties prioritising their issues, and suddenly transition can become the most important thing in the world.

People with ADHD can often be immature and consequently feel like they don't belong among their peers. Just like with other neurodiverse people, this can lead to a pervasive sense of loneliness that might be alleviated somewhat by an online community. The fast nature of online interaction can suit the person with ADHD, and they might feel like they have finally found their tribe.

Typically, a person with ADHD might have difficulties focusing on or completing any given task, and so they can feel attracted to the specific pathway offered by transition. Yet people with ADHD can often become just as hyperfixated as other neurodiverse individuals, and we have often seen an obsessive focus on a trans identity among neurodiverse people. They often feel on the edge of chaos, and the strict rules and guidelines associated with the transition pathway can seem to offer a calming solution for the inner chaos the ADHD individual often experiences.

The excessive activity and restlessness that is a common trait among people with ADHD can also be channelled into a desire to transition. These young people often have a low tolerance for frustration and have difficulties handling stress. Their emotions can be overpowering and so they might become very angry very quickly. Frequent mood swings are already a common issue in adolescence, and the extreme emotion of the ADHD adolescent leads many to perceive ADHD as a turbocharged version of adolescence.

Parents with an ADHD child can feel utterly exhausted by the relentless campaigning, and so self-care is more important than ever. The very same rules that apply to every other aspect of the child's life also apply to their desire to transition – they need to learn to control their impulsive behaviour and improve their distress tolerance. It is valuable for parents to become experts on ADHD so that they can teach their child the different facets of this complex condition.

OBSESSIVE–COMPULSIVE DISORDER (OCD)

OCD is a chronic condition which can lead a person to have uncontrollable, reoccurring thoughts ('obsessions') and/or behaviours ('compulsions') that he or she can feel compelled to repeat over and over. Rumination is a core feature of OCD that can cause the individual to spend an inordinate amount of time thinking about a particular thought or theme. OCD can be extremely distressing as the sufferer can spend their life worrying in a near-constant state of anxiety and worry. Some people appear to ruminate compulsively over their gender identity and how they appear to other people. This obsessive thought process can be followed by compulsive behaviour such as binding, tucking or hair removal.

It can be helpful if children are taught about OCD with a course of psychoeducation. They might need to learn the value of distraction; others find that visualisation or meditation works better for them. As gender dysphoria can be diagnosed alongside OCD, it can become very difficult for anyone to ascertain how much a fixation on their gender identity is a symptom of an OCD rumination. Again, the more the parents know about this difficult condition, the more likely it is that they can help equip their child with useful knowledge.

DISORDERED EATING

An eating disorder is characterised by abnormal eating behaviours that have a negative impact on a person's life. It is arguable that many teenage girls who would perhaps have developed an eating disorder had they lived in a previous generation have instead developed gender dysphoria today. However, we have also seen in our practices that many trans-identified young people may also have an eating disorder such as anorexia or bulimia. Disordered eating may include restrictive eating, compulsive eating and/or inflexible patterns of eating. Gender dysphoria and eating disorders share in common a deep sense of dissatisfaction with one's body. Both issues involve a desire to alter the body in extreme ways. Just like those with eating disorders, people with gender-related distress can become very absorbed by how they 'should' look. Biological girls can feel thrilled as they watch their fat turn to muscle under the influence of testosterone. They might become obsessed with their physical appearance and continue with their disordered eating but with an additional component of gender rumination.

It is recommended that you seek professional help for your child if you believe she has disordered eating patterns. This can be a very fraught challenge that requires a lot of sensitivity and understanding, and further support is usually necessary.

BODY DYSMORPHIA (BDD)

Body dysmorphic disorder (BDD), also known as body dysmorphia, is a mental health condition where a person spends an inordinate amount of time worrying about perceived flaws in their appearance. These flaws can be any aspect of their body and/or face and might be unnoticeable to others. It can be difficult to figure out what's going on if a teenage girl has BDD and is fixated upon her hatred of her breasts and her desire for a mastectomy. Indeed, this thought rumination can feel like a combination of gender dysphoria, OCD and BDD. It is important for parents to remind their child about how little we know about the brain and how difficult it can be to understand what is going on for a young person who hates their body hair and spends hours every day removing all traces of it.

GIFTEDNESS

Young people who are gifted demonstrate an advanced ability or potential in one or more specific areas when compared to their peers. Many children who experience gender distress are also gifted. People who are highly cerebral can be attracted to complex new ideas that require a good deal of thought and reflection. The utopian impulse – the propensity to seek out a better world – can make the esoteric nature of queer theory alluring to a gifted person, as they believe that it might reduce unfairness in the world. It is notable that many highly intelligent people are often more likely to join a cult that their less intelligent counterparts because they are driven by a utopian impulse and drawn in by the challenging thought processes required for them to become part of the community. Gifted people also tend to feel more lonely than others, as they are statistically less likely to find people who can easily understand them, and so they are more likely to seek out a community that offers a range of new ideas and concepts.

GLOSSARY

Language in this area is highly politicised. The following terms are those you may hear your child use. Items in quotes are activist language that are based in ideological concepts. We offer this glossary as a resource for parents who may feel confused by the new terms their child is using. These terms continue to change and expand.

'AFAB': 'Assigned female at birth'. We recommend using the term 'female' instead.

affirmative approach: A therapeutic and medical approach arguing that adults and children, no matter what age, should be affirmed in their chosen gender and supported in social and medical transition if desired. The affirmative approach generally sees exploration and differential diagnosis (i.e. seeing gender dysphoria as a symptom of distress rather than its cause) as undesirable.

'agender': A person who feels themselves to be neither male nor female.

'AMAB': 'Assigned male at birth'. We recommend using the term 'male'.

'asexual': Someone who is uninterested in sexual activity or is not sexually attracted to others.

autogynephilia (or AGP): A diagnosable paraphilia listed in the *DSM-5*, which refers to a male's sexual fixation on the thought of himself as a female. A man who has autogynephilia is termed an 'autogynephile'.

'cis, cisgender': A term used to denote people who do not identify as trans. Many people object to this term because it implies a belief in innate gender identity.

'cis-het': Short for 'cisgender' and 'heterosexual'. Often used derogatorily.

'deadname': The process of referring to someone by the birth name with which they no longer identify.

desistance: The process of reversing a transition that was only social (e.g. by reverting to a birth name). Desistance typically implies that an individual who was once considering or seeking medical transition is no longer doing so.

detransition: The process of changing a person's gender identification back to his or her biological sex by seeking to cease or reverse an earlier medical transition. Detransition may involve changing presentation, reversing a name change and legal documents, ceasing hormones, and in some cases reversing surgeries such as breast implants (female) or a mastectomy (male).

developmental approach: A therapeutic and medical approach arguing that many factors (biological, psychological and social) can lead an individual to experience distress around gender.

DSDs: DSDs (differences of sexual development) are more than forty different conditions where sexual development does not rigidly adhere to the typical male or female pathway. DSDs are also known as intersex conditions, and the terms 'VSD' (variation of sexual development) and 'CCSD' (congenital condition of sexual development) are also in use. The proportion of people with DSDs is 0.018%.[1]

'femme boy': Initially this term described a male who is very feminine, but it can now describe a person who has been born a girl, identifies as male and now presents as a feminine boy.

FTM: 'Female to male' can mean either social or medical transition.

gender: Once used interchangeably with 'sex' to mean male or female. Now denotes a person's social or cultural status as masculine, feminine or something else.

'gender-affirming': A way of describing gender reassignment procedures. We recommend avoiding this term, as it implies that medical interventions are the only means by which people suffering with gender incongruence or gender dysphoria might address these feelings.

gender critical: An outlook that believes gender is a social construct and (unlike biology, which is an objective reality) is neither an innate, essential nor deterministic quality.

gender dysphoria: The distress caused by the discrepancy between one's experienced gender and one's primary or secondary sex characteristics. This is a diagnostic category in the *DSM-5*.

'gender identity': An internal sense of one's own gender, which may or may not be at odds with one's biological sex. Make sure not to assume that everyone has a gender identity, as many people do not ascribe to this notion for themselves.

Gender Identity Disorder: A term that appeared in the *DSM-3* and *DSM-4* to describe what is now termed 'gender dysphoria'. This term is now disfavoured, and should only be used to describe diagnoses made before the terminology shift to 'gender dysphoria'.

gender ideology: A belief that everyone has an innate gender identity that may be misaligned with biological sex, and that ought to take precedence over biological sex. Gender ideology undergirds such statements as 'trans women are women', and is one of the rationales for medical intervention to align one's body with one's felt sense of gender.

gender incongruence: Where an individual's sex and gender are experienced to be at odds with one another. This is a diagnostic category in the *International Classification of Diseases (ICD-11)* defined as a marked and persistent discrepancy between an individual's sex and experienced gender.

gender-questioning: Describes someone who is asking questions about or otherwise exploring his or her own gender identity. We recommend this term be used in lieu of 'trans' or 'transgender' for young people whose identity is still in a formative stage.

gender reassignment: Also known as sex reassignment. Refers to any of the hormonal or surgical interventions undertaken as part of medical transition.

internalised homophobia: The shame or discomfort a gay, lesbian or bisexual person feels about their sexual orientation.

intersex: An umbrella term for the more than forty different conditions where sexual development does not rigidly adhere to the typical male or female pathway. Given that this word has entered common parlance, we recommend you include the term 'DSD' in parentheses afterwards, as many people with DSDs find 'intersex' to be an ambiguous or contentious label – and vice versa.

LGB: An acronym that unites same-sex-attracted people (i.e. lesbians, gay men and bisexual women and men).

LGBT (or LGBTQ, LGBTQ+, LGBTQI, etc.): An acronym that unites same-sex-attracted people (i.e. lesbians, gay men and bisexual women and men) with trans people – and, in some iterations, with other groups, such as people with DSDs, or 'queer' people. We urge caution when using such acronyms, as many same-sex-attracted people (or people with DSDs) do not consider themselves to be part of this community and prefer to remain distinct.

medical transition: A range of medical interventions (such as hormones and surgeries) undertaken in order to present as a different gender.

'misgender': The process of referring to someone using a pronoun that does not correspond to the gender with which they identify.

'mis-sex': The process of referring to someone using a pronoun that does not correspond with their biological sex.

MTF: 'Male to female' can refer to medical or social transition.

'non-binary': A gender identity where an individual's sense of self is neither male nor female.

'pansexual': Attraction towards people regardless of their sex or gender identity.

'queer': Used by some as a general way of describing sexualities and/ or gender identities that are seen as counter-normative. 'Queer' was used as a slur against same-sex-attracted people for decades, and remains an offensive word to some homosexuals, lesbians and bisexuals. It refers to people who are same-sex-attracted and same-gender-attracted. Some people consider it to be shorthand for promoting gender ideology above the rights of lesbians, gays and bisexuals.

Rapid Onset Gender Dysphoria (ROGD): A description of a relatively new phenomenon whereby adolescents (girls especially) are experiencing starkly elevated rates of gender dysphoria, mediated by peer influence, and with high levels of co-occurring mental health conditions.

retransition: The term used when a person who has previously detransitioned decides to revert back to a trans identity.

sex: The system by which humans are classified as male or female in utero or at birth, based on reproductive functions and bodily characteristics such as chromosomes and hormones.

'skoliosexual': Someone attracted to a non-binary or trans person.

social transition: The process of changing your name, asking people to use different pronouns to refer to you, or changing aspects of your appearance (such as your clothing or your hairstyle) to present as a different gender.

trans or transgender: An umbrella term for both transgender people and transsexual people that is not related to their sexual orientation. Given the ambiguity about this term, we advise it not be used to describe young people whose identity is still in a formative period.

'trans-fem/trans-feminine': A biological man who identifies as feminine.

'trans kid', 'trans child': We strongly advise you not to use these terms, as they can concretise a young person's identity while that identity is still in a formative stage. Instead, we recommend saying 'a child who has undergone medical transition' or 'a gender-questioning child', according to the circumstance.

transition: The process of changing a person's gender presentation and/or sex characteristics to accord with their internal sense of gender identity. Transition can be social and/or medical.

'transman' (aka a trans-identified woman): A natal female, whether heterosexual, bisexual or same-sex-attracted, who may have undergone medical intervention to appear male and/or who has adopted a male identity. Some transmen consider themselves to be gay men.

'trans-masc/trans-masculine': A biological woman who identifies as masculine.

'transphobia': originally a term to describe people who are prejudiced against the trans community, this has become a catch-all word to describe opposition to issues related to trans rights, such as self-ID or the use of compelled pronouns.

transsexual (or 'transexual', with one 's'): A now outdated term that describes individuals who have modified their bodies through hormones or surgery to present as a member of the opposite sex.

'transwoman' (aka a trans-identified man): A natal male, whether heterosexual, bisexual or same-sex-attracted, who may have undergone medical intervention to appear female and/or who has adopted a female identity. Some transwomen consider themselves lesbians.

RESOURCES

BOOKS

Attwood, Tony, *The Complete Guide to Asperger's Syndrome*

Bailey, J. Michael, *The Man Who Would Be Queen: The Science of Gender-Bending and Transsexualism*

Barnes, Hannah, *Time to Think: The Inside Story of the Collapse of the Tavistock's Gender Service for Children*

Brunskell-Evans, Heather, and Michele Moore (eds), *Inventing Transgender Children and Young People*

Brunskell-Evans, Heather, and Michele Moore (eds), *Transgender Children and Young People: Born in Your Own Body*

Coleman, Joshua, *Rules of Estrangement: Why Adult Children Cut Ties and How to Heal the Conflict*

Davies, James, *Cracked: Why Psychiatry is Doing More Harm Than Good*

Davis, Lisa Selin, *Tomboy: The Surprising History and Future of Girls Who Dare to Be Different*

Evans, Susan and Marcus Evans, *Gender Dysphoria: A Therapeutic Model for Working with Children, Adolescents and Young Adults*

Haidt, Jonathan and Greg Lukianoff, *The Coddling of the American Mind: How Good Intentions and Bad Ideas Are Setting Up a Generation for Failure*

Hakeem, Az, *Trans: Exploring Gender Identity and Gender Dysphoria*

Hassan, Steve, *Combating Cult Mind Control: The Guide to Protection, Rescue, and Recovery from Destructive Cults*

Hendrickx, Sarah, *Women and Girls with Autism Spectrum Disorder: Understanding Life Experiences from Early Childhood to Old Age*

Jongeling, Nele Peer and Elie Vandenbussche, *Gender Detransition: a path towards self-acceptance* [PDF booklet], https://post-trans.com/ Detransition-Booklet

Joyce, Helen, *Trans: Gender Identity and the New Battle for Women's Rights*

Kreger, Randi et al., *Stop Walking on Eggshells for Parents: How to Help Your Child (of Any Age) with Borderline Personality Disorder without Losing Yourself*

Kübler-Ross, Elisabeth, *On Death and Dying: What the Dying Have to Teach Doctors, Nurses, Clergy and Their Own Families*

Lawrence, Anne A., *Men Trapped in Men's Bodies: Narratives of Autogynephilic Transsexualism*

Marchiano, Lisa, *Motherhood: Facing and Finding Yourself*

Neff, Kristin, *Self-Compassion: Stop Beating Yourself Up and Leave Insecurity Behind*

Neufeld, Gordon and Gabor Maté, *Hold on to Your Kids: Why Parents Need to Matter More Than Peers*

O'Malley, Stella, *Bully-Proof Kids: Practical Tools to Help Your Child to Grow Up Confident, Resilient and Strong*

O'Malley, Stella, *Cotton Wool Kids: What's Making Irish Parents Paranoid?*

O'Malley, Stella, *Fragile: Why We Feel More Stressed, Anxious and Overwhelmed than Ever (And What We Can Do About It)*

O'Malley, Stella, *What Your Teen is Trying to Tell You*

Ostertag, Bob, *Sex Science Self: A Social History of Estrogen, Testosterone, and Identity*

Pluckrose, Helen and James Lindsay, *Cynical Theories: How Activist Scholarship Made Everything About Race, Gender, and Identity – and Why This Harms Everybody*

Robinson, Max, *Detransition: Beyond Before and After*

Shrier, Abigail, *Irreversible Damage: Teenage Girls and the Transgender Craze*

Soh, Deborah, *The End of Gender: Debunking the Myths about Sex and Identity in Our Society*

Stock, Kathleen, *Material Girls: Why Reality Matters for Feminism*

Vedantam, Shankar, *The Hidden Brain: How our Unconscious Minds Elect Presidents, Control Markets, Wage Wars, and Save Our Lives*

Vedantam, Shankar and Bill Mesler, *Useful Delusions: The Power and Paradox of the Self-Deceiving Brain*
Watters, Ethan, *Crazy Like Us: The Globalization of the American Psyche*
Watters, Ethan and Richard Ofshe, *Making Monsters: False Memories, Psychotherapy, and Sexual Hysteria*

BOOKS FOR CHILDREN

Alcott, Louisa May, *Little Women*
Blyton, Enid, *The Famous Five* (series)
O'Neill-Sheehan, Elizabeth, *Grace O'Malley: The Queen of the Sea*
Rooney, Rachel, illustrated by Jessica Ahlberg, *My Body is Me!*
Schefer, Valorie, *The Care and Keeping of You: The Body Book for Younger Girls*
Walliams, David, *The Boy in The Dress*

BOOKS FOR ADOLESCENTS

Cole, Joanna, *Asking About Sex and Growing Up: A Question-and-Answer Book for Kids*
Elkan, Sophie, Laura Chaisty and Dr Maddy Podichetty, *The Girls' Guide to Growing Up Great: Changing Bodies, Periods, Relationships, Life Online*
Hill, Milli, *My Period: Find Your Flow and Feel Proud of Your Period!*
Todnem, Scott, *Growing Up Great! The Ultimate Puberty Book for Boys*

PARENTING GUIDANCE

Sasha's Parent Membership Group: https://www.subscribestar.com/sashalpc
Stella's Parent Coaching Site: https://substack.com/profile/13204233-stella-omalley

PODCASTS

Calmversations, with Benjamin Boyce, https://www.youtube.com/c/
BenjaminABoyce

Gender: A Wider Lens, with Sasha Ayad and Stella O'Malley, www.
widerlenspod.com

Heterodorx, with Nina Paley and Corinna Cohn, https://www.
heterodorx.com/

Transparency Podcast, https://link.chtbl.com/0pxmTbEP

This Jungian Life, with Lisa Marchiano, Joseph Lee and Deb Stewart,
https://thisjungianlife.com/podcast

The Unspeakable Podcast, with Meghan Daum, https://www.theun-
speakablepodcast.com/

FILMS

Affirmation Generation: The Lies of Transgender Medicine

The Detransition Diaries: Saving Our Sisters

Dysphoric: Fleeing Womanhood Like a House on Fire [four-part documentary series]

The Social Dilemma

This World: Transgender Kids [BBC2]

Transgender Kids: Who Knows Best?

Trans Kids: It's Time to Talk [Channel 4]

Trans Mission: What's the Rush to Reassign Gender?

The Trans Train [four-part documentary series]

What Is a Woman?

The Wrong Body [video series – viewing requests available from the
British Film Institute. Part 1 (1997), https://www2.bfi.org.uk/
films-tv-people/4ce2b80c5d9ba; part 2 (1996), https://www2.bfi.
org.uk/films-tv-people/4ce2b7f121f1b]

FOREIGN TRAVEL OPPORTUNITIES

Adolesco, https://adolesco.org/: helps arrange immersive language
experiences of up to three months.

En Famille, https://www.enfamille.com/en/: a French non-profit which arranges longer language exchanges.

Semester at Sea, https://www.semesteratsea.org/: a multi-country study abroad programme which is based on a ship.

WWOOF (World Wide Opportunities on Organic Farms), https://wwoof.net/: allows young people to volunteer on farms.

Workaway, https://www.workaway.info/: a community for cultural exchange, working holidays and volunteering in 170 countries.

ORGANISATIONS

The Clinical Advisory Network for Sex and Gender (CAN-SG) is a group of UK and Ireland-based clinicians calling for greater understanding of the effects of sex and gender in healthcare: https://can-sg.org/

Critical Therapy Antidote (CTA) is a platform for talking therapists and allied mental health professionals who are concerned about the negative impact of Critical Social Justice (CSJ) on their professions: https://criticaltherapyantidote.org/

dsdfamilies is an information and peer support charity for families with children who have been diagnosed with differences of (or, as doctors might say, disorders of) sex development (also known as 'intersex'): https://www.dsdfamilies.org/

FAIR (Foundation Against Intolerance and Racism) is a US non-partisan organisation dedicated to advancing civil rights and liberties for all Americans, and promoting a common culture based on fairness, understanding and humanity: https://www.fairforall.org/

Fightthenewdrug helps raise awareness about the harmful effects of porn and exploitation: https://fightthenewdrug.org/

The Gender Dysphoria Alliance (GDA) was formed by a small group of community members concerned about the direction that gender medicine and activism has taken: https://www.genderdysphoriaalliance.com/

The Global Exploratory Therapy Association (GETA) is an organisation of mental health clinicians committed to providing ethical individualised agenda-free care for those struggling with gender-related distress: https://genderexploratory.com/

Genspect is an international organisation of professionals, parent groups, trans people, detransitioners and others who seek a healthy approach to sex and gender: https://genspect.org/

The Institute for Comprehensive Gender Dysphoria Research (ICGDR) is a non-profit corporation created to conduct, support and communicate quality research about gender dysphoria: https://icgdr.org/

The LGB Alliance exists to provide support, advice, information and community to UK men and women who are same-sex-attracted: https://lgballiance.org.uk/. There are also groups in Australia, Brazil, Canada, Germany, Iceland, Ireland, Mexico, Norway, Poland, Serbia, Spain and the US.

Sex Matters is a UK organisation that campaigns to establish that sex matters in rules, laws, policies, language and culture: https://sex-matters.org/

The Society for Evidence-based Gender Medicine (SEGM) aims to promote safe, compassionate, ethical and evidence-informed healthcare for children, adolescents and young adults with gender dysphoria: https://www.segm.org/

Thoughtful Therapists is a group of psychotherapists and counsellors who have come together with a shared concern about the impact of gender identity ideology on children and young people. Thoughtful Therapists seek to protect the integrity of open-ended, exploratory and ethical therapy: https://thoughtfultherapists.org/

Transgender Trend is an organisation of parents, professionals and academics based in the UK who are concerned about the current trend to diagnose children as transgender, including the unprecedented number of teenage girls suddenly self-identifying as 'trans' (Rapid Onset Gender Dysphoria or ROGD): https://www.transgendertrend.com/

Wider Lens Consulting provides support for parents, including in-person retreats that offer parents the opportunity to replenish their energy and some practical help so that gender-expansive children in their care can flourish: https://widerlens.consulting/

PARENT COMMUNITIES

4thWaveNow is a community of people who question the medicalisation of gender-atypical youth: https://4thwavenow.com/

Amanda Familias (Agrupación de Madres de Adolescentes y Niñas con Disforia Acelerada) is based in Spain with a presence in Argentina, Chile, Colombia, Costa Rica, Mexico and Peru: https://www.amandafamilias.org/

The Gender Critical Support Board is a public forum for parents: https://gendercriticalresources.com/

The Gender Dysphoria Support Network (GDSN) is an international group that aims to offer psychoeducation and support to families of individuals affected by gender dysphoria. The GDSN has a presence in Australia, Canada, France, Germany, Ireland, Italy, the Netherlands, New Zealand, Spain, Switzerland, the UK, the US and more: https://genderdysphoriasupportnetwork.com/

Our Duty is an international support network for parents who wish to protect their children from gender ideology. Our Duty has a presence in Australia, Canada, the UK and the US: https://ourduty.group/

Parents of ROGD Kids is a group of parents whose children have suddenly decided they identify strongly with the opposite sex and are at various stages in transitioning. Parents of ROGD Kids has a presence in Australia, Canada (six groups), Germany, the UK and the US (eighty-five groups): https://www.parentsofrogdkids.com/

PITT (Parents with Inconvenient Truths about Trans) publishes stories written and edited exclusively by parents with first-hand experience in the world of gender ideology: https://pitt.substack.com/

COUNTRY-SPECIFIC SUPPORT

Argentina

Amanda Familias: https://www.amandafamilias.org/

Australia

Gender Dysphoria Support Network: https://genderdysphoria-supportnetwork.com/
Parents of ROGD Kids: https://www.parentsofrogdkids.com/
Our Duty: https://ourduty.group/

Belgium

Cry For Recognition: https://cryforrecognition.be/

Brazil

No Corpo Certo: https://nocorpocerto.com/

Canada

Canadian Gender Report: https://genderreport.ca/
Gender Dysphoria Support Network: https://genderdysphoria-supportnetwork.com/
Parents of ROGD Kids: https://www.parentsofrogdkids.com/
Our Duty: https://ourduty.group/

Chile

Amanda Familias: https://www.amandafamilias.org/

Colombia

Amanda Familias: https://www.amandafamilias.org/

Costa Rica

Amanda Familias: https://www.amandafamilias.org/

Finland

Kirjo: https://www.ihmistenkirjo.net/

France

Observatoire La Petite Sirène: https://www.observatoirepetitesirene.org/
Ypomoni: https://ypomoni.org/

Germany

Transteens Sorge berechtigt: https://transteens-sorge-berechtigt.net/
Gender Dysphoria Support Network: https://genderdysphoria-supportnetwork.com/
Parents of ROGD Kids: https://www.parentsofrogdkids.com/
Our Duty: https://ourduty.group/

Italy

GenerAzioneD: https://www.generazioned.org/

Mexico

Amanda Familias: https://www.amandafamilias.org/

New Zealand/Aotearoa

Aotearoa Support: https://aotearoasupport.nz/

Norway

Genid Gender Identity Challenge Norway: https://genderchallenge.no/

Peru

Amanda Familias: https://www.amandafamilias.org/

Spain

Amanda Familias: https://www.amandafamilias.org/

Sweden

Genid: Gender Identity Challenge Sweden: https://genid.se/

Switzerland

AMQG: Association pour une Approche Mesurée des Questionnements de Genre chez les Jeunes: https://www.amqg.ch/

United Kingdom

Bayswater Support Group: https://www.bayswatersupport.org.uk/
Gender Dysphoria Support Network: https://genderdysphoria-supportnetwork.com/
Parents of ROGD Kids: https://www.parentsofrogdkids.com/
Our Duty: https://ourduty.group/

United States

Cardinal Support Network: https://www.cardinalsupportnetwork.
com/

Child and Parental Rights Campaign: https://childparentrights.org/

Gender Dysphoria Support Network: https://genderdysphoria-
supportnetwork.com/

Parents of ROGD Kids: https://www.parentsofrogdkids.com/

Our Duty: https://ourduty.group/

REFERENCES

PREFACE

1 Cass, H. (2022), 'Independent review of gender identity services for children and young people', https://cass.independent-review.uk/publications/interim-report/, p. 36.

1. IS MY CHILD TRANS?

1 Block, J. (2023), 'Gender dysphoria in young people is rising – and so is professional disagreement', *British Medical Journal*: 380–2. doi: 10.1136/bmj.p382.
2 Singh et al. (2021), 'A follow-up study of boys with gender identity disorder', *Frontiers in Psychiatry* 12. doi:10.3389/fpsyt.2021.632784; Steensma, T.D. et al. (2013a), 'Factors associated with desistence and persistence of childhood gender dysphoria: a quantitative follow-up study', *Journal of the American Academy of Child and Adolescent Psychiatry* 52 (6):582–90. doi: 10.1016/j.jaac.2013.03.016; Zaliznyak, M. et al. (2021), 'How early in life do transgender adults begin to experience gender dysphoria? Why this matters for patients, providers, and for our healthcare system', *Sexual Medicine* 9 (6):100448. doi: 10.1016/j.esxm.2021.100448.
3 Winnicott, D.W. (1960), 'Ego distortion in terms of true and false self'. In: D.W. Winnicott, *The Maturational Process and the Facilitating Environment: Studies in the Theory of Emotional Development*, pp. 140–57. New York: International Universities Press, Inc.
4 Li, Gu et al. (2017), 'Childhood gender-typed behavior and adolescent sexual orientation: a longitudinal population-based study', *Developmental Psychology* 53 (4): 764–77. doi:10.1037/dev0000281.
5 Yu, J. et al. (2021), 'Which boys and which girls are falling behind? Linking adolescents' gender role profiles to motivation, engagement, and achievement', *Journal of Youth and Adolescence* 50: 336–52. https://doi.org/10.1007/s10964-020-01293-z.
6 Hilgenkamp, K.D. and Livingston, M.M. (2002), 'Tomboys, masculine characteristics, and self-ratings of confidence in career success', *Psychological Reports* 90 (3) (pt 1):743–9. doi: 10.2466/pr0.2002.90.3.743.

7 Aitken, M. et al. (2015), 'Evidence for an altered sex ratio in clinic-referred adolescents with gender dysphoria', *Journal of Sexual Medicine* 12 (3): 756–63. https://doi.org/10.1111/jsm.12817.

8 Kurth, F. et al. (2022), 'Brain sex in transgender women is shifted towards gender identity', *Journal of Clinical Medicine* 11 (6):1582. doi: 10.3390/jcm11061582.

9 Maudsley Hospital National and Specialist OCD, BDD and Related Disorders Service (2019), *Appearance Anxiety: A Guide to Understanding Body Dysmorphic Disorder for Young People, Families and Professionals*. London: Jessica Kingsley Publishers.

10 Littman, L. (2018), 'Parent reports of adolescents and young adults perceived to show signs of a rapid onset of gender dysphoria', *PLOS One* 14 (3). doi: 10.1371/journal.pone.0202330.

11 Littman, L. (2021), 'Individuals treated for gender dysphoria with medical and/or surgical transition who subsequently detransitioned: a survey of 100 detransitioners', *Archives of Sexual Behavior* 50 (8): 3353–69. https://doi.org/10.1007/s10508-021-02163-w.

12 National Health Service (2020), 'Treatment: gender dysphoria', https://www.nhs.uk/conditions/gender-dysphoria/treatment/.

13 Singh et al. (2021); Steensma et al. (2013a).

2. SOCIAL CONTAGION AND RAPID ONSET GENDER DYSPHORIA (ROGD)

1 Kravetz, L.D. (2018), *Strange Contagion: Inside the Surprising Science of Infectious Behaviors and Viral Emotions and What They Tell Us About Ourselves*. New York: Harper Wave.

2 Müller-Vahl, K.R. et al. (2021), 'Stop that! It's not Tourette's but a new type of mass sociogenic illness', *Brain* 145 (2): 47680. doi:10.1093/brain/awab316.

3 Littman, L. (2018), 'Parent reports of adolescents and young adults perceived to show signs of a rapid onset of gender dysphoria', *PLOS One* 14 (3). doi: 10.1371/journal.pone.0202330.

4 Shrier, A. (2020), *Irreversible Damage: Teenage Girls and the Transgender Craze*, p. xxi. Washington DC: Regnery Publishing.

5 Shorter, E. (1993), *From Paralysis to Fatigue: A History of Psychosomatic Illness in the Modern Era*. New York: Free Press.

6 Hacking, I. (1995), *Rewriting the Soul: Multiple Personality and the Sciences of Memory*. Princeton, NJ: Princeton University Press, p. 238.

7 Hacking, I. (1995).

8 Still, T. (2022), 'The truth about trans murders', *UnHerd*, https://unherd.com/2022/01/the-truth-about-trans-murders/.

9 Heino, E. et al. (2021), 'Transgender identity is associated with bullying involvement among Finnish adolescents'. *Frontiers in Psychology* 11. doi: 10.3389/fpsyg.2020.612424.

10 O'Malley, S. (2021), *Bully-Proof Kids: Practical Tools to Help Your Child Grow up Confident, Resilient and Strong*. London: Swift Press.

11 Heino et al. (2021); Macaskill, M. (2022), 'Primary pupils are being bullied and called transphobic for using wrong pronoun', *The Times*, https://www.thetimes.co.uk/article/primary-pupils-are-being-bullied-and-called-transphobic-for-using-wrong-pronouns-f0v5w9rmg?t=ie.

12 35%: Butler, G. et al. (2018), 'Assessment and support of children and adolescents with gender dysphoria', *Archives of Disease in Childhood* 103 (7):631–6. doi: 10.1136/archdischild-2018-314992; 48%: Churcher Clarke, A. and Spiliadis, A. (2019), '"Taking the lid off the box": the value of extended clinical assessment for adolescents presenting with gender identity difficulties', *Clinical Child Psychology and Psychiatry*, 24 (2): 338–52. doi: 10.1177/1359104518825288.

13 Fulton, A.M. et al. (2012) 'The female profile of autism: an examination of friendships' [conference paper], https://www.researchgate.net/publication/268129052_The_Female_Profile_of_Autism_An_Examination_of_Friendships.

14 Obsessive behaviours: Zucker, K.J. et al. (2017), 'Intense/obsessional interests in children with gender dysphoria: a cross-validation study using the Teacher's Report Form', *Child and Adolescent Psychiatry and Mental Health* 11 (51). doi: 10.1186/s13034-017-0189-9; body dysmorphic disorder: Vasudeva, Sara B., and Hollander, E. (2017) 'Body dysmorphic disorder in patients with autism spectrum disorder: a reflection of increased local processing and self-focus', *American Journal of Psychiatry* 174 (4): 313–16. https://doi.org/10.1176/appi.ajp.2016.16050559.

15 Cass, H. (2022), 'Independent review of gender identity services for children and young people', https://cass.independent-review.uk/publications/interim-report/, p. 17.

16 Kabat-Zinn, J. (2004) (reprint edition), *Wherever You Go, There You Are: Mindfulness Meditation for Everyday Life*. London: Piatkus.

17 Ayad, S. and O'Malley, S. (2022), 'Borderline personality: distorted attempts to integrate – a conversation w/ Lisa Duval' [podcast], *Gender: A Wider Lens Podcast*, https://gender-a-wider-lens.captivate.fm/episode/75-borderline-personality-distorted-attempts-to-integrate-a-conversation-w-lisa-duval.

18 Littman (2018).

19 Fox, A. (2021), 'When sons become daughters: parents of transitioning boys speak out on their own suffering', *Quillette*, https://quillette.com/2021/04/02/when-sons-become-daughters-parents-of-transitioning-boys-speak-out-on-their-own-suffering/.

20 Kerschner, H. (2019), 'Tumblr – a call-out post', *4thWave Now*, https://4thwavenow.com/2019/03/20/tumblr-a-call-out-post/.

21 Transgender Trend (n.d.), *The Transmission of Transition* [booklet]. Available at https://www.transgendertrend.com/product/the-transmission-of-transition/.

22 Genspect (2021), 'The collapse of gender medicine into customership', ROGD Webinar [video], YouTube, https://youtu.be/uIVwPFcGYJM.

3. SEXUALITY

1 Tuerk, C. (2011), 'Considerations for affirming gender nonconforming boys and their families: new approaches, new challenges', *Child and Adolescent Psychiatric Clinics of North America* 20 (4): 767–77. doi: 10.1016/j.chc.2011.07.005.

2 Amici, F. et al. (2019), 'Growing into adulthood – a review on sex differences in the development of sociality across macaques', *Behavioral Ecology and Sociobiology* 73 (2). doi: 10.1007/s00265-018-2623-2.

3 Littman, L. (2021), 'Individuals treated for gender dysphoria with medical and/or surgical transition who subsequently detransitioned: a survey of 100 detransitioners', *Archives of Sexual Behavior* 50 (8): 3353–69. https://doi.org/10.1007/s10508-021-02163-w.

4 American Psychiatric Association (2022), 'Gender dysphoria'. In: *Diagnostic and Statistical Manual of Mental Disorders* (5th ed., text rev.) Washington DC: American Psychiatric Association Publishing.

5 Blanchard, R. (1989), 'The classification and labeling of nonhomosexual gender dysphorias', *Archives of Sexual Behavior* 18 (4): 315–34. doi:10.1007/bf01541951.

6 Fisher, K.A. and Marwaha, R. (2022), 'Paraphilia'. In: *StatPearls* [Internet]. Treasure Island, FL: StatPearls Publishing.

7 Kerschner, H. (2022), 'By any other name', Prude Posting [blog], https://lacroicsz.substack.com/p/by-any-other-name.

8 Richards, S. A. (2022), 'Purification rites: an autobiographical essay', Semantic Sorcery [blog], https://cutdowntree.substack.com/p/purification-rites.

9 Bischmann et al. (2017), 'Age and experience of first exposure to pornography: relations to masculine norms', discussed in 'Age of first exposure to pornography shapes men's attitudes toward women', American Psychological Association, https://www.apa.org/news/press/releases/2017/08/pornography-exposure#:~:text=%E2%80%9CWe%20found%20that%20the%20younger,to%20engage%20in%20playboy%20behavior.%E2%80%9D.

10 Vera-Gray, F. et al. (2021), 'Sexual violence as a sexual script in mainstream online pornography', *British Journal of Criminology* 61 (5): 1243–60. https://doi.org/10.1093/bjc/azab035.

11 Psychoducks [thread starter] (2020), 'Sexual confusion: Sissy addiction: Crossdressing help', NoFap® [web forum], https://forum.nofap.com/index.php?threads%2Fsexual-confusion-sissy-addiction-crossdressing-help.296639%2F.

12 'Let's talk about porn – a conversation blueprint by Fight the New Drug' (n.d.), Fight the New Drug, https://fightthenewdrug.org/lets-talk-about-porn/topic/?to=child.

4. PARENTING ALTERNATIVES TO AFFIRMATION

1 Olson-Kennedy, J. et al. (2018), 'Chest reconstruction and chest dysphoria in transmasculine minors and young adults', *JAMA Pediatrics* 172 (5): 431. doi: 10.1001/jamapediatrics.2017.5440.

2   Cantor, J. (2016), 'Do trans- kids stay trans- when they grow up?', *Sexology Today* (blog), from http://www.sexologytoday.org/2016/01/do-trans-kids-stay-trans-when-they-grow_99.html.

3   Li, G. et al. (2017), 'Childhood gender-typed behavior and adolescent sexual orientation: a longitudinal population-based study', *Developmental Psychology* 53 (4), 764–77. doi: 10.1037/dev0000281.

4   Steensma, T.D. et al. (2011), 'Desisting and persisting gender dysphoria after childhood: a qualitative follow-up study', *Clinical Child Psychology and Psychiatry* 16 (4), 499–516. doi: 10.1177/1359104510378303.

5   Jargon, J. (2021), 'TikTok diagnosis videos leave some teens thinking they have rare mental disorders', *Wall Street Journal*, https://www.wsj.com/articles/tiktok-diagnosis-videos-leave-some-teens-thinking-they-have-rare-mental-disorders-11640514602.

5. SOCIAL TRANSITION

1   Zucker, K.J. (2020), 'Debate: different strokes for different folks', *Child and Adolescent Mental Health* 25: 36–7. doi: 10.1111/camh.12330; Olson, K.R. et al. (2022), 'Gender identity 5 years after social transition', *Pediatrics* 150 (2):e2021056082. doi: 10.1542/peds.2021-056082.

2   Steensma, T.D. et al. (2011), 'Desisting and persisting gender dysphoria after childhood: a qualitative follow-up study', *Clinical Child Psychology and Psychiatry* 16 (4): 499–516. doi: 10.1177/1359104510378303.

3   Peitzmeier, S. et al. (2017), 'Health impact of chest binding among transgender adults: a community-engaged, cross-sectional study', *Culture, Health & Sexuality* 19 (1): 64–75. doi: 10.1080/13691058.2016.1191675.

4   Cumming, R. et al. (2016), 'Understanding the effects on lung function of chest binder use in the transgender population', *Thorax* 71: A227. doi: 10.1136/thoraxjnl-2016-209333.400.

5   Peitzmeier et al. (2017).

6   Peitzmeier, S. et al. (2021), 'Time to first onset of chest binding-related symptoms in transgender youth', *Pediatrics* 147 (3): e20200728. doi: d10.1542/peds.2020-0728.

7   Poteat, T., (2018), 'Understanding the health effects of binding and tucking for gender affirmation', *Journal of Clinical and Translational Science* 21 (2) (S1): 76. doi: 10.1017/cts.2018.268.

8   Cass, H. (2022), 'Independent review of gender identity services for children and young people', https://cass.independent-review.uk/publications/interim-report/, pp. 62–3.

6. MEDICAL INTERVENTIONS

1   Ostertag, B. (2016), *Sex Science Self: A Social History of Estrogen, Testosterone, and Identity.* Amherst, MA: University of Massachusetts Press.

2 Barnes, H. (2023), *Time to Think: The Inside Story of the Collapse of the Tavistock's Gender Service for Children*. London: Swift Press, p. 167.

3 Andersson, J. and Rhoden-Paul, A. (2022), 'NHS to close Tavistock child gender identity clinic', BBC News, https://www.bbc.com/news/uk-62335665.

4 Society for Evidence-Based Gender Medicine (2022), 'Summary of key recommendations from the Swedish National Board of Health and Welfare (Socialstyrelsen/NBHW)', https://segm.org/segm-summary-sweden-prioritizes-therapy-curbs-hormones-for-gender-dysphoric-youth.

5 Society for Evidence-Based Gender Medicine (2021), 'One year since Finland broke with WPATH "Standards of Care": Finland prioritizes psychotherapy over hormones, and rejects surgeries for gender dysphoric minors', https://segm.org/Finland_deviates_from_WPATH_prioritizing_psychotherapy_no_surgery_for_minors.

6 Carbonaro, G. (2023), 'Republicans are trying to ban transgender health care in these 26 states', *Newsweek*, https://www.newsweek.com/republicans-trying-ban-transgender-health-care-these-states-1780316.

7 Respaut, R. and Terhune, C. (2022), 'Putting numbers on the rise in children seeking gender care. Reuters Investigates', *Reuters*, https://www.reuters.com/investigates/special-report/usa-transyouth-data/.

8 Olson-Kennedy, J. et al. (2018), 'Chest reconstruction and chest dysphoria in transmasculine minors and young adults', *JAMA Pediatrics* 172 (5): 431. doi: 10.1001/jamapediatrics.2017.5440.

9 Block, J. (2023), 'Gender dysphoria in young people is rising – and so is professional disagreement', *BMJ* 380L 382. doi: 10.1136/bmj.p382.

10 Nainggolan, L. (2022), 'WPATH removes age limits from transgender treatment guidelines', *Medscape*, https://www.medscape.com/viewarticle/980935.

11 Arain, M. et al. (2013), 'Maturation of the adolescent brain', *Neuropsychiatric Disease and Treatment* 9: 449–61. doi: 10.2147/NDT.S39776.

12 de Vries, A.L.C. et al. (2014), 'Young adult psychological outcome after puberty suppression and gender reassignment', *Pediatrics* 134 (4): 696–704. doi: 10.1542/peds.2013-2958.

13 Barnes (2023), p. 118.

14 van der Loos, M.A. et al. (2022), 'Continuation of gender-affirming hormones in transgender people starting puberty suppression in adolescence: a cohort study in the Netherlands', *The Lancet Child & Adolescent Health* 6 (12): 869–75. doi: 10.1016/s2352-4642(22)00254-1.

15 Tavistock and Portman NHS Foundation Trust (2021), 'Early Intervention Study shows puberty blockers are a well-received intervention in carefully selected patients', https://tavistockandportman.nhs.uk/about-us/news/stories/early-intervention-study-shows-puberty-blockers-are-well-received-intervention-carefully-selected-patients/.

16 BSPED [website] (2005), 'Guidelines for the management of Gender Identity Disorder (GID) in adolescents and children: specific endocrinological recommendations approved by the British Society of Paediatric Endocrinology & Diabetes', archived at https://web.archive.org/web/20051214002955/bsped.org.uk/professional/guidelines/docs/BSPEDGIDguidelines.pdf; quoted in Barnes (2023), pp. 40–1.

17 Jewett, C. (2017), 'Drug used to halt puberty in children may cause lasting health problems', *STAT*, https://www.statnews.com/2017/02/02/lupron-puberty-children-health-problems/.

18 Reid, S. (2022), 'Leo's shattered body and the horror story from Sweden that reveals spinal fractures, stunted growth and porous bones are linked to life-changing trans treatments… so when WILL Britain wake up to the danger of giving puberty blockers to children?', *Daily Mail*, https://www.dailymail.co.uk/news/article-10768707/When-Britain-wake-danger-giving-puberty-blockers-children.html.

19 Hough, D. et al. (2017), 'A reduction in long-term spatial memory persists after discontinuation of peripubertal GnRH agonist treatment in sheep', *Psychoneuroendocrinology* 77: 1–8. doi: 10.1016/j.psyneuen.2016.11.029.

20 Biggs, M. (2020), 'Gender dysphoria and psychological functioning in adolescents treated with GnRHa: comparing Dutch and English prospective studies', *Archives of Sexual Behavior* 49 (7): 2231–6. doi: 10.1007/s10508-020-01764-1.

21 The FDA's warning is discussed in AAP News (2022), 'Risk of pseudotumor cerebri added to labeling for gonadotropin-releasing hormone agonists', https://www.fda.gov/media/159663/download.

22 Cheng, P.J. et al. (2019), 'Fertility concerns of the transgender patient', *Translational Andrology and Urology* 8 (3): 209–18. doi: 10.21037/tau.2019.05.09.

23 Shrier, A. (2021), 'Top trans doctors blow the whistle on "sloppy" care,' Common Sense [blog], https://www.thefp.com/p/top-trans-doctors-blow-the-whistle.

24 BBC News (2020), 'Puberty blockers: under-16s "unlikely to be able to give informed consent"', https://www.bbc.com/news/uk-england-cambridgeshire-55144148.

25 American College of Cardiology (2023), 'Hormone therapy for gender dysphoria may raise cardiovascular risks', *EurekAlert!*, https://www.eurekalert.org/news-releases/980465.

26 Mayo Foundation for Medical Education and Research (2023), 'Feminizing hormone therapy', https://www.mayoclinic.org/tests-procedures/feminizing-hormone-therapy/about/pac-20385096.

27 Grand View Research (n.d.), 'U.S. sex reassignment surgery market size, share and trends analysis report by gender transition (male to female, female to male), and segment forecasts, 2022–2030', https://www.grandviewresearch.com/industry-analysis/us-sex-reassignment-surgery-market.

28 GoFundMe (2022), 'Gender-affirming care fundraising', https://www.gofundme.com/c/gender-confirmation-surgery-fundraising.

29 Coleman, E. et al. (2022), 'Standards of care for the health of transgender and gender diverse people, version 8', *International Journal of Transgender Health* 23 (sup 1): 1–259. doi: 10.1080/26895269.2022.2100644.

30 Hysto.net (n.d.), 'FTM hysterectomy frequently asked questions', https://www.hysto.net/faq/.

31 Parkinson's disease: Abdelzaher Ibrahim, A. et al. (2022), 'The risk of Parkinson's disease in women who underwent hysterectomy before the age of menopause',

Menopausal Review 21 (3): 185–90. doi: 10.5114/pm.2022.119634. Dementia: Gong, J. et al. (2022), 'Reproductive factors and the risk of incident dementia: a cohort study of UK Biobank participants', *PLOS Medicine* 19 (4). doi: 10.1371/journal.pmed.1003955.

32 Madueke-Laveaux, O.S. et al. (2021), 'What we know about the long-term risks of hysterectomy for benign indication – a systematic review', *Journal of Clinical Medicine* 10 (22): 5335. doi: 10.3390/jcm10225335.

33 Crane, C. (2016), 'Phalloplasty and metoidioplasty – overview and postoperative considerations', UCSF Transgender Care, https://transcare.ucsf.edu/guidelines/phalloplasty.

34 Bekeny, J.C. et al. (2021), 'Breast augmentation in the transgender patient: narrative review of current techniques and complications', *Annals of translational medicine* 9 (7): 611. doi: 10.21037/atm-20-5087.

35 Schardein, J.N. and Nikolavsky, D. (2022), 'Sexual functioning of transgender females post-vaginoplasty: evaluation, outcomes and treatment strategies for sexual dysfunction', *Sexual Medicine Reviews* 10 (1): 77–90. doi: 10.1016/j.sxmr.2021.04.001.

36 Bustos, S. S. et al. (2021), 'Complications and patient-reported outcomes in transfemale vaginoplasty: an updated systematic review and meta-analysis', *Plastic and Reconstructive Surgery – Global Open* 9 (3): e3510. doi: 10.1097/gox.0000000000003510.

37 de Vries, A.L.C. et al. (2014).

38 Crane Center for Transgender Surgery (2022), 'Non-binary surgery', https://cranects.com/non-binary-surgery/.

39 Chapman, M. (2022), 'Activist doctors are urging GPs to prescribe cross-sex hormones', *The Economist*, https://www.economist.com/britain/2022/02/19/activist-doctors-are-urging-gps-to-prescribe-cross-sex-hormones.

40 Williams, G. (2019), 'A grand conspiracy to tell the truth: an interview with 4thWaveNow founder & her daughter Chiara of the Pique Resilience Project', *4th Wave Now*, https://4thwavenow.com/2019/02/27/a-grand-conspiracy-to-tell-the-truth-an-interview-with-4thwavenow-founder-her-daughter-chiara-of-the-pique-resilience-project/.

41 Ayad, S. and O'Malley, S. (2022), 'Mother-daughter story: "I didn't want to be yours anymore" w/ Dr. Maggie Goldsmith' [podcast], *Gender: A Wider Lens Podcast* (2 Sep. 2022), https://gender-a-wider-lens.captivate.fm/episode/85-mother-daughter-story-i-didnt-want-to-be-yours-anymore-w-dr-maggie-goldsmith.

7. DEALING WITH THERAPISTS, SCHOOLS, UNIVERSITIES AND OTHER PROFESSIONALS

1 Watters, E. (2022), 'The forgotten lessons of the recovered memory movement', *New York Times*, https://www.nytimes.com/2022/09/27/opinion/recovered-memory-therapy-mental-health.html.

2 Persistence of gender-related distress: Steensma, T.D. et al. (2013a), 'Factors associated with desistance and persistence of childhood gender dysphoria: a quantitative follow-up study', *Journal of the American Amademy of Child and Adolescent Psychiatry* 52 (6): 582–90, doi: 10.1016/j.jaac.2013.03.016; Zucker, K.J. (2020), 'Debate: different strokes for different folks', *Child and Adolescent Mental Health* 25: 36–7. doi: 10.1111/camh.12330; Singh et al. (2021), 'A follow-up study of boys with gender identity disorder', *Frontiers in Psychiatry* 12. doi:10.3389/fpsyt.2021.632784. Interference: de Vries, A.L.C. and Cohen-Kettenis, P. (2012), 'Clinical management of gender dysphoria in children and adolescents: the Dutch approach', *Journal of Homosexuality* 59 (3): 301–20. doi: 10.1080/00918369.2012.653300; Wren, B. (2019), 'Reflections on "Thinking an ethics of gender exploration: against delaying transition for transgender and gender variant youth"', *Clinical Child Psychology and Psychiatry* 24 (2):237–40. doi: 10.1177/1359104519838591.
3 Arnett, J. (2006), *Emerging Adulthood: The Winding Road from the Late Teens through the Twenties.* Oxford: Oxford University Press.

9. MANAGING CONFLICT WITH YOUR CHILD

1 National Center for Transgender Equality (n.d.), 'The report of the 2015 U.S. Transgender Survey', https://transequality.org/sites/default/files/docs/usts/USTS-Full-Report-Dec17.pdf.
2 Dhejne, C. et al. (2011), 'Long-term follow-up of transsexual persons undergoing sex reassignment surgery: cohort study in Sweden', *PLOS ONE* 6 (2). doi: 10.1371/journal.pone.0016885.
3 Biggs, M. (2022), 'Suicide by Clinic-Referred Transgender Adolescents in the United Kingdom', *Archives of Sexual Behavior* 51, 685–90. doi: 10.1007/s10508-022-02287-7.
4 de Graaf, N.M. et al. (2020), 'Suicidality in clinic-referred transgender adolescents', *European Child & Adolescent Psychiatry* 31 (1): 67–83. doi: 10.1007/s00787-020-01663-9.
5 Barnes, H. (2023), *Time to Think: The Inside Story of the Collapse of the Tavistock's Gender Service for Children.* London: Swift Press, p. 131.
6 Society for Evidence Based Gender Medicine (2020), 'Correction of a key study: no evidence of "gender-affirming" surgeries improving mental health', https://segm.org/ajp_correction_2020.
7 Dhejne et al. (2011).
8 Wiepjes, C.M. et al. (2020), 'Trends in suicide death risk in transgender people: results from the Amsterdam Cohort of Gender Dysphoria study (1972–2017)', *Acta Psychiatrica Scandinavica* 141 (6): 486–91. doi: 10.1111/acps.13164.
9 This is some wisdom that we learned from one of Lisa's colleagues.
10 Toomey, R.B. et al. (2018), 'Transgender adolescent suicide behavior', *Pediatrics* 142 (4): e20174218. doi: 10.1542/peds.2017-4218.
11 Nock, M.K., and Kessler, R.C. (2006), 'Prevalence of and risk factors for suicide attempts versus suicide gestures: analysis of the National Comorbidity

Survey', *Journal of Abnormal Psychology* 115 (3), 616–23. doi: 10.1037/0021-843X.115.3.616.

12 Savin-Williams, R.C. (2001), 'Suicide attempts among sexual-minority youths: population and measurement issues', *Journal of Consulting and Clinical Psychology* 69 (6): 983–91. doi: 10.1037/0022-006X.69.6.983.

13 Biggs, M. (2022), 'Suicide by Clinic-Referred Transgender Adolescents in the United Kingdom', *Archives of Sexual Behavior* 51, 685–90. doi: 10.1007/s10508-022-02287-7.

14 Turban, J.L. et al. (2020), 'Pubertal suppression for transgender youth and risk of suicidal ideation', *Pediatrics* 145 (2): e20191725. doi: 10.1542/peds.2019-1725.

15 Biggs, M. (2022), 'The Dutch Protocol for juvenile transsexuals: origins and evidence', *Journal of Sex & Marital Therapy*: 1–21. doi: 10.1080/0092623X.2022.2121238.

16 Bränström, R. and Pachankis, J.E. (2020), 'Toward rigorous methodologies for strengthening causal inference in the association between gender-affirming care and transgender individuals' mental health: response to letters', *American Journal of Psychiatry* 177 (8), 769–72. doi: 10.1176/appi.ajp.2020.20050599.

10. SELF-CARE FOR PARENTS

1 Pickhardt, C. (2010), 'The disenchantment of adolescence: when adolescence begins the old parent and child relationship ends', *Psychology Today*, https://www.psychologytoday.com/us/blog/surviving-your-childs-adolescence/201002/the-disenchantment-adolescence.

2 Kübler-Ross, E. (2011), *On Death and Dying: What the Dying Have to Teach Doctors, Nurses, Clergy and Their Own Families*. New York: Scribner.

3 Self-Compassion: Dr. Kristin Neff (2022), 'About Dr. Kristin Neff', https://self-compassion.org/about-kristin-neff/.

4 Frankl, V.E. (2015). *Man's Search for Meaning: The Classic Tribute to Hope from the Holocaust*. Boston, MA: Beacon Press, p. 63.

11. ALIENATION AND ESTRANGEMENT

1 Ro, C. (2019), 'The truth about family estrangement', BBC Future, https://www.bbc.com/future/article/20190328-family-estrangement-causes.

2 Coleman, J. (2021), 'A shift in American family values is fueling estrangement', Joshua Coleman Ph.D. [website], https://www.drjoshuacoleman.com/post/a-shift-in-american-family-values-is-fueling-estrangement.

3 Halverson, J.R., and Way, A.K. (2012), 'The curious case of Colleen LaRose: social margins, new media, and online radicalization', *Media, War & Conflict* 5 (2), 139–53. doi: 10.1177/1750635212440917.

4 Coleman, J. (2022), *Rules of Estrangement: Why Adult Children Cut Ties and How to Heal the Conflict*. London: Sheldon Press, p. 50.

5 Coleman (2022), p. 209.

12. DESISTANCE

1   Zucker, K.J. (2018), 'The myth of persistence: response to "A critical commentary on follow-up studies and 'desistance' theories about transgender and gender non-conforming children" by Temple Newhook et al. (2018)', *International Journal of Transgenderism* 19 (2): 231–45, https://www.tandfonline.com/doi/abs/10.1080/15532739.2018.1468293?journalCode=wijt20; Ristori, J. and Steensma, T.D. (2016), 'Gender dysphoria in childhood', *International Review of Psychiatry* 28 (1): 13–20. doi: 10.3109/09540261.2015.1115754; Cantor, J. (2016), 'Do trans-kids stay trans- when they grow up?' *Sexology Today!*, http://www.sexologytoday.org/2016/01/do-trans-kids-stay-trans-when-they-grow_99.html.
2   Wallien, M.S. and Cohen-Kettenis, P.T. (2008), 'Psychosexual outcome of gender-dysphoric children', *Journal of the American Academy of Child and Adolescent Psychiatry* 47 (12): 1413–23. doi: 10.1097/CHI.0b013e31818956b9.

13. DETRANSITION

1   Bustos, V.P., Bustos, S.S., Mascaro, A., Del Corral, G., Forte, A.J., Ciudad, P., Kim, E.A., Langstein, H.N., & Manrique, O.J. et al. (2021), 'Regret after gender-affirmation surgery: a systematic review and meta-analysis of prevalence', *Plastic and Reconstructive Surgery – Global Open*, 9 (3). doi: https://doi.org/10.1097/gox.0000000000003477.
2   Expósito-Campos, P. and D'Angelo, R. (2021), 'Letter to the editor: regret after gender-affirmation surgery: a systematic review and meta-analysis of prevalence', *Plastic and Reconstructive Surgery – Global Open* 9 (11). doi: 10.1097/gox.0000000000003951.
3   Littman, L. (2021), 'Individuals treated for gender dysphoria with medical and/or surgical transition who subsequently detransitioned: a survey of 100 detransitioners', *Archives of Sexual Behavior* 50 (8): 3353–69. https://doi.org/10.1007/s10508-021-02163-w.
4   Irwig, M.S. (2022), 'Detransition among transgender and gender-diverse people – an increasing and increasingly complex phenomenon', *Journal of Clinical Endocrinology and Metabolism* 107 (10): e4261–62. doi: 10.1210/clinem/dgac356.
5   Boyd, I. et al. (2022), 'Care of transgender patients: a general practice quality improvement approach', *Healthcare* 10 (1): 121. doi: 10.3390/healthcare10010121; Hall, R. et al. (2021), 'Access to care and frequency of detransition among a cohort discharged by a UK national adult gender identity clinic: retrospective case-note review', *BJPsych Open* 7 (6). doi: 10.1192/bjo.2021.1022.
6   Barker, E. (1983), 'The ones who got away: people who attend Unification Church workshops and do not become Moonies'. In: Barker, E. (ed.), *Of Gods and Men: New Religious Movements in the West.* Macon, GA. Mercer University Press; Galanter, M. (1983), 'Unification Church ("Moonie") dropouts: psychological readjustment after leaving a charismatic religious group', *American Journal of Psychiatry* 140 (8): 984–9. doi: 10.1176/ajp.140.8.984.

14. HOW TO ROW BACK AFTER AFFIRMATION

1 Ault, A. (2022), 'Gender surgeons on TikTok, Instagram: appropriate or not?', *Medscape*, https://www.medscape.com/viewarticle/976863.
2 Biggs, M. (2022), 'The Dutch Protocol for juvenile transsexuals: origins and evidence', *Journal of Sex & Marital Therapy*: 1–21. doi: 10.1080/0092623X.2022.2121238.

APPENDIX 1. WHAT IS GENDER?

1 Jaffe, S. (2018), 'Queer time: the alternative to "adulting"', *JSTOR Daily*, https://daily.jstor.org/queer-time-the-alternative-to-adulting/.
2 Keo-Meier, C. and Ehrensaft, D. (eds) (2018), *The Gender Affirmative Model: An Interdisciplinary Approach to Supporting Transgender and Gender Expansive Children*. Washington, DC: American Psychological Association.
3 Stock, K. (2021), *Material Girls: Why Reality Matters for Feminism.* Boston, MA: Little, Brown Book Group, p. 56.

APPENDIX 2. SOCIAL AND CULTURAL MOVEMENTS THAT CAN SHAPE GENDER-RELATED DISTRESS

1 Cullen, P., Hoose, B. and Mannion, G. (eds) (2007), *Catholic Social Justice: Theological and Practical Explorations.* London: T & T Clark.
2 Pérez-Garzón, C.A. (2018), 'Unveiling the meaning of social justice in Colombia', *Mexican Law Review* 10 (2): 27–66. ISSN 2448-5306.

APPENDIX 3. GENDER DYSPHORIA: DIAGNOSIS AND DEFINITIONS

1 World Health Organization (2022), 'Gender incongruence and transgender health in the ICD', https://www.who.int/standards/classifications/frequently-asked-questions/gender-incongruence-and-transgender-health-in-the-icd.
2 Griffin, L. and Clyde, K. (2019), 'Challenging stigma in sexuality and gender', *World Psychiatry*, https://www.cambridge.org/core/journals/bjpsych-international/article/stigma-in-psychiatry-seen-through-the-lens-of-sexuality-and-gender/FF24E21150B556BD429F39102B7FF2CE?fbclid=IwAR36t2CBsUc-2Aw6k_lyUzhHo5LmNOBStmbQx9NxjMcK3mC6ZFApQdX8C1E#comments. (Note that you will need to sign in and go to the letters section to see the comment in question.)
3 World Health Organization (2022).
4 American Psychiatric Association (2022), *Diagnostic and Statistical Manual of Mental Disorders* (5th ed.), text revision (*DSM-5-TR*), p. 822.

5 American Psychiatric Association (2022).

6 American Psychiatric Association (2022); Singh et al. (2021), 'A follow-up study of boys with gender identity disorder', *Frontiers in Psychiatry* 12. doi:10.3389/fpsyt.2021.632784.

7 American Psychiatric Association (2022).

8 Turban, J. (2022), 'What is gender dysphoria?', American Psychiatric Association [website], www.psychiatry.org/patients-families/gender-dysphoria/what-is-gender-dysphoria.

APPENDIX 4. APPROACHES TO TREATMENT

1 Butler, J. (1990), *Gender Trouble: Feminism and the Subversion of Identity*. Abingdon: Routledge Classics.

APPENDIX 5. CHILD AND ADOLESCENT DEVELOPMENT

1 Erikson, E. and Erikson, J. (1998). *The Life Cycle Completed: Extended Version*. New York: W.W. Norton.

2 Devon Children and Families Partnership (2020), 'Radicalisation and extremism – how children may be at risk', https://www.dcfp.org.uk/child-abuse/radicalisation-and-extremism/.

3 Denworth, L. (2020), 'The outsize influence of your middle-school friends', *The Atlantic*, https://www.theatlantic.com/family/archive/2020/01/friendship-crucial-adolescent-brain/605638/.

4 Gilman, J.M. et al. (2014), 'Impulsive social influence increases impulsive choices on a temporal discounting task in young adults', *PLoS ONE* 9 (7): e101570. doi: 10.1371/journal.pone.0101570.

GLOSSARY

1 Sax, L. (2002), 'How common is intersex? A response to Anne Fausto-Sterling', *Journal of Sex Research* 39 (3): 174–8. doi: 10.1080/00224490209552139.

ACKNOWLEDGEMENTS

Writing a book takes a village. This book would not have come together without the help of many and we are grateful for their support. First, we are thankful to Mark Richards at Swift Press for believing in this project and for his endless good-humoured patience with us – dealing with three co-authors is not easy! We'd also like to thank the entire Swift Press team who helped us shape and edit the manuscript. Gratitude is due to all of the contributors who generously offered sidebars – your perspectives have greatly enriched and enlivened the book and made it much more valuable. We are grateful to all the parents we have consulted with over the years, especially those who have attended our retreats. We are so honoured that we can now pass onto others all you have taught us over the years. And lastly, thank you to our spouses, partners and families. We really couldn't have done this without you.

INDEX